TEACHER
EDUCATION

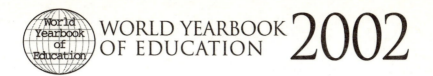

WORLD YEARBOOK
OF EDUCATION 2002

TEACHER

EDUCATION

DILEMMAS AND PROSPECTS

EDITED BY
ELWYN THOMAS

KOGAN
PAGE

First published in 2002

Apart from any fair dealing for the purposes of research or private study, or criticism or review, as permitted under the Copyright, Designs and Patents Act 1988, this publication may only be reproduced, stored or transmitted, in any form or by any means, with the prior permission in writing of the publishers, or in the case of reprographic reproduction in accordance with the terms and licences issued by the CLA. Enquiries concerning reproduction outside these terms should be sent to the publishers at the undermentioned addresses:

Kogan Page Limited
120 Pentonville Road
London N1 9JN
UK

Stylus Publications Inc.
22883 Quicksilver Drive
Sterling VA 20166-2012
USA

British Library Cataloguing in Publication Data

A CIP record for this book is available from the British Library.

ISBN 0 7494 3574 7

Typeset by Saxon Graphics Ltd, Derby
Printed and bound in Great Britain by Clays Ltd, St Ives plc

Contents

List of contributors

Dr Ian Andrews, Associate Professor, Simon Fraser University, Canada

Dr Chris Berry, Research Officer, Multigrade Teaching Project, Education and International Development Group, Institute of Education, University of London, UK

Professor Roy Carr-Hill, Education and International Development Grouping, Institute of Education, University of London, UK

Dr Robert Cowen, Reader in Education, Institute of Education, University of London, UK

Professor Lynn Davies, Centre for International Education and Research, University of Birmingham, UK

Professor Teresa Davis, Rector, Instituto de Ensenamza Superior en Lenguas, Buenos Aires, Argentina

Professor Felix Etxeberria, University of the Basque Country, Faculty of Education Science, Spain

Dr Sassia Ghedjghoudj, Senior Lecturer, Ecole Normale Supérieure, Algiers, Algeria

Dr Norma Martin Goonen, Dean of Undergraduate Studies, Nova Southeastern University, Fort Lauderdale, USA

Professor S Gopinathan, National Institute of Education, Nanyang Technological University, Singapore

Professor Peter Grimmett, Simon Fraser University, Canada

Dr Ken Howey, Former Director of the UNITE Project, University of Wisconsin–Milwaukee, USA

Dr George L Iber, Associate Professor, Nova Southeastern University, Fort Lauderdale, USA

Professor In Whoe Kim, Director, Institute of Korean Studies, Yonsei University, Korea

Professor Terri Kim, Institute of Asia Pacific Development, Seoul National University, Seoul, Korea

Dr Molly N N Lee, Associate Professor, School of Educational Studies, Universiti Sains, Penang, Malaysia

Dr Relebohile Moletsane, Senior Lecturer, School of Education, University of Natal, Durban, South Africa

Richard Moreno, Adjunct Professor, Nova Southeastern University, Fort Lauderdale, USA

Anita Pincas, Senior Lecturer, Institute of Education, University of London, UK

Dr Linda Post, Chair, Departments of Curriculum and Instruction, University of Wisconsin–Milwaukee, USA

Professor V K Raina, NCERT, New Delhi, India

Dr Luciola L Santos, Lecturer, Faculty of Education, Federal University of the State of Minas Gerais, Brazil

Dr Ladislaus M Semali, Associate Professor of Education, The Pennsylvania State University, USA

Dr Leslie Sharpe, Associate Professor, National Institute of Education, Nanyang Technological University, Singapore

Professor Shin'ichi Suzuki, Graduate School of Education, Waseda University, Tokyo, Japan

Dr Elwyn Thomas, Senior Lecturer, Institute of Education, University of London, UK and Visiting Professor/Senior Fellow, Nanyang Technological University, Singapore

Janusz Tomiak, Senior Lecturer, Institute of Education and School of Slavonic Studies, University of London, UK

Professor Marvin Wideen, Simon Fraser University, Canada

Dr Evie Zambeta, Lecturer in Education, Department of Early Childhood Education, University of Athens, Athens, Greece

Dr Tikva Zohar, Lecturer, The Open University of Israel and Kibbutzim College of Education, Israel

Series Editors' foreword

Teacher education lies behind education as a whole. It is crucial to the success of the enterprise and yet we still do not do it well, as many of the chapters in this year's *World Yearbook of Education* reveal. Indeed, the *World Yearbook*s have had several previous volumes on the topic, indicating both its importance and its constantly changing nature.

Globalization and the demands of the knowledge economy would imply that a common model is developing to position teachers to deal effectively and efficiently with these new social forces. However, as the four sections of this *Yearbook* indicate, there is much still to debate and much innovative theory and practice on which to report.

The themes of state control and cultural reproduction are central to any understanding of teacher education. Increasingly, states are understanding the importance of teacher education to their patterns of control and reproduction. With this understanding has come increased state involvement.

Anyone seeking to find out about what is happening globally in relation to teacher education will find in this volume, as we did, a great deal of interesting and diverse information on this important topic.

David Coulby and Crispin Jones
Series Editors

Preface: Dilemmas and prospects unravelled – an overview

Dilemmas are about situations in which choices have to be made between two or more alternatives, both of which may have an element of doubt or even undesirability about them. Prospects, on the other hand, have a more underlying positive connotation, and are about expectations and something favourable to look forward to in the future. When these two words are discussed in the context of education, and particularly teacher education, there is little doubt that both are to be found aplenty in the past and recent literature. In choosing these words to be part of the title of the present *Yearbook of Education* as a guide for the contributors to the volume, the author of this overview was mindful of the fact that professionals from all sectors of education and throughout the world are, and have been, facing dilemmas for many years. Some dilemmas have been tougher to resolve than others and, as the reader will discover from the various contributions in this volume, in most countries the development of teacher education is facing many tough and varying types of dilemmas.

As an antidote to the ethos of 'the problematic', by surveying the future of teacher education from the standpoint that 'things will hopefully get better', the formulation of sets of expectations and aspirations under the rubric of future prospects provides an opportunity for educators to supply some realistic strategies to help solve at least some of the dilemmas they identify. The reader will find that many of the 29 contributors to this book have identified dilemmas that are of common concern across national and regional boundaries. This is not surprising as the pace of globalization and the greater role of information communication technology (ICT) informs more of the public. On the other hand some dilemmas appear to be country-specific.

However, whether these dilemmas have universal or particularistic characteristics, the need for mapping out the prospects for the future of teacher education to meet such dilemmas is clearly a priority. In some cases, it is more difficult to spell out precise prescriptions for resolving dilemmas than it is for others. For example, training teachers to meet the problem of combating HIV/AIDS through education is clearly a much more difficult task than planning more classrooms and providing extra teaching materials. The contributors have reflected such disparities in their proposals and strategies for change. Gauging the prospects of success of projects to improve class teaching or teacher training depends on many factors. These would include a thorough knowledge of the workings of socio-cultural contexts, understanding the nuances of political control, the commitment, expertise and competency of significant personnel involved in the projects, the possible effects of external events and the role of international aid agencies. These and other factors emerge in the various chapters, as authors aim to link the dilemmas they raise with realistic and valid propositions to meet the challenges inherent in many dilemmas concerning the future improvement of teacher education.

Why four themes?

To assist in unravelling the dilemmas facing teacher education and the prospects for their resolution, four themes were selected, not only to make the compilation of this volume a more manageable task, but to consider from an international perspective key issues facing teacher educators and education policy makers that will ultimately affect children's opportunities to learn and develop their potential. There are areas of inevitable overlap between the four themes discussed, as all focus on the common aim of developing sound, effective and creative teacher educators. This can only be achieved if teachers and their trainers are given support and trust that enhances their development as professionals. Each of the four themes will be discussed below with reference to the contributions made to this volume.

Control of teacher education by the state with reference to schools and higher education

This theme provides different dilemmas and prospects for both teachers and teacher educators. For instance, too much government influence strikes at the heart of professional autonomy and the role of training institutions to do their job effectively. This issue was elaborated upon comparatively, and with reference to the United Kingdom in particular, by Robert Cowen in his chapter. Teresa Davis writing about Argentina and Evie Zambeta on Greece underlined the gradual changes that marked the evolution of more openness by government towards teacher professionalism, and a move away from the authoritarianism of the past.

A more relaxed interest and commitment on the part of government means a lack of direction and responsibility for the social and economic development of the nation, and a possible erosion of national and cultural identity. Kim and Kim, writing about developments in South Korea, see the need for a balance to be struck between the interests of the state and the professional autonomy of teachers. Gopinathan and Sharpe discuss the close collaboration between the state and teacher education in Singapore, which has resulted in a highly competent and dynamic system of teacher education; this collaboration has certainly contributed to both economic success and a cohesive society. Balancing the control of teacher education by the state with the demands of teacher educators, teachers, parents and the wider community is indeed a dilemma of major concern. While all governments are ultimately responsible for the education and training of teachers, a balance between control and a trust in teacher professionalism should be forged between the policy makers and the professionals in which schools, higher education and ultimately the state would be the beneficiaries.

Change and reform in teacher education

Change and reform in teacher education is not a new subject, for it has been written about in much of the teacher education literature previously. However, globalization has brought with it immense social, political, cultural, economic and technological change, which already impinges on the lives of people throughout the world.

How successfully schools, colleges and universities prepare students to meet these changes depends on developing new patterns of teacher training, as discussed by Molly Lee in her chapter on Malaysian teacher education. In Malaysia, new patterns involving twinning institutions with those from countries like Australia and the United Kingdom reflect a need to upgrade the quality of lecturers and school teachers. Luciola Santos writing about reform of the Brazilian teacher education system also refers to the development of closer links between teacher training institutions and universities for the purposes of upgrading teachers and thereby improving their professionalism.

Both Lee and Santos also discuss approaches to fostering new learning and teaching styles that need to be developed within existing socio-cultural contexts. However, Santos is cautious about the help that organizations such as the World Bank offer to reform teacher education, as they overemphasize modernization and economic factors at the expense of local needs of teachers and pupils. Shin'ichi Suzuki, discussing developments within Japanese teacher education, also describes the need to improve teacher and teacher educator effectiveness. He refers to the reform of the training curriculum to embrace ICT, provide more enlightened forms of assessment and better opportunities for researching key educational issues concerning the future of Japanese education.

Ideas for the reform of teacher education can also be directed towards changing former training patterns that were tied to undemocratic and authoritarian government control. For instance, Relebohile Moletsane, writing about recent changes in South African teacher education, makes a strong point that restructuring teacher training without reconceptualization is insufficient. Without reconceptualization, social reconstruction of teacher education suffers, and with it the empowerment of students and staff alike to participate fully in decisions affecting teacher professionalism. Janusz Tomiak writing about reform and reassessment of teacher education in post-communist Poland also raises the need for greater openness on the part of government, to encourage teacher educators to develop new approaches to learning and teaching.

Teachers and teacher educators in South Africa and Poland are devising new ways by which they can reconcile differences between a former austere educational authoritarianism, and a recently introduced open form of teaching and learning. There is also a need for such countries to be exposed to new ideas and methods that have originated from research and development in the West, and to which hitherto they had little or no access. Furthermore, in order that these countries can develop their own research capacity, reform of the university postgraduate curriculum for education researchers would mean that innovative strategies can be developed to investigate local problems, researched *by* local researchers.

So far, the contributions to this theme have examined reforms and innovations covering areas such as new patterns of training, teacher upgrading and developing more relevant curricula to meet changes in the context of social and political change. In some of the chapters, new modes of teacher assessment and stronger links affecting training institutions and universities, between countries and within them, have also figured. However, how reforms may be implemented according to a set of principles that could assist the reform process is an area that has so far received little attention.

In their chapter, Marvin Wideen, Peter Grimmett and Ian Andrews from Canada's Simon Fraser University discuss their original framework to deal with a set of five dilemmas associated with educational reform in Jamaica, and Trinidad and Tobago, which included changes to teacher education in these small island states. The framework they put forward goes some way to help translate 'ideas into action'. The authors also examined the role of outsiders in planning and implementing a particular reform in a cultural context different from their own. This leads us to a discussion of the next theme, which relates specifically to the cultural context of teacher education.

Cultural perspectives and the education of teachers

While reform, change and innovation have become a feature of past attempts to improve the delivery of education worldwide, a constant criticism expressed by those who try to implement the ideas (mainly the teachers) is that failure of reform can be equated with an ignorance of the socio-cultural context of a particular country or region. These criticisms have been directed towards the development of curricula that do not meet sufficiently the needs, expectations and aspirations of local communities. For instance, subject content and methods of its delivery are often ineffective, irrelevant and impractical. This also applies to the teaching of immigrants and minority groups and the related role of language in these situations.

The chapter written by Felix Etxeberria of Spain makes a strong case for a training curriculum that addresses the issues of cultural diversity and development of minority languages, to meet the needs of immigrant pupils and other minorities. For him, the development of pedagogy as an intercultural tool in the training of teachers would be a major step in maintaining the cultural identity of the minority, while enriching Spanish cultural diversity as a whole. The chapter by George L Iber, Norma Martin Goonen and Richard Moreno from the United States also deals with the cultural context surrounding the teaching of immigrants and minority groups in the state of Florida. They examined the various challenges facing non-English speakers. The quantitative and qualitative data that they collected from schoolchildren and their teachers exposed that many problems were both linguistically and culturally resulting in poor educational achievement. The authors suggest that the training curriculum should cater for better opportunities for English for speakers of other languages (ESOL) and exposure to courses about understanding cultural diversity.

Sassia Ghedjghoudj from Algeria, in her chapter about Algerian teacher education, also discusses the need for a teacher education curriculum that will address cultural issues, especially those relating to modernity and traditionalism in the context of religion, and the Arabic and Berber languages. She makes a strong plea for relevance in both subject content and teaching methodologies, so that a proper melding of modernity and traditionalism can be achieved. This will hopefully produce a more culture-sensitive teaching profession.

The need for pedagogies that are culture-sensitive, which can be combined with other pedagogical models when necessary, is the basis of the argument put forward by Elwyn Thomas in his chapter about the prospects for a culture-sensitive teacher education. It would be the task of teacher educators under these circumstances to develop teaching strategies for their trainees, so that they could meet the cultural needs of pupils in multicultural classrooms. The chapter written by Tanzanian-born Ladislaus M Semali, now living in the United States, continues along a similar theme, of making pedagogies and school curricula in countries like Tanzania more culturally relevant. However, he emphasizes the value of indigenous knowledges and pedagogies, which have in most cases been ignored in the pursuit of Western knowledge. He makes the case for the legitimization of indigenous pedagogies to be part of the training curriculum, as it would provide teachers who would be more in tune with their African culture and so provide relevance to schooling in Tanzania.

Finally, cultural perspectives influencing teacher education are not confined only to the classroom. A number of authors whose works were not specifically included under this theme also observed that cultural influences extend to school management styles, power relationships within training organizations, relationships between school and community, and between training institutions and government. The role of external agents such as international consultants comes in for particular criticism, in their apparent insensitivity to local norms, modes of discourse and culture-specific forms of decision making. A thorough knowledge of socio-cultural contexts together with an awareness of the cultural intricacies of the way governments operate would provide a much healthier base from which change and innovation can take root. More important, however, is that research about the cultural bases underpinning teacher education would go some way in ensuring the sustainability of new and worthwhile ideas for improving teacher quality.

Training challenges for teachers and teacher educators: ongoing projects

Chapters that have been included under this theme examine the dilemmas and consequent training challenges for teachers and teacher educators in a number of ongoing projects in teacher education. The projects include multigrade teaching in the Caribbean, preparation for HIV / AIDS teaching in Africa, a project on teacher education democratization in the Gambia, training teachers for urban settings in North America, so-called borderless education as a consequence of ICT in higher education in the United Kingdom, restructuring Indian teacher education for improving the quality of both rural and urban teachers and, finally, the role of reflective methods in training Israeli teachers.

All the ongoing projects underline the need for training that is on the job, relevant and integral to the wider role of teachers in the community. The notion of partnership in its various guises is a sub-theme that runs through many of the projects discussed, because it has become a key concept in meeting the challenges of effective teacher training in many countries.

In Chris Berry's chapter about multigrade teaching in the Caribbean, he discusses his experience of training teachers for this type of teaching. He argues that, while multigrade teaching may be seen as an alternative to monograde teaching in countries where there are teacher shortages, it also has several overarching advantages, which include developing teachers who are competent at curriculum design, who use more imaginative assessment procedures and are better at class management. These advantages emerge because the multigrade situation imposes quite stringent demands on teachers. Therefore, the training for this type of teaching will need to reflect how trainees meet such demands by developing effective instructional and organizational skills.

The chapter by Roy Carr-Hill deals exclusively with the problems of training teachers to confront the challenge of HIV / AIDS education. He argues that existing content and methodologies used in the training curriculum require a different approach. He advocates the use of new materials and content, and an emphasis on how to communicate with children and adolescents on the topic of AIDS. A key requirement is that teachers need to be trained to have the right attitudes before they tackle the task of teaching about the danger of HIV / AIDS.

The increasing concerns for the respect of human rights and discrimination against gender and sexual orientation, and the need for a greater degree of openness and democratization amongst teachers and teacher educators have also emerged as issues in teacher education in several countries. The chapter by Lynn Davies from Birmingham, UK on the democratization of teacher education refers to a unique project in this field, in which she and her colleagues are developing materials and methods to involve Gambian teacher trainees in citizenship education. The project emphasizes the need for local participation, and takes seriously the importance of socio-cultural contexts in developing this type of training.

The problems of training teachers who can accommodate the special needs of urban and rural schools, while not entirely a new issue, remain a cause for concern for education professionals in many parts of the world. The chapter by Ken Howey and Linda Post from the United States describes the development of a prototype mixed partnership in teacher preparation for high-need urban schools in their part of the United States. This ongoing and longest-running teacher education study in the United States is called UNITE (Urban Network to Improve Teacher Education), and sets out to recruit, prepare and retain teachers by learning about the problems of urban schooling on the job, and in the framework of an inter-organizational support system. Urban issues also emerged for Vijay Raina in his chapter about teacher education in India but, unlike the mainly urban-focused work of Howey and Post, Raina examines the urban and rural divide and its implications for quality teacher education. He describes the prospects of the current restructuring of teacher education, which attempts to address such disparities as the urban–rural contrasts in schooling. The role of special institutes to upgrade teachers for primary and secondary schools in India is already part of ongoing measures designed to meet the challenges that Raina identifies.

The chapter by Anita Pincas from the United Kingdom discusses an ongoing project in the use of ICT. Pincas argues that ICT is having a marked effect on traditional approaches to teaching and learning in higher education, including teacher training. She raises the intriguing notion of a 'borderless education' at the tertiary level, which entails a rethinking of the way knowledge and skills are sourced and subsequently used by students through computer screens. Knowledge taught in conventional higher education institutions need not only come from the university teacher any more. The impact of ICT has already affected the interaction between the university teacher and his or her student, so that the university lecturer is less of an instructor and more of a facilitator and mentor.

Finally, the chapter by Tikva Zohar from Israel deals with the changing face of teacher education in her country, with reference to a country-wide, ongoing internship programme. In the context of this programme, Zohar discusses her research on reflective techniques in teacher preparation. She shows that, by improving the quality of teachers through intensive fieldwork that employs reflective techniques, the professional prospects for a more sensitive and yet effective teaching force will be realized in the not-too-distant future.

In summary, the prospects discussed by contributors to this theme give hope and encouragement to those who seek change for the sake of improved educational practice, and the development of a more reflective teaching force.

The emergence of common issues

A chapter-by-chapter analysis by the author of common issues relating to teacher education that transcend national boundaries indicated that a number of areas emerged as current concerns in developing teacher education in the various countries that appeared in this volume. The issues of *socio-cultural context* to teacher education and the need for a *training curriculum that is relevant* and practical figured highly with many authors. Both issues were discussed mainly under the themes of reform, cultural perspectives on teacher education and ongoing programmes for teacher education improvement. In many instances these two issues were seen as being related, as a lack of knowledge of the social and cultural context of a society by the planners of reform inevitably invites criticisms of irrelevance and insensitivity towards the educational needs of that society, leading ultimately to reform failure.

The subject of developing *appropriate pedagogies* to make teaching and learning more effective, and the implication these would have for training was also an issue of common concern. It was pointed out that, from both a cultural viewpoint and that of the growing influence of ICT, teaching and learning styles will have to change to meet the demands of learners, whether they are in higher education or in schools. Accompanying the issue of developing pedagogical skills, several authors raised the issue of *developing reflective techniques* as part of pre-service and in-service education, while still maintaining the need to give trainees a sound technicist training as well. Issues such as the *changing nature of knowledge* and a *meaningful link between theory and practice* were also perceived by some authors as part of the wider debate about training teachers to be effective, up to date and relevant in times of rapid change.

The issues of *professionalization* and *the role of universities* involved in the process were also discussed widely by many authors. The essential role of universities in upgrading the quality of teacher education was seen as crucial to the future of sound teacher professionalism, especially in countries like Argentina and Singapore, where there has been a concerted effort to link teacher education more closely to the tertiary sector. Closely related to the role of universities in teacher training is the issue of *partnership*. This subject emerged with considerable frequency, the main focus being on links between training institutions and schools.

However, other forms of partnership such as involving schools, community and training institution, between institutions/faculties of teacher training and those training doctors and engineers, and more equitable partnerships with government were also discussed. The issue of *government control of teacher education*, which was seen as integral to the notion of partnership and the need for change and reform, was discussed from mainly two opposing viewpoints. In countries such as Korea, Japan and Singapore, a softer and more positive view is taken of government control, as it is closely bound with economic success and national identity, issues that are close to the heart of policy makers in these countries. This is in contrast to countries like the United Kingdom and the United States where government intervention is viewed by professionals with much scepticism and in some cases with open hostility.

Finally, the *historical and political context* that forms the background to many changes and reforms in teacher education in all countries was another issue that emerged. In the case of Poland, the communist past had coloured many of the rigid approaches to teacher training. In countries like Malaysia, South Africa, Tanzania and the Gambia, colonial and neo-colonial influences still affect, to some extent, existing structures and processes of the education system and, by implication, teacher education. However, modernization and globalization have meant that such narrow influences have become weakened over the years, although both positive as well as negative features of the past still continue to be recognized by these countries.

Section I

Control of teacher education by the state with reference to schools and higher education

1. Socrates was right? Teacher education systems and the state

Robert Cowen

If by any chance the young teacher still had any spirit left in him after this course of training, the conditions under which he was expected to practise his profession were calculated to grind it out of him, for in most of the Australian colonies in the last quarter of the nineteenth century teachers were engaged under a system of 'payment by results' whereby their livelihood was made dependent upon their success in beating the three R's into their unfortunate charges. (Austin, 1961: 237)

Introduction

Once upon a time, in the United Kingdom of Great Britain and Northern Ireland at least, we knew where we were and where we were going. Teachers would become a profession. The universities, with the tacit agreement of the state, were working hard to improve the status and the potential remuneration of teachers, through improvements in their qualifications and the knowledge base of initial teacher education. This was the situation in the 1960s. Currently, in 2001, we know where we are and where we are going, in England at least. Teachers are going to become a 'new profession'; and the state, with the uneasy agreement of the universities, is working hard to improve the status, the remuneration and the recruitment of teachers, and the knowledge base of initial teacher education. The difference between the 1960s and the contemporary moment is that the power relations (and the trust) between teachers, the universities and the English state have been altered dramatically. There are also new definitions of what counts as the knowledge fit for teachers. This has produced new dilemmas and some strange prospects for teacher education in England.

What happened in England, why this happened and the consequences of the current situation are the indirect concern of this chapter – but the theme is approached comparatively. An understanding of the extreme case of England, which is only briefly sketched, is sought through a comparative perspective. What are some of the signifiers of the struggles between states, teachers and universities about the proper education (or training) of teachers, which put the English case into perspective? How have definitions of what counts as 'educational knowledge' altered? Are there any implications of the reform of the training of teachers in England for the education of teachers elsewhere? The chapter is structured around three areas, professions and states, discourses on mass teacher education and educational knowledge.

Professions and states

It is well known that professions have particular sociological characteristics: they perform an essential public service; they possess esoteric knowledge based on intellectual principles; they control entry and exit to the profession; and they have a code of ethics that can be used for expulsion from the profession in cases of violation of the code (Lieberman, 1956). Sociological and comparative accounts of teaching as a profession typically arrive at the conclusion that teachers are a 'semi-profession' (Jackson, 1970). Within such assumptions about the nature of a profession, debates about the quality of teachers were partly construed in terms of the knowledge that teachers possessed. How strong was their initial training in providing academic knowledge? How thorough and lengthy was their preparation in the acquisition of 1) theories of how to teach (*didactics*), 2) their actual experience of teaching under observation and in controlled conditions (*teaching practice*) and 3) their knowledge of the philosophical, historical and sociological framing of educational ideas, processes and institutions, understood in social context or contexts (*the foundations of education*)?

The US debate of the 1960s for example contained a strong critique of the inadequate knowledge that teachers were alleged to have of the academic subjects (eg history, mathematics, etc) that they would teach in the schools (Conant, 1963; Koerner, 1963). The English debate of the 1960s was very much about how to strengthen the 'foundations' of teacher education, including psychology and the theoretical underpinnings (Herbart, Piaget, Mead, Dewey and so on) of the pedagogic act (Tibble, 1966). Also in dispute was how much observation and practical teaching experience in the schools should be packed into initial teacher education (Taylor, 1990: 112). In the 1960s these debates were criss-crossed by anxieties about teacher supply, problems over how to finance teacher education, and concern about class sizes and the levels of remuneration for teachers.

However, this was a particular historic moment in the countries of north-west Europe and in the United States. Controls by central or regional surveillance agencies of the state were relatively light-handed. The universities were important in defining what was a 'good teacher'. There was an understanding that the academic qualifications awarded by universities or colleges of education would be turned into state-issued licences to teach. The reform efforts of the 1960s were not about how to increase state surveillance of the details of teacher education. They centred on how to improve the status of teachers and teacher education by absorbing initial training into the university sector, or placing it under university influence. Thus the code phrase of the period was the expression 'an all-graduate profession'; and some of the literature tended to assume that organizing this properly would solve quality problems in teacher education (Holmes, 1973).

What such a phrase and such assumptions hide is the actual power relations between states and the teaching profession. Aspirations and policies for an 'all-graduate profession' in Australia, Canada, England, France, West Germany, New Zealand and the United States could be held only within a certain set of cultural assumptions and stable power relations: the concern of ministries of education or their equivalents was mainly about the supply of a fairly well-qualified teaching force in sufficient numbers, at costs judged to be reasonable. In other words, these 'liberal democratic' states working within an ideology of equality of educational opportunity concentrated on the infrastructure of provision for teacher education. *De jure*, such states licensed teachers; *de facto*, academics controlled access to the teaching force through university-dominated examination and certification systems.

However, these ways of thinking about teacher education are bad comparative education. They generalize a particular moment in the history of teacher education in the second half of the 20th century in a particular selection of countries – as if these patterns of relation between the state and teachers were and are normal. The assumption that academics and universities are normally in charge of the selection and training of teachers is parochial. And the explicit assumption that ideal-typical models of a profession (of the kind illustrated above) have a unique power of explanation is dangerous. At best such models of a profession permit a simplistic – more precisely a jejune – comparative education. At worst they hide the history of the construction of professions (Larson, 1977) and the power relations that define the knowledge to be given to teachers.

Power relations between states, universities and teachers vary. Even 'normal states' have complex histories that continually (but not linearly and sequentially) redefine the relationships between the state, the university, and teachers and their education. Other states have even more dramatic histories. *Transformative radical states* cull and co-opt the professions, including teachers. These are states that, to an explicit view of the future, redefine the relations between politics, the economy and civil society. The economy becomes subordinated to political principle. *Transformative conservative states* confirm the status and power of professions, but within clear ideological parameters. These are states that, around an explicit vision of a selected past, reconfirm religious principle, and try to stabilize the economy and a traditional social order, not least by affirming the status of professions and teachers. *Recuperating states* cull and reliberate the professions, including teachers. Discursive space is opened up for them (and the university) to redefine an education, including an education for teachers, which is appropriate for that recuperation. 'Recuperative states' include Japan and West Germany after 1945, Brazil from about 1980, Argentina, Chile, Greece, Portugal and Spain after their encounters with 'men on horseback', and the countries of Central Europe after 1990 – such as Hungary, Latvia, Poland, the former East Germany and so on. Thus illustratively, after 1945, with different degrees of determination and efficiency, the occupying powers in Japan and Germany culled the teaching force: teachers were subjected to a minimum test of political identity. In Japan, teachers associated with 'militarism' had to leave teaching (Duke, 1973). In the British zone of Germany, teachers strongly affected by the ideology of the National Socialist Party were dismissed within the broader policy of 'de-Nazification' of public institutions (Hearnden, 1978).

Thus (and without assuming that all states in the world can be forced into three or four categories) there is a complex range of relations between states and the university, and the education of teachers. In particular, the discursive space that is defined by the interaction of the political principles and actions of the state, the universities and teacher education varies sharply. That space may be opened up, as it was by US people in Japan after 1945 although to their distaste a left-wing teacher education movement emerged rapidly (Duke, 1973). Or discursive space may be tightly demarcated. Supervisory agents (such as the People's Liberation Army) may penetrate the universities. Similarly agencies such as Narkompros, strongly influenced by particular political theories, may redefine the responsibilities of the universities, as in the USSR (Fitzpatrick, 1970); or the All-Union Academy of Pedagogical Sciences may define closely what is good (and useful) educational research in, say, psychological theory or curriculum. It could, in contrast, be argued that there are many societies, 'liberal democratic societies', that permit on the basis of political principle major discursive freedoms for the definition of genuinely professional concerns in education. It is in these societies that teaching is a profession, or has the possibilities to become one.

Discourses on mass teacher education

Inventing the new social technology of the mass elementary schools and the parallel social technology for mass teacher education needed considerable feats of imagination and some practical work in institutional creation; or borrowing, because the discursive space was international. The Prussian model was an attractive one for such educational leaders as Horace Mann in the United States, Victor Cousin in France, Kay-Shuttleworth in England and Egerton Ryerson in Canada. The finance of the new teacher education systems, what should be learnt, the preferred teaching styles, textbooks and examination systems were all matters for invention. Who would train the teachers, what should they learn, who would certify them as teachers and which schools would they teach in? All these problems had to be addressed and solved in different historical contexts characterized by different political and cultural agendas for the construction of mass teacher education systems.

From various starting points, the 19th century was marked by struggles over which institutions should train teachers. There was tension between church and state in many countries; and there were choices to be made (in a variety of vocabularies) between a range of monitorial and pupil-teacher models of training, and efforts to construct 'normal schools'. It was not always the case that the 'normal school model' became dominant (though it tended to be strong in places influenced by France – such as Argentina and Brazil).

Sometimes the normal school model lost momentum. For example, although the state of Massachusetts in 1838 established four normal schools, the schools became awkwardly caught between the community college movement and the university – and the increasing tendency for their students to use them as routes of upward social mobility (Herbst, 1989). In contrast in England the 'teachers college' had gained support by the end of the 19th century. The monitorial and pupil–teacher apprenticeship models of teacher preparation had tended to trap the future elementary school teacher in the elementary schools themselves and by the end of the century these systems were being severely criticized in public reports (Dent, 1977). A slow growth of residential training colleges had begun earlier. By 1890, there were about 40 and they had supplied about a quarter of the elementary school teaching force, as a system of day-training colleges came into place at the end of the century (Aldrich, 1990). So, the development of institutions for the training of elementary school teachers, although it was patterned, was by no means similar in all countries.

However, there was a greater consensus on the correct image of 'conduct, character and manner' (to use one of Basil Bernstein's classic phrases) and the knowledge that was appropriate for elementary school teachers. In (Upper) Canada, the training of teachers was extracted from community influence and, in the schools and in teacher training, Ryerson's sophisticated theories on moral education and discipline informed both technical instruction (eg in reading) and the building of attitudes of moral self-control in teachers and taught. Sound moral character – recognized by a minister of religion – was a requirement for entry to the teachers' examination itself (Curtis, 1988). In the English teacher training colleges, the emphasis on moral training and comportment was very strong, even to the point perhaps where it was taken as the 'chief business'; the training of men and women tended to take place in separate institutions, and the colleges themselves became closed and insulated and very practical cultures (Rich, 1933). For the United States, Cubberley's classic text paints a detailed picture of a simple and formal curriculum for both teachers and taught. Cubberley also points to some straightforward moral rules: teachers were required to 'refrain from all spirituous liquors while engaged in this school, and not to enter the schoolhouse when intoxicated, nor to lose time through such intemperance' (Cubberley, 1947: 326).

The point, however, is not the rehearsal of detailed examples of the social control of teachers – this has already been done brilliantly by Willard Waller (1965) for the United States. The point is, rather, that with this creation of these major and administered systems for the training of a mass teacher force for the 19th century elementary schools, a subsequent problem was being created. Clear distinctions were being created among teachers, in terms of their qualifications, their salaries, the gendered nature of their professional careers and their opportunities for further study. The answer to the mid-19th-century question as to how the education of teachers might be institution-alized and who would control that system had been given. New institutions would be created, curricula for teacher training devised and qualification systems invented.

But this answer subsequently created another layer in the complex problems of the relations between the state, the university and other institu-tions of teacher education.

In Europe at least, in the *lycée*, in the *Gymnasium*, in the grammar schools and especially in the 'public schools' of England, there had gradually emerged a well-qualified teaching corps, educated in a different way and in a different tradition. These teachers were certified for teaching by the possession of a bachelor's degree (or its equivalent in, say, Germany), rather than training in pedagogy and the knowledge content of an advanced version of the elementary school curriculum.

Thus by the 1920s in most countries of north-west Europe and in the United States there were two relatively distinct cohorts in the national teaching force. One group possessed certificates (based on a year or two years' training) in a specialist normal school or teacher training college. Typically this group would be female, be paid less, have lower social status and work in the elementary sector of the school system. Other teachers – typically male with bachelor degrees from universities, with higher social status and higher pay – would work in the academic secondary schools of their countries (Bereday and Lauwerys, 1963).

These structures established *de facto* not merely two 'professions' but two 'circulation systems' for teachers. One group came out of the elementary schools and after training in a 'normal school' went back into the elementary school. The other group, after long-cycle secondary education in a *lycée*, *Gymnasium* or grammar school and experience of 'the university', went back into the academic secondary sector.

These dual-track systems of teacher education took their full formation in the period between the two world wars. During or after the war, at different speeds in different countries, the dissonance between these two career tracks, training institutions, qualification patterns, remuneration levels and social status became visible. An important turning point was World War Two itself, for many of the north European countries and the United States and Canada. Clearly some of the pressures for a reform of teacher education (and the schools) grew out of the concern for constructing 'democratic' societies (Bereday and Lauwerys, 1963).

Thus the basic themes of the post-war teacher education crisis were in place, rapidly compounded by the 'common school movement' in northern Europe in the 1960s. The common school movement highlighted the division of labour in the teaching forces of those countries. The closed circulation system of teachers' educational origins, and their school destinations, and the inadequacies of seeing teachers in post-war democracies as moral guardians and agents of social control for the working class were dealt with rapidly by a wave of reforms. The new solution was to 'upgrade' the teacher education traditionally linked to the 'elementary school' by absorbing it into – or placing it firmly under – the influence of the university sector (Judge *et al*, 1994).

However, this brought into sharp focus the beginnings of the tension over the forms of knowledge that should be transmitted to teachers: the craft knowledge associated with the pupil–teacher tradition and even the teachers' colleges; the work done in universities as 'educational studies'; and later the links of teacher education with educational research itself. This third theme in the post-war reforms of teacher education had taken a long time to develop and it is still with us. It is this aspect of teacher education, the knowledge judged fit for teachers and the contestation for the discursive space in which that will be decided and re-decided, that is a vital dilemma in the contemporary teacher education situation in a number of countries.

Educational knowledge

The third issue, the relationship between the practical and the common-sense knowledge required for school work and the creation of 'educational studies', required almost a hundred years to become clear. Teacher education was more and more closely linked to the universities. The education of teachers was increasingly organized in three academic layers: training in an academic subject; a formal initial cycle of teacher education organized around the 'foundations' of education; and a second cycle of teacher education linked to formal academic study of education celebrated in a range of diplomas and MA degrees offered by the universities. The shift had occurred. Vocabularies changed and included terms such as 'reflective practitioners' (Schön, 1983, 1987). In Australia, Canada, England and Wales, Scotland and the United States, the universities in their role as the providers of the initial knowledge base of traditional professions (such as the church, the law and medicine) were given freedoms to define this knowledge base and to construct it in disciplinary form.

The problem was that in some countries discordant voices identifying incompetence were emerging. Teachers were perhaps reflective but they were not yet competent. Discourses about the education of teachers in terms of 'professionalism' can easily tip into discourses about 'competence'. This began to happen in the United States in the early 1970s and in England also about that time, but with greater speed in the 1980s. The US solution was initially expressed in the competency-based teacher education movement (Burton, 1977). The pressures in England were initially expressed through the Council for the Accreditation of Teacher Education (CATE) (Taylor, 1990). In England the pressures rapidly led (with a new, aggressive and reforming Conservative administration) to increased surveillance of all teacher performance, including that within universities; the weakening of university influence on teacher education; partnerships with the schools; and ultimately the creation of the Teacher Training Agency. Similar processes occurred and are occurring in Australia and New Zealand in particular (Scott and Freeman-Moir, 2000). The basic pattern is that the state itself ceases to agree with the traditional assumptions about the creation of 'a profession'. It disputes that the universities can be trusted to deliver a cadre of 'reflective professionals'. It may be questioned whether in contemporary Australia, England and New Zealand the governments want 'reflective practioners' as this concept – in different vocabularies – has been understood since 1945.

Currently both that which teachers learn and that which specialists in education in the university consider good research become subject to the tests of immediate use and applicability. Criteria for admission to the teaching force become more and more based on practical experience; teacher education becomes teacher training; teacher training is increasingly school-based; and teacher training approximates more and more to immersion in daily school practice (which has pedagogic actors and pedagogic actions that are also increasingly under state surveillance).

Overall, a new political ideology, in some countries, has melded a concern for teacher competence into a powerful new discourse about excellence in education, managerialism, surveillance and new professionalism. 'Quality control' is the key ideological concept here – along with the equation of educational excellence with 'standards and assessment'. The point is interestingly opaque. Clearly it applies in principle to Nazi Germany, to the United States, to contemporary Iran and France, and to apartheid South Africa – just as its analogue ($E = mc^2$) applies to the universe.

The steps towards this version of excellence – after the existence of contemporary incompetence among teachers has been asserted – are to find solutions in 1) the correct management of schools, 2) objective standards of performance and 3) agencies of surveillance external to the schools (and the universities). A version of this efficiency movement was visible in the United States in the 1920s (Callahan, 1962) and in England from the mid-1970s (Stoll, 1992; Mortimore *et al*, 1988). The third and final step – carried out strenuously in England – is to separate teacher training from the universities, and establish a state quango for the definition and delivery of teacher training on a school-dominated model.

Conclusion

This historical shift and the current sociological and political process are a combination of the state power with an ideology of managerialism, competence and efficiency movements, and anticipatory socialization for teachers into school cultures that are themselves dominated by such credos. One relevant theoretician – to begin to assess how we have moved from the discourse of reflective practitioner, to the idea of a competent practitioner, to the concepts of 'new professionalism' and *fonctionnaires* – is Foucault. How was the discursive space closed? The new discourse is deeply penetrative, and has already affected the daily practices and pedagogies of schools of education in England.

As a university academic, I am fascinated by the politics and sociology embedded in the details of these processes. As a practising university teacher, I am appalled. As a citizen, I am angry at the cash costs of state surveillance exercises. As I no longer teach in schools, I cannot hope to be accused of corrupting the young of Athens or London. Perhaps I should be accused of permitting the corruption of the old: the visions of thinkers such as Socrates, Dewey and Freire of what a good education is and what teachers are for.

Acknowledgements

I am grateful to colleagues at the Institute of Education, David Lambert, Denis Lawton and Michael Totterdell, for drawing my attention to bibliographic materials on teacher education in contemporary England; and to Marianne Larsen for advising me about materials on teacher education in 19th-century Canada.

References

Aldrich, R (1990) The evolution of teacher education, in *Initial Teacher Education: Policies and progress*, ed N J Graves, Kogan Page, London

Austin, A G (1961) *Australian Education 1788–1900: Church, state and public education in colonial Australia*, Pitman, Melbourne

Bereday, G Z F and Lauwerys, J A (1963) *The Education and Training of Teachers: The yearbook of education*, Evans Brothers, London

Burton, A (1977) Competency-based teacher education in the United States, *Compare*, 7 (1), pp 31–39

Callahan, R E (1962) *Education and the Cult of Efficiency*, University of Chicago Press, Chicago

Conant, J (1963) *The Education of American Teachers*, McGraw-Hill, New York

Cubberley, E (1947) *Public Education in the United States: A study and interpretation of American educational history*, Houghton Mifflin, Cambridge, MA

Curtis, B (1988) *Building the Educational State: Canada West, 1836–1871*, Falmer Press, London

Dent, H C (1977) *The Training of Teachers in England and Wales, 1800–1975*, Hodder & Stoughton, Sevenoaks, Kent

Duke, B C (1973) *Japan's Militant Teachers*, University Press of Hawaii, Honolulu

Fitzpatrick, S (1970) *The Commissariat of Enlightenment: Soviet organization of education and the arts under Lunacharsky*, Cambridge University Press, Cambridge

Hearnden, A (1978) *The British in Germany: Education reconstruction after 1945*, Hamish Hamilton, London

Herbst, J (1989) Teacher preparation in the nineteenth century: institutions and purposes, in *American Teachers: Histories of a profession at work*, ed D Warren, Macmillan Publishing Company, New York

Holmes, B (1973) Teacher education in England and Wales: a comparative view, in *The Education of Teachers in Britain*, ed D E Lomax, John Wiley, London

Jackson, J A (1970) *Professions and Professionalisation*, Cambridge University Press, Cambridge

Judge, H *et al* (1994) *The University and Teachers: France, the United States, England*, Oxford Studies in Comparative Education, vol 4 (1/2), Triangle Books, Oxford

Koerner, J (1963) *The Miseducation of American Teachers*, Houghton Mifflin, Boston

Larson, M S (1977) *The Rise of Professionalism: A sociological analysis*, University of California Press, Berkeley

Lieberman, M (1956) *Education as a Profession*, Prentice Hall, New York

Mortimore, P *et al* (1988) *School Matters: The junior years*, Open Books, Wells

Rich, R W (1933, 1972) *The Training of Teachers in England and Wales during the Nineteenth Century*, Cedric Chivers, Bath, Cambridge University Press, Cambridge

Schön, D A (1983) *The Reflective Practitioner*, Temple Smith, London

Schön, D A (1987) *Educating the Reflective Practitioner*, Jossey-Bass, London

Scott, A and Freeman-Moir, F (2000) (eds) *Tomorrow's Teachers: International and critical perspectives on teacher education*, Canterbury University Press, Christchurch, NZ

Stoll, L (1992) Teacher growth in the effective school, in *Teacher Development and Educational Change*, ed M Fullan and A Hargreaves, Cassell, New York

Taylor, W (1990) The control of teacher education: the Council for the Accreditation of Teacher Education, in *Initial Teacher Education: Policies and progress*, ed N J Graves, Kogan Page, London

Tibble, J W (ed) (1966) *The Study of Education*, Routledge, London

Waller, W (1965) *The Sociology of Teaching*, John Wiley & Sons, New York

2. Teacher education in Argentina: at a crossroads or at a loss?

Teresa Davis

Introduction

Since the origins of Argentina as a nation in the 19th century, education has been a relevant issue, and the legislation at the time marked the way for future developments ever since. Governments of different ideologies made a point of expressing their commitment to education as a subject close to the hearts of people. Hence, in the 1990s, marked by an overall concern in the world about education, the state in Argentina was not an exception and sought to adapt to the times and extend the reach of education as a force for development. The first section of this chapter will describe the legal background that framed the debate during the last decade. This is followed by an account of some of the positions taken by specialists in the last 30 years.

The legal and historical background

To understand the present and future context of Argentine teacher education, it is necessary to examine both the legal and the historical background. Let us therefore first examine the legal background and then the historical context.

Education laws, teachers and teacher training

The passing of the Federal Law of Education (1993) and the subsidiary Law for Higher Education (1995), in particular, caused deep concern with those involved in teacher education in Argentina. This mistrust was due to a long spell of authoritarian governments and a costly return to democracy that slowed the process of restoring confidence about the intentions of those in authority. This lack of confidence translated itself into the question whether politicians produced reforms in education to reduce public expenses or, as they proclaimed, to improve the quality of education in general and of teaching in particular (Alliaud, 1997). The Federal Education Law extended compulsory education to nine years, and redesigned the primary and secondary school system, with a consequent demand for teachers specifically trained for the new levels and modalities.

Behind these legal aspects lies the fact that the Federal Law of Education aimed at introducing a profound transformation in education, and challenged the definition of the role of teachers. The professional teacher was seen in a new light as one who should be prepared to find solutions to teaching and even administrative problems, and autonomous to act within the new organization, be it public or private. The term autonomy, though, required redefinition to suit the new organizations that demanded independent decision-making abilities and accountability.

Tracing the historical context

In 1970, during the military government that ruled under the name of the Argentine Revolution, teacher education was transformed: normal secondary schools became non-university tertiary-level institutes, that is, they were to be dependent on the National Higher Education Department. In their origin, normal schools had had as a main objective to train officials not intellectuals. They were teaching centres, not centres for the production of knowledge. Even after their inclusion within higher education, these centres for initial teacher training continued to be organized as the traditional schools were.

In the early 1970s, teachers defended their position as corporate workers and refused to be seen as independent professionals. They reinforced their positions as civil servants dependent on the state and as such claimed their rights as workers, losing in the new status the degree of autonomy associated with being a professional. With the advent of democracy in the 1980s, and released from the fear of military repression, collective claims, channelled in strikes for better salaries, indicated that teachers wished to confirm themselves as workers.

The lack of reliability of the state school system and the indifference of the public led to a drop in the quality of teaching and pointed to a process of deterioration in the image of the teacher. This process went hand in hand with the need of the new democratic government to manage the last and probably most crucial stage in the crisis of the welfare state that had started in the 1970s. It faced the implementation of policies that minimized the intervention of the state in the funding of the school system and caused the transference of its responsibilities to agents that were not prepared to assume them. However, in the late 1980s, the National Ministry of Education presented a project to bring the education of primary school teachers back into secondary school. In order to extend programmes of studies that were considered insufficient, the project continued only two more years after secondary school, thus not upsetting the ratio between time devoted to studies and salary expectations. Hence, the proposal restored the four-year preparation but with the disadvantage of starting at an earlier point in secondary school (Southwell, 1995).

The new curriculum implemented the initial education of teachers for basic education in the last two years of secondary school oriented to teaching and linked it with specific training in two subsequent years of higher education. The attempt failed to achieve country-wide acceptance since only a hundred normal schools joined the experience in 1988 and registered the last cohort in 1990. By that time, there was large agreement about the need to preserve the education of teachers within higher education.

Meanwhile, as was stated earlier, the democratic government of the 1980s had to administer the last stages of the welfare state within the context of a post-authoritarian model. This implied difficulties in restoring the power of intervention for the state in education and in changing the authoritarian discourse at the same time. With this in mind, modifications were introduced to the contents of subjects such as citizenship education, as a constant reminder for people of the importance of preserving democracy.

Reform and the role of external influences

As in many other developing countries, external agencies came to the rescue of economies that were not ready to face the challenges of the time. The guidelines of action were that post-social, neo-liberal governments like the one in Argentina ceased to act on the economy. Their role was to guarantee the rules of the game, transferring leadership, development and the distribution of assets to the marketplace (Filmus, 1996).

Hopes and aspirations?

Some of this dependency on funding agencies was evident in a strong tendency towards restricting public expenses, in particular those assigned to social policies. That implied not only suppressing welfare institutions but also reducing the value of their products by reducing the quality of services rendered. In this context, marketization missed the logic of education as a public service, since the school had proved to be a crucial element in the construction and consolidation of democracy and a strategy for socio-economic development. In Argentina as well as in the rest of Latin America, educational reforms were dependent on their sources of funding. As an emerging country Argentina depended on the World Bank lending policies that were followed up by policy and decision makers. The Bank advocated educational policies based on neo-classical economic principles that had been relevant 20 years earlier – efficiency and a transparent and competitive market – and evaluated schools as companies. This appreciation of education was a package to be adopted by receiving nations that in many cases, like Argentina, were not able to reply with reasonable alternative proposals (Coraggio, 1997).

The implementation of these policies was detached from reality: they were imposed top down, negotiated and communicated to those in charge of carrying them out, who had not had any part in their design. It is in this general context that teacher education takes place. The reform in the education of teachers is still slowly growing as a strategic component in the educational reforms, together with the power of collective negotiations of the unions and their development as recognized interlocutors with the different governments.

The reality of thwarted expectations

A strengthened democracy in 1992 allowed a joint confrontation – by teachers, parents and students – against the central government for a common right: quality in the education received by their children. The demand against the Ministry of Education for better salaries and overall investment produced an interesting effect: teachers had come out of their cocoon and made contact with the outside world, integrating themselves with the community they served. In spite of this, the interest in improving the teaching profession – with adequate salaries and working conditions and with solid teacher education – has not matched the decisive importance it has in educational changes. To go back to the historical development of the debate, the transformations proposed by external agencies were not implemented in the 70s but they were raised 20 years later. The military regime did not enforce them since it would not have been viable to impose market-focused policies openly. Nevertheless, the conditions were intentionally created to allow this viability in later years through a pattern of lack of interest in education, low investment and resulting low quality.

With the application of neo-liberal strategies within a framework of profound socio-economic and political transformations and a diminishing role of the state, the pattern succeeded. The welfare state failed to supply the needs of the majority, and the belief that investing in education was not attractive in a context of low economic growth strengthened the idea that the state should not participate in education. After the process of hyperinflation, stabilizing and privatizing strategies in agreement with new models of globalization found the support of large numbers of people; thus, marketplace policies generated wide consensus. The loans from international agencies, such as the World Bank, were accompanied by strong recommendations about the administration of education. These recommendations were closely followed owing to the lack of alternative democratic proposals rather than the strength of the requirements (Filmus, 1997). Large sectors, teacher unions in particular, criticized the decisions but their criticism outweighed their capacity for proposing new guidelines for transformation in education.

In this respect, decentralization turned out to be key to transformation, and it was proposed on four principles: financial convenience, bureaucratic simplification, quality improvement and equality in decision making. Later assessment by international agencies proved financial convenience overrode the other principles, and the ensuing reduction in investment resulted in diminishing quality and equality. According to union leaders, teacher education should not be excluded from the general picture since the teaching profession acted as a hinge in any attempt at transformation. Whereas decentralization proved an asset at first, in that the salaries of teachers appeared at an advantage, this advantage turned into an element of negotiation later with teachers standing at the losing end of the deal (Maffei, 1997). This fed mistrust in the profession and discouraged prospective candidates from becoming teachers.

The fact was that the solution offered in the 1980s had only been an attempt at designing new courses of studies that would match the type of job and recognition attainable on graduation, not a true curricular improvement. Again in the 1990s, the overall educational reform in progress conditioned any programme of initial or continuing teacher education. However, teacher education had not become, as expected, one of the most important strategies for educational success. Those prospects also discouraged candidates from taking up studies that only seemed to attract students who performed poorly in secondary school or who came from a low-income or low-motivation background (Messina, 2000).

In the process of overall reform, the questions were many. Two main ones were how to transform a school conceived 300 years before to answer the needs of a globalized world, and how to respect cultural differences in a school that had a homogenizing structure. A third one was unavoidable: how best to train teachers who would be faced daily with the uncertainties of present situations that bring together the problems of the past and the demands of the future. According to Popkewitz (1994), reform programmes constitute an answer to change; they are not isolated occurrences and they appear as nations face transformations in different sectors of society. In Argentina, at a time of social awareness after the repressive years of the military governments, education was not going to be able to avoid becoming an element of discussion in the demands to the state for action.

In this debate, teacher education appeared to show a strong tendency towards becoming one of the myths of the end of the century. Teachers should be educated to be able to counter all queries, disorders and anxieties of individuals and of different groups baffled and displaced by a constantly changing world and a deep economic crisis (Diker and Terigi, 1997). There was the assumption that an education of this kind was not available and probably had never existed, even in a past full of certainties; nevertheless, something had to be attempted.

Old questions about new reforms

Faced with the rethinking of teacher education, two questions asked at the end of the 19th century were still valid. What do teachers need to know? How are they going to be trained (Diker, 1997)? The answers would be linked to the definition of the mission of a teacher at any particular time. In the 1880s, the teacher was meant to battle against ignorance in primary school armed with a fixed set of knowledge. The normal schools were the answer to teacher training at the time, though later they raised the question of how much time should be devoted to developing pedagogical knowledge against the time devoted to practice. Evidently, the discussion repeated itself, this time for the sake of a new demand for professionalization of teachers.

Throughout the 1990s, social problems cut across all approaches to teacher education with strong urgency. Some governments showed some interest in these aspects when they approached the transformation of teacher education, while others complied with the requirements of the Federal Law, superficially modifying content and leaving the curriculum untouched. For some, the lack of clear political and social objectives in the national government and the need to appear democratic allowed for a variety of responses. In 1991, even before the issue of the Federal Law of Education in 1993, the Ministry of Education had set the framework for the design of a curricular and institutional organization that would provide continuing education for teachers. Ten provinces implemented this relatively short-lived proposal, interrupted by the new Federal Law. It was an attempt at looking into the past as a source of experience, but not with the purpose of re-implanting old models for a society that was becoming increasingly hetero-geneous socially and culturally.

Furthermore, all attempts at evaluating the performance of teachers at the time were based on the assumption that teachers in the past had been autonomous professionals who enjoyed social status, possessed expert knowledge and responded to the demands of society. This assumption was never challenged and present teachers lost out in the comparison. The purpose behind the assessment was not to revert to the past but an effort to restore the old certainties. Nobody could possibly believe in the viability of transporting into the 21st century models that answered to political and peda-gogical objectives of the 19th century.

In 1992–93, national non-university institutes were transferred to provincial jurisdiction, thus contributing to the enormous variety of locations for teacher education, which by then also included universities. At the time that the Federal Law of Education was passed, teacher education in Argentina was carried out in multiple unconnected institutions, depending on different agencies and offering varied plans of studies (Braslavsky and Birgin, 1995). This heterogeneity was an obstacle to any attempts at transforming rapidly the content and format of teacher education. At that stage of development, the weight of initial education was borne by state institutions. The private sector produced larger numbers of primary and pre-primary teachers than secondary teachers, and was practically non-existent for physical and artistic education and education for the disabled. In general, the state did not provide in-practice postgraduate studies for teachers. Furthermore, all these institutions showed strong traces of the normal school movement, with the implications of decades of dejection, lack of materials and the desire to look into a glorious past when schools stood for cultural authority.

According to Mariano Narodowski (1997), in the 1990s the school culture was no longer a monopoly or hegemonic but had to adapt to its context. Schools had to accommodate to the community in the same way that the community had to adapt to schools before. That implied fragmentation and diversity in teacher education, since teachers would have to adapt to communities that might be different in social and cultural backgrounds. In this variety of demand, students required teachers who were not only specialists in one field of knowledge but also able to integrate subject matters and adopt a critical position when selecting and treating them. Furthermore, teachers needed to be able to research collectively the nature of knowledge and ways of transmitting and using it. In fact, existing programmes of teacher education did not produce professionals capable of mediating difficulties with esoteric knowledge and operating creatively in a context marked by uncertainties, plurality of thought and proliferation of cultural input.

At this stage, a generalized consensus was voiced by experts, politicians and even teachers themselves about the deficiencies in the education of teachers. Not only was the initial education questioned but also the lack of systematic and appropriate in-service training. As an answer to this, the National Ministry of Education designed and enforced the Federal Network of Continuing Teacher Education (1994), widely known as 'The Net', and embarked on an attempt at setting national standards for in-service training. 'The Net' was an effort to allow communication among different institutions: universities, non-university institutes and schools. Furthermore, there was particular interest in encouraging institutions to perform multiple functions such as initial education, in-service training and research since most of the institutions devoted themselves to one model.

This established an obstacle in the communication process and in the essential feedback between the training institutions and the schools they served. In fact, if reforms build and distribute pedagogical identities (Messina, 2000), this communication was essential in order that teachers should not take the reforms as an imposition and a waste of time but as an answer to their needs. State policy based on the principle of continuing education still lacks, in 2000, sound implementation policies, in particular for initial training programmes in each region. This link would allow for a better distribution of resources to provide for the multiple demands on teachers in their social roles. It is necessary to balance scientific and professional formation, individual and institutional cooperation, and learning about new technologies, evaluation and the relationship between theory and practice.

The prospects with caution!

To sum up, each time the need appears to introduce changes in education, the poor preparation of teachers is seen as the most significant cause of failure. The situation at present is not an exception and the urge to professionalize teachers accompanies every effort to implement the reforms introduced by the Federal Law of Education (1993). This movement was preceded by two clearly marked currents involved in defining the role of teachers, that of normalism at the end of the 19th century and professionalism in the late 1960s.

The normal school movement as well as technocratic professionalism advocated teacher models, 'the role model' and 'the educational technician' respectively. Although these models are chronologically differentiated, they still rule jointly at present in a state of confrontation that becomes an obstacle in the debate. The two sides share similarities and even agreements; they both confine teachers to transmitting their role in knowledge, values or norms produced and validated by others, external to and ignorant of the everyday teaching–learning situation in the classroom (Suarez, 1994). As the new law advocates continuing education for teachers based on the idea that initial and continuing education constitute one single process, the two confronting models fail to respond to the challenge. They propose initial teacher training as a final stage. However, in the new approach, there is no one step to becoming a professional. Nor is in-service training only destined to make up for the deficiencies of initial education. Moreover, an in-service training model that lacks a preceding initial training designed along open and critically oriented lines runs the risk of creating dependency of the teacher on fixed school models.

Later, in 1995, the Law of Higher Education, complementary to the Federal Law and in accordance with international tendencies, confirmed the position of teacher education exclusively within higher education and even stated the need to move it into the university. Why were eyes set on the university to introduce changes in teacher education? In an attempt at moving away from a model that was too homogeneous to respond to a globalized society, accelerated change and the need to elaborate flexible proposals, the university framework appeared to offer different opportunities. The production of knowledge and research associated with universities should provide the means to find answers to the problems posed by a complex social context. This context is characterized by a globalized economy, a gradual loss of national identity, a marketplace demanding a flexible labour force, the crisis of the ideal of progress, explosive developments in science and technology, and mass-media culture.

The role of education in the search for answers to the new problems seems to be crucial, and requires that the teaching profession recover its prestige if it is to be accepted as an active agent. Recognizable qualifications provided by universities would ensure continuing education and guarantee the research requirements leading to the production of knowledge appropriate to the characteristics of the present social context.

Nevertheless, the university, as it stands today, could not provide an adequate training for primary and secondary school teachers since it has always been under attack for its detachment from schools. It lacks the conditions necessary to obtain feedback on its actions. However, it could ensure professionalization in the eyes of the public.

In addition, according to Daniel Filmus (1996), the withdrawal from action of the state implies a wider field of action for the marketplace, but it also allows for greater possibilities for the development of new social agents and movements. This was made evident during the debate about the Federal Law of Education, when these movements were taken into account, for they represented the educational interests of different social actors as well as the significance of specific regional problems. Accordingly, education should be restored to its role of a link between the public and the private, between the individual and society, between the institutions and their agents. It is in this context that we would rather be 'at a loss than at a crossroads' where we would be forced to choose between the two proposals represented by the confronting models (Beltrán Llavador, 1997), that of the teacher as a role model and the teacher as a technician. Otherwise, the sense of being at a loss allows room for the desire to search for different ways based on what we know, exercising creativity to modify existing patterns and taking advantage of the fact that the way is also opened by the latest resolutions of the Federal Council of December 2000. Those resolutions allowed jurisdictions to make their own provisions as to the overall implementation of the law, the only restriction being that of respecting the main guidelines related to the number of compulsory years of education and minimum basic contents.

The search for a lost sense of direction in teacher education involving policies, institutions and various new agents should channel creative efforts to find multiple answers to the questions under discussion. For some, this search builds a maze where they find themselves tightly entangled and, for others, it poses the question of what brought about the loss. Unfortunately, in both cases, it is producing few concrete results. Finally, it is of extreme importance to point out that teachers consider futile any discussion about transforming teacher education and teacher participation in the democratization of education if there is no political will to introduce radical changes in the material conditions in which teaching practice is carried out in Argentina.

References

Alliaud, A (1997) Formación docente y universidad: superando dicotomías, *Revista del Instituto de Investigaciones Educativas en Ciencias de la Educación*, **VI** (10), pp 70–76

Beltrán Llavador, F (1997) Las instituciones en el cruce de caminos, in *Políticas, Instituciones y Actores en Educación*, ed G Frigerio, M Giannoni and M Poggi, Ediciones Novedades Educativas, Buenos Aires

Braslavsky, C and Birgin, A (1995) Quienes enseñan hoy en la Argentina, in *Las Transformaciones de la Educacion en Diez Años de Democracia*, ed G Tiramonti, C Braslavsky and D S A Filmus, Grupo Editorial Norma, Argentina

Coraggio, J L (1997) Economistas y educación, in *Políticas, Instituciones y Actores en Educación*, ed G Frigerio, M Giannoni and M Poggi, Ediciones Novedades Educativas, Buenos Aires

Diker, Gabriela (1997) Historia, coyunturas y futuros de la formacion docente, in *La Formacion Docente: Explorando problematicas teoricas*, Secretaria de Educacion, GCBA, Argentina

Diker, G and Terigi, F (1997) *La Formación de Maestros y Profesores: Hoja de ruta*, Editorial Paidos, Buenos Aires

Filmus, Daniel (1996) *Estado, Sociedad y Educación en la Argentina de Fin de Siglo*, Editorial Troquel, Argentina

Filmus, D (1997) La educación latinoamericana: entre la transformación y el ajuste, in *Políticas, Instituciones y Actores en Educación*, ed G Frigerio, M Giannoni and M Poggi, Ediciones Novedades Educativas, Buenos Aires

Maffei, M (1997) Sobre la situación de los docentes en Argentina, in *Políticas, Instituciones y Actores en Educación*, ed G Frigerio, M Giannoni and M Poggi, Ediciones Novedades Educativas, Buenos Aires

Messina, Graciela (2000) La renovacion de la formacion docente: instituciones y sujetos, in *Cuadernos de Gestion Institucional No. 3*, Novedades Educativas, Buenos Aires

Narodowski, Mariano (1997) La formacion docente en el discurso pedagogico, en *La Formacion Docente: Explorando problematicas teoricas*, Secretaria de Educacion, GCBA, Argentina

Popkewitz, T (1994) *Modelos de Poder y Regulación Social en Pegagogía: Crítica comparada de las reformas contemporáneas de la formación del profesorado*, Pomares-Corredor, Barcelona

Southwell, Myriam (1995) Historia y formación docente, *Revista del Instituto de Investigaciones Educativas en Ciencias de la Educación*, **IV** (7), pp 10–16

Suarez, Daniel (1994) Normalismo, profesionalismo y formacion docente: notas para un debate inconcluso, in *American Review of Educational Development*, Departamento de Asuntos Educativos, Secretaria General de la OEA, **XXXVIII** (118), p II

3. The teacher is the key: professionalism and the strategic state

S Gopinathan and Leslie Sharpe

Introduction

Education systems, nested within nation states, are everywhere coping with the challenges of globalization and technological innovation. We argue that, in Singapore, reforms to teacher education need to be understood as part of a general strategy to align the education system as a whole to meet the needs of a globalized, knowledge-based economy. We believe they point the teaching profession towards more promising and empowering directions. While changing conceptions of the work of teachers and of teaching, and drives to professionalize teaching will necessarily create stress and contradiction, coherent policy, adequate resourcing and innovative practice can limit strain. Career- and service-enhancing strategies, emphasis on opportunities for professional development, and encouragement to build productive partnerships have created a more enabling culture for teacher preparation in Singapore. This chapter will briefly examine the notions of partnership, pedagogy and professionalism in the context of teacher education, followed by a discussion of recent developments in Singapore. The final section of the chapter will examine the role of universitization and the prospects for the future of teacher education in Singapore in the context of state strategy.

Partnership, pedagogy and professionalism

It is in Britain that recent changes to the form and content of initial teacher training (ITT) have been the most far-reaching and where debate has been the most intense. We are not so much interested here in the domestic political ramifications of the changes as in the consequences for training institutions, the individuals training to be teachers and for policy makers elsewhere contemplating changes to their systems. Many ex-colonies, such as Singapore, have modelled their ITT on Britain's and any changes to the British system are naturally followed closely, with an eye to portability (Singapore Teachers' Union, 2001). With its long history of excellence in ITT, it is no small matter when radical changes are made in Britain, especially when they are made in the name of producing a world-class education system capable of meeting the challenges of globalization and the knowledge-based economy. The obvious question that springs to policy makers' minds elsewhere is, 'Should we be doing the same things?'

We believe that such reforms signal a profound misreading of the challenges of globalization and the knowledge-based economy. The qualities required in a knowledge-based economy are flexibility, risk taking, entrepreneurship, the ability to change and a commitment to lifelong learning. It seems paradoxical that preparation for this sort of future should be built upon setting limits to teacher knowledge and skills, with hopes for an empowered teaching force resting on a discourse of blame and derision (Ball, 1990). We hope to show that by contrast Singapore is moving away from restrictiveness, even though the state is still in charge.

Recent developments in Singapore

In 1997 the Prime Minister, Goh Chock Tong, launched a 'Thinking Schools, Learning Nation' initiative. It aims to reform the education system to enable it to develop in all schools a critical and creative thinking culture that will promote innovation and divergent practices, cater more adequately to pupils' multiple intelligences and aptitudes, and encourage entrepreneurship and risk taking. It seeks to achieve this through 1) the explicit teaching of critical and creative thinking skills, 2) the use of instructional technology, 3) the reduction of subject content, in some cases up to 30 per cent of existing coverage, 4) greater encouragement to group-based multidisciplinary project work, 5) the inclusion of a wider range of assessment modes and 6) a greater emphasis on processes instead of outcomes when appraising schools. A noteworthy aspect of the changes is the resourcing that was made available to bring about the changes. The government, for example, committed S $2 billion over five years. The government funded changes to physical infrastructure, provided computers and broadband access to the Internet, and set a target of one computer to two teachers and one computer to two students, which has been largely met.

These school-focused reforms were accompanied by changes to system governance, through the adoption of a school excellence model, as the Ministry of Education (MOE) sought to move from a bureaucracy-dominated education system to one characterized by greater autonomy at school level. School clusters headed by superintendents were introduced to exploit strengths that individual schools possessed. School leaders, both principals and heads of departments, were provided with seminars using the learning organization framework as a means of reculturing schools. What is also remarkable is that the effort to reform schools was undertaken, not to fix a failing system, but to build upon a legacy of success. After all, it was only in 1999 that the results of the Third International Mathematics and Science Study showed how well Singaporean pupils had been tutored in science and mathematics.

At the same time that curricular-based reforms were being implemented in the schools, the Ministry also acknowledged that reforms are only likely to be successful if teachers have the capacity and desire to change. The Ministry has made available, as an entitlement to all teachers, a 100-hours-per-year in-service entitlement paid for by the Ministry. In 1998 the Ministry established a Teachers' Network to facilitate professional development through exchange and learning, dissemination of innovation and support for beginning teachers. In 2001 the Ministry undertook a comprehensive review of teachers' careers (Teo, 2001). Three career tracks, one for teaching, a leadership track and a senior specialist track, are to be introduced, coupled with both pay increases and an innovative scheme to reward those who stay on in the profession; the longer they stay in service, the greater the financial incentives.

How does all this impact on teacher preparation? The National Institute of Education (NIE) is a specialized institute of the Nanyang Technological University and the sole teacher training agency in Singapore, providing courses from early childhood, through initial teacher training at diploma, degree and postgraduate levels, a wide array of in-service courses, leadership programmes and postgraduate and doctoral programmes. Most of the educational research done in Singapore is done at the NIE. The link with changes in the education system was clearly set out by Dr Aline Wong, Senior Minister of State, who is responsible for teacher education (Wong, 2001).

In 1999, NIE undertook a major review of governance, resources, programmes and research to seek ways to align itself better to the changing expectations of schools. The review was jointly undertaken by the Ministry and NIE, signalling the strong interest and involvement the Ministry wished to have with equipping NIE for its new challenges. As a result of the review, the vision of 'An Institute of Distinction' was adopted and three strategic thrusts identified, namely 1) developing and delivering quality teacher training programmes centred on a model that emphasizes commitment and professionalism on the part of teachers, 2) the development of centres of excellence and flagship centres to produce educational research that meets national needs and merits international recognition and 3) the adoption of a programme-driven matrix structure. We noted earlier the responsibilities given to a senior policy maker, Dr A Wong, for overseeing NIE's development. The Director of NIE is a full member of the Ministry's top policy-making committee, the Ministerial Committee Meeting. In addition, following the review, the Permanent Secretary of the Ministry of Education was appointed to NIE's Council, replacing the President of Nanyang Technological University as Chairman. To facilitate better linkages and dialogue, the Permanent Secretary set up an MOE–NIE Coordinating Committee to examine and decide on matters of mutual interest.

Accompanying these changes was an enhanced flow of additional resources. NIE moved into a new purpose-built campus in December 2000, a campus built at a cost of some US $200 million and providing both hostel accommodation for students and enhanced access to NTU's resources. In line with the policy of exploiting ICT, NIE was given an IT budget to provide enhanced computing facilities for students and staff. Finally, in line with the Ministry's desire to place policy making and educational practice on an evidence-based footing, the budget was doubled to S $2 million.

The NIE review mentioned above considered the situation and recommended a new professionally oriented programme for teaching in primary schools, with an emphasis on one academic subject (rather than the two in the former programme). Greater emphasis is placed in this programme on aligning academic content to the needs for primary school teaching, and to ensure that all teachers are able to teach the four core curricular subjects, English, mathematics, science and social studies. NIE is also offering for the first time a degree programme to train Malay-language secondary teachers. Both programmes were set to begin in July 2001. The repositioning of the degree programme also took into account the need to accommodate new clienteles, especially polytechnic diploma holders, and the need to provide upgrading opportunities to the large majority of non-graduate primary teachers.

The Ministry's commitment to preparing the teachers to be capable of implementing the reforms had to be met by the NIE gearing up to provide a large number of new in-service courses. Accordingly, a number of new advanced postgraduate diplomas have been developed that have been designed as routes via accreditation to degree and postgraduate qualifications. NIE has recognized that teachers now have access to a multitude of training opportunities and that a system of accreditation is necessary if teachers are to benefit fully from such opportunities.

NIE has also reviewed and introduced new leadership programmes. The one-year Further Professional Diploma in Education was replaced by the Diploma in Departmental Management programme. More significantly, the successful Diploma in Educational Administration was replaced by the Leaders in Education programmes (LEP) with the aim of preparing school leaders committed to innovation, and thus ready 'in an education context that is dynamic, complex and uncertain... to help schools develop as innovative learning communities' (*LEP Handbook*).

The magnitude of the curriculum development undertaken to date and the decision to reorganize the Institute into a programmes-driven structure signals the very serious effort to align teacher preparation better to the needs of the new education environment. Considerable attention has been given to the attitudinal dimension in teacher professionalism. Singapore is a young nation with a recent history of fragmentation as a result of its multi-ethnic character. School-based socialization and identification with state and nation is still a core aim of schooling. The state, however, recognizes that the opportunities created by economic success and globalization will create pressures on the socialization process. The Ministry and NIE have jointly agreed that teacher preparation should pay serious attention to cultivating desirable moral attitudes. For several years now NIE and MOE have sought to foster greater schools–NIE partnership in teacher preparation. The principal impulse for this move lies in the recognition that teacher training will benefit if it draws more fully upon the practical wisdom of school personnel; it is not, as in the current UK reform moves, based on perceived inadequacies of university-based teacher preparation or an attempt to reduce resources.

Universitization, prospects and the strategic state

The changes to ITT that we have described suggest a distinctively Singaporean configuration of partnership, pedagogy and professionalism. NIE has moved towards a more collaborative form of partnership with the schools to involve school practitioners more centrally in ITT, both in the university and in the schools. However, the traditional block teaching practice has been retained and the majority of the trainees' time is still spent in the university. Though the Ministry of Education has set broad goals for ITT, university staff still retain overall control of their courses, and these include a large foundations component dealing with issues such as education policies, the socio-psychological basis for learning and academic achievement, assessment, counselling and ICT.

In line with changes in the schools, NIE is seeking to create a more learner-centred environment through an emphasis on independent study, multidisciplinary group work and critical and creative thinking skills. A model of teacher professionalism has been adopted that emphasizes attitudes, values and integrity over and above content mastery and specific teaching competencies, which, as we have argued, seeks to return teaching to its origins as a moral activity. Furthermore ITT is underpinned by generous funding, including a doubling of funding for educational research, and positive public recognition of NIE's efforts. Taken together, these policies appear different from those being pursued elsewhere, notably in Britain, and raise for us the central questions of whether they represent a more coherent and viable alternative to those being pursued elsewhere, why it has been thought necessary to pursue them in Singapore and what kinds of obstacles there might be.

We believe that an explanation for the distinctiveness of Singaporean ITT policy needs to be sought at two levels: firstly, as part of a general reading of and response to universal processes of globalization; and secondly, in terms of local conditions and histories. The notion of the state as 'strategic trader' is particularly useful (Brown and Lauder, 1997; Green, 1990). As a strategic trader, the state is actively involved in investing in human capital and national infrastructure to create a magnet economy that will attract, and retain, high-skilled, high-waged employment. Its fundamental task is to strike a 'correct' balance between the market and the democratic state, so as to guarantee economic success, freedom and social justice. Only under such circumstances, it is argued, can the market be aligned to necessary social ends. Only under such circumstances is it possible to generate the trust that forms the 'social glue' necessary for national success to be generated and sustained. Green and Sakamoto-Vandenberg (2001) deployed this concept to help explain the success of Singapore's economic strategy since independence.

Before proceeding to a discussion of the Singapore case, however, it will be useful to locate the concept of strategic trader in the broader discussion of the relationship of state and market in recent times, especially since the state's control of education is being challenged. Middleton (2000) argues that the central 'conundrum' for theorists is to explain how a market can be mobilized for strategic political ends when 'by common agreement its function is to reconcile an infinite variety of individual ends' (p 550). He identifies three permutations of the balance between the state and the market in the political economy literature: a 'quasi market' analysis; theories of the free economy and the strong state; and 'varieties of neo-liberalism and steering at a distance'.

The notion of the state as strategic trader fits in most clearly with steering at a distance analysis which, as Middleton points out, allows us to see that market relations are not simply 'managed' but 'mobilised' (p 551). We would add that this is an important sociological insight that helps explain current trends not only in Britain but also in Singapore. Mobilization implies an element of voluntarism in human affairs and draws attention to the human face of strategic trading. Furthermore, it ties in well with Brown and Lauder's influential typology of 'neo-Fordist' and 'post-Fordist' responses to globalization and the knowledge-based economy.

Given their daily experience of strong state tactics over the last few years it is understandable that British educationalists are for the most part sceptical of New Labour's embracing of human capital arguments and of the recent introduction of the General Teaching Council in England. They have seen what in an earlier paper we termed 'market universitization' (Sharpe and Gopinathan, 1993) harden into 'franchise universitization' and their role has been progressively shaped around marketplace competition for certificates of entitlement (licences) to train the state's teachers. Though there is some evidence that with greater standardization and uniformity trainees feel better prepared for the job of classroom teaching than before (Furlong *et al*, 2000), critics allege that trainees are being inducted into a narrow, 'technicized' version of teaching (Mahony and Hextall, 1998; Tickle, 2000); the focus on content knowledge and pedagogic skills produces trainees who lack the capacity to 'interrogate their practice' (Furlong *et al*, 2000) and make independent judgements; school mentors are reluctant to induct their mentees into a broader 'public' or 'ecological' role (Bottery and Wright, 2000). As a response to this and tighter budgets, universities are seriously questioning whether they should continue to be involved in ITT (Reid, 2000; Nixon *et al*, 2000). Overall, Smyth (2000) finds highly questionable whether such low trust and 'commercialised professionalism' are capable of delivering the 'world class education system capable of competing in the globalised world' that was the major intent of the reforms.

There are two fundamental criticisms here. The first is economic and centres on the apparent paradox of ITT in Britain, namely the preparation of teachers in a narrow and highly prescriptive way for a rapidly changing and unpredictable future. The second is social and raises fundamental questions about autonomy, accountability and trust in a democratic state. As Giddens (1993), following Held, has pointed out, autonomy is perhaps the key concern in all interpretations of modern democracy. Autonomy means 'the capacity of individuals to be self-reflective and self determining', 'to deliberate, judge, choose and act upon different courses of action'. The 'principle of autonomy' asserts that individuals should 'enjoy equal rights (and, accordingly, equal obligations) in the specification of the framework which generates and limits the opportunities available to them, so long as they do not deploy this framework to negate the rights of others' (p 307).

Of all the criticisms levelled at the changes to British teacher training and to the manner in which the changes have been made, it has been the lack of trust shown in the profession that has arguably been the most damaging (Halstead, 1994). The narrowing of skills is one thing but the lack of trust and positive recognition makes teachers less likely to act as change agents. New Labour's policies in education hold out the prospect of a different balance, with the state as strategic trader taking on the role of mobilizer, but it remains to be seen if teachers will embrace change more positively.

As Green (1990) argues, national education systems were established first in countries where the process of state formation has been the most intense. As commentators such as Gopinathan (2001) have pointed out, in the case of Singapore, from its earliest days the developmental state used the education system as a central instrument of nation building. The economic crisis that propelled educational restructuring in the United States and Britain was experienced in Singapore in the 1950s as well, but the socio-political implications were more significant for Singapore (Sharpe and Gopinathan, 1995).

In the name of survival, the state in Singapore sought to mobilize the population to what most saw as an impossible project, namely that a dot on the map recently evicted by a larger, hostile neighbour could survive and prosper. For the state acting as strategic trader, mobilization is crucial to the success of the societal project. The sense of vulnerability led the state to invest much in education and to see its success as crucial to the achievement of the state's goals. Essential control had to be fought for in the 50s and 60s and, in our view, the Ministry has used the power responsibly as attested by the quality that is evident in the system. This in turn has led to teaching and teachers being valued, thus making the building of a trusted partnership between the Ministry and NIE both necessary and possible.

Giddens (1998) asks whether it is possible for affiliation to the nation to be a benign force. In asking the question, he poses the central dilemma for all tightly knit nation states in a globalized world. As critics (Boshier, 1994) of Singapore have pointed out, the strategies for achieving social solidarity that has fuelled economic growth could become a major hindrance to future survival. Such comments have not been lost on the government and since the economic downturn of the mid-80s there has been a concerted effort to decentralize the education system whilst at the same time the government has moved to provide a framework more in line with globalized conditions. We have argued elsewhere that it has pursued a distinctive mixture of neo-Fordist and post-Fordist strategies (Sharpe and Gopinathan, 2001). Professionalism, partnership and pedagogy are structured differently in Singapore and we have located the reason for this in the way the state in Singapore has read the challenges posed by globalization and in its own history, which provided a strong rationale for state control over education and, equally important, the success of the state in building a credible education system. The state has been a successful mobilizer – indeed it could not otherwise have survived the trauma of its political birth and the deep fissures inherent in a multi-ethnic society.

We are not unmindful of the fact that in all systems seeking radical change there are tensions and contradictions. A flurry of initiatives and the need to learn new skills, especially in ICT, do lead to an intensification of work, adding to teacher stress. Singapore's educational success is founded largely on a coherent, well-resourced system that emphasized content mastery and rewarded effort rather than enterprise. A strategy founded on giving students more scope for non-conformist behaviour, on application and problem-solving skills, and on making teachers facilitators is bound to disorient some of them; some will adapt to the needed change better than others. It is how well the system is supported in making the changes and how trusted the teachers feel that will determine prospects for success.

Equally, the view of professionalism offered to trainee teachers and teachers is not one that is built upon freewheeling autonomy. A balance is being sought between knowing how to instruct well and to understanding teaching as a social enterprise (Carnoy, 1999). Even as the system remains competitive, collegiality and networking to share experiences are fostered through the cluster schools concept, Teacher Network and annual teachers' conferences. This approach perhaps best meets the needs of a system in which the exercise of the state's authority is seen as legitimate, while at the same time there is recognition that the changes sought must mean more space to act professionally on the part of teachers.

A half-century ago Singapore's education and teacher training system reflected the tensions and conflicts of a divided multi-ethnic society; teachers were leaders in the anti-colonial struggle and teacher unionism rather than professionalism was the focus of debate. A strong state has effectively mobilized the citizenry and built a credible education and teacher training system.

Today, it is responding to the prospects of the globalization challenge from a position of strength and ample resources, and the odds are that the desired new era of teacher preparation will be realized.

References

Ball, S (1990) *Politics and Policy Making in Education: Explorations in policy sociology*, Routledge, London

Boshier, R (1994) Education and docility, in *Education in Urban Areas: Cross-national dimension*, ed N P Stromquist, Praeger, Westport, CT

Bottery, M and Wright, N (2000) The National Curriculum for Teacher Training: playing politics or promoting professionalism?, *British Journal of In-Service Education*, **23** (2), pp 163–78

Brown, P and Lauder, H (1997) Education, globalisation and economic development, in *Education, Culture, Economy, Society*, ed A H Halsey *et al*, Oxford University Press, Oxford

Carnoy, M (1999) *Globalisation and Educational Reform: What planners need to know*, UNESCO International Institute for Educational Planning, Paris

Furlong, J *et al* (2000) *Teacher Education in Transition: Re-forming professionalism?*, Open University Press, Buckingham

Giddens, A (1993) The nature of modernity, in *The Giddens Reader*, ed P Cassell, Macmillan, Basingstoke

Giddens, A (1998) *The Third Way: The renewal of social democracy*, Polity Press, Cambridge

Gopinathan, S (2001) Globalisation, the state and education policy in Singapore, in *Education and Political Transition: Themes and experiences in East Asia*, ed Mark Bray and W O Lee, Comparative Education Research Centre, The University of Hong Kong Publications, Hong Kong

Green, A (1990) *Education and State Formation: The rise of education systems in England, France and the USA*, Macmillan, London

Green, A and Sakamoto-Vandenberg (2001) The place of skills in national competition strategies in Germany, Japan, Singapore and the UK, Paper presented at the Institute of Policy Studies Forum on 'Achieving a High Skills Society and Economy', 21 February, Singapore

Halstead, M (1994) Accountabilities and values, in *Accountabilities and Control in Educational Settings*, ed D Scott, pp 146–65, Cassell, London

Mahony, P and Hextall, A (1998) Social justice and the reconstruction of teaching, *Journal of Education Policy*, **13** (4), pp 545–58

Middleton, C (2000) Models of state and market in the 'modernisation' of higher education, *British Journal of the Sociology of Education*, **21** (4), pp 537–54

Nixon, J *et al* (2000) University-based initial teacher education: institutional re-positioning and professional renewal, *International Studies in Sociology of Education*, **10** (3), pp 243–62

Reid, I (2000) Accountability, control and freedom in teacher education: towards a panopticon, *International Studies in Sociology of Education*, **10** (3), pp 213–26

Sharpe, L and Gopinathan, S (1993) Universitisation and the reform of teacher education: the case of Britain and Singapore, *Research in Education*, November, pp 5–16

Sharpe, L and Gopinathan, S (1995) Effective island, effective schools: repairing and restructuring in the Singapore school system, *International Journal of Educational Reform*, **4** (2), pp 394–402

Sharpe, L and Gopinathan, S (2001) After effectiveness: new directions in the Singapore school system, Paper presented at the International Forum on Education Reforms in the Asia Pacific Region, 14–16 February, Hong Kong

Singapore Teachers' Union (STU) (2001) *Vision, Leadership and Learning: Impact of recent educational initiatives in England (1998–2000)*, Singapore Teachers' Union, Singapore

Smyth, J (2000) Review symposium, teacher education in transition: reforming professionalism, *British Journal of Sociology of Education*, **21** (4)

Teo, Chee Hean (2001) A high quality teaching force for the future: good teachers, capable leaders, dedicated specialists, Speech delivered at the Senior Education Officer Promotion Ceremony, Singapore

Tickle, L (2000) *Teacher Induction: The way ahead*, Open University Press, Buckingham

Wong, A (2001) Speech by Aline Wong at the Singapore NIE Corporate Seminar, 10 February, Singapore

4. Globalization and *dirigisme*: teacher education in South Korea

In Whoe Kim and Terri Kim

Introduction

This chapter sketches the South Korean history of teacher education during the second half of the 20th century, and reviews the future prospects of teacher education. Three questions will be raised. First, what purposes did and do institutions for teacher education serve in the Republic of Korea? Second, what roles were and are school teachers expected to play in society? Third, what is the philosophy behind recent teacher education reforms? The conclusion will note the pressures that shape the future of the teacher education system, given the complex political and socio-economic relations of South Korea.

Historical types of conformity: the roles of school and teacher education

The formation of the modern teacher education system in South Korea can be traced to the Japanese colonial period. During the 36 years of the colonial period (1910–45), the national education system was developed for the colonial goals of assimilation and colonial industrialization. The first separate institution for teacher training was established in Seoul in 1922 during Japanese rule. Later, each province attempted to found its own normal school. These normal schools were, however, soon absorbed by a few strategically located government normal schools for teacher training, which became narrower in purpose and task, ie the cultural assimilation and modernization of Korea to support the Japanese industrializing colonial economy. Particularly towards the end of colonial rule, when Japan was deeply involved in the Second World War, teacher training in Korea took on a more militaristic character. Overall, the Japanese colonial government effectively used educational incentives for upward socio-economic mobility. Students in teacher training were given full scholarships, and their educational certificates could be upgraded to the same level as higher education diplomas (Kim, 2001).

Immediately after the end of World War II, the subsequent political independence and the national partition of Korea, the US Military Governance (USMG) (1945–48) clearly influenced the political and economic purposes of teacher education: to convert Koreans to the US model of liberal capitalist democracy and to provide useful skill training for the newly independent nation (Mason, Kim and Cole, 1980). However, many of the US military advisers lacked cultural understanding of Korean circumstances, yet initiated radical educational reforms to eradicate the Japanese colonial system. Accordingly, grand plans to reorganize the 6–3–3–4 schooling system were put into practice; textbooks were printed in the Korean script, a new curriculum was installed, and in-service and pre-service teacher training programmes were initiated to raise the professional level of the teaching personnel. The official USMG reports describe these efforts as 'democratizing' and 'modernizing' Korean education. Ironically, however, the US Military Government operated all these reform activities through the infrastructure inherited from the Japanese colonial government (Kim, 1993).

In this period, teachers, classified as civil servants, were poorly paid and, given the periodic bursts of inflation, dissatisfaction in the teaching profession and even resignations were the result. The students and teaching staff often became embroiled in political conflicts, which disrupted the normal operation of schooling. Accompanying these problems was an upward surge in enrolment at all school levels. Gradually the US concept of democracy was accepted among the Korean people, along with more democratic ideas about equality of educational opportunity, in contrast to Japanese 'colonial' meritocracy and educational elitism. However, more Korean people were able to pursue upward social mobility through schooling.

The anti-communist stance of the US military government was another pressure for conformity in the Republic of Korea. The South Korean alliance with the United States was firmly consolidated after the Korean War ended in 1953 (Cole and Lyman, 1971). The North Korean communist threat then made it possible to legitimate strong nationalistic, autocratic governance for the rest of the century, at least until the so-called 'People's Government' led by the incumbent President Kim Dae Jung took power in 1998.

In this period, the government maintained its control over teacher training with strong emphasis on moral, anti-communist education and vocational education. Vocational education, in particular, reflected the nation's need to expedite economic growth as a way out of poverty, especially after the Korean War. Accordingly, from 1952 to 1958, special teacher training programmes were implemented on a massive scale, to produce or to reorient vocational education teachers (Ministry of Education and Human Resources Development, 2000). Education law in the period of the military regimes (1961–91) maintained the colonial philosophy of teacher training in terms of educational uniformity and conformity, and aimed to keep the supply of teachers under government control. Despite some efforts to implant US methods of instruction in the teacher training programme, school culture itself still reflected the inherited Japanese pedagogic model (Kim, 1993). Structural reforms followed the US model on the surface to encourage wider educational opportunities. However, the pedagogic discourse in schooling was still continuous from the period of Japanese colonialism (1910–45). More precisely, while following the US model on the surface, the teacher education system in South Korea has been based on the inherited authority of the Confucian Chinese examination system and the pedagogic modes of Japanese colonialism.

The military *coup d'état* led by General Park Jung Hee in 1961 was another moment to redefine new norms of conformity for teachers. It was during Park's military dictatorship (1961–79) that South Korea emerged as a 'developmental state' in East Asia and its economy started to 'take off'. Since then, South Korea has made considerable progress in building a strong nation with economic modernization through consecutive five-year economic development plans. The purpose of school education was explicitly linked to governmental labour planning. Despite weaknesses in the techniques of labour planning, the government's position has maintained its basic premises. Education has always been viewed from an input–output standpoint. The dominance of neo-classical economic perspectives, such as rates of return analysis, was and still is powerful in interpreting educational performance in South Korea. Corresponding to its characteristics as a 'developmental state', South Korea has maintained its preference for a policy of cost-effectiveness, aiming to get the most in educational results for the least cost in public money.

Thus, with a continuing Cold War anti-communistic stance and the stress on political conformity imposed by the South Korean government, the Japanese *dirigiste* colonial infrastructure has survived in South Korea. In effect, unlike many other countries in the 'Third World' of the time, South Korea managed successfully to provide an industrious, literate workforce to meet the rapid increase in the demand from industry, through its education system. The military autocratic regimes of South Korea used successful strategies to build a newly industrializing 'family state' that met the interests of families in using the educational ladder as a route to success.

Numerous higher education reforms were made in the period of military governance during Park's regime and that of his successors, Chun Doo Hwan (1981–87) and Roh Tae Woo (1988–91). The rationale behind these reforms was to check the expansion of higher education and keep it within the narrowly focused economic development plans led by strong military governments.

The government's control of teacher education: university admission and recruitment of teachers

The university entrance examination system was revised many times as a result of higher education reforms. The national university entrance examination system has been a notable mechanism for the government's quality control of higher education in South Korea. University admission is determined by the student's high school records and national standardized test results. Since 1996, individual colleges and universities have been allowed to require an additional entrance essay test, administered at the institutional level and separate from the national university entrance examination.

The ways to recruit candidates for teacher education are basically similar to those of the national university entrance examination. The candidates are evaluated on scholastic aptitude test scores (50 per cent), high school grade point average (GPA) (40 per cent), personality and aptitude for the teaching profession (5 per cent) and interview (5 per cent) (Lee and Pang, 1998).

Teacher education is offered at universities that provide education courses, colleges of education and departments of education. There are teaching certificate courses in general colleges and universities, the Korea National University of Education, junior vocational colleges, the Air and Correspondence University, and graduate schools of education, which altogether recruit approximately 40,000 teachers annually (MoE, 1998a). Primary teacher education is provided at 11 national institutions of teacher education and at Ewha Women's University, which is the only private university offering primary teacher training. Secondary teacher education is offered by teachers' colleges at 13 national universities, and by 23 private universities and 128 graduate schools of education. Table 4.1 shows the increase in numbers of institutions for formal education, and of teachers since 1965.

As a unique national university for teacher education, the Korean National University of Education (KNUE) was established in 1985. The KNUE provides pre-service teacher training at all levels, kindergarten, primary and secondary school, and also in-service education and educational research. The university offers a variety of special privileges for its students, such as exemption from

Table 4.1 Numbers of schools and institutions for teacher education, and of teachers

Year	1965		1980		1995		2000	
	Schools	Teachers	Schools	Teachers	Schools	Teachers	Schools	Teachers
Kindergarten	423	1,402	901	3,339	8,960	25,576	8,494	25,576
Primary School	5,125	79,164	6,487	119,064	5,772	138,369	5,267	128,012
Middle School	1,208	19,067	2,100	54,858	2,683	99,931	2,731	140,000
High School	701	14,108	1,353	50,948	1,830	99,067	1,957	92,589
Univ. of Education	13	305	11	564	11	766	11	698
University	70	5,305	85	14,458	131	45,087	161	41,943

Source: Ministry of Education and Human Resources Development (2000)

entrance and tuition fees (free for the first two years and modest for third- and fourth-year students). In-service teachers at the KNUE compose more than 80 per cent of the graduate student body.

As illustrated above, in order to recruit good candidates to the national institutions of teacher education, the government created a reward system including exemption from tuition fees and guaranteed job opportunities without examinations, whereas those who enrolled at private institutions for teacher education were required to take examinations before recruitment, and had to compete for vacancies. However, this reward system was abolished in 1990, when it was judged to violate equal job opportunity rights that were protected by the Constitution. Accordingly, since 1991 all teacher candidates have been recruited through open competition based on examinations (MoE, 1998a).

The open education policy

The examination-oriented mode of school teaching did not change, and the severe competition in university entrance examinations continued, even though the government's policy on 'open education' was aimed to adapt education for a globalized knowledge economy. However, the government announced in 1998 the abolition of university entrance examinations from the year 2002 as a remedy for the malfunctioning of school education. This drastic measure was based on the government's reforming policy of a 'new learner-centred open education system', announced in *The Vision for Education in 2002* (MoE, 1998c). The Ministry of Education has produced detailed measures to achieve those goals, stressing that they are not just slogans. The actual plans include new student evaluation schemes, mandatory computer education, and pupil-oriented education through a diversified and expanded curriculum to nurture creativity and character development. In implementing this open education policy, the government has devised new in-service and pre-service teacher training programmes. The establishment of teacher training institutions is authorized by the Minister of Education and the superintendents of regional offices of education. There are 95 teacher training institutes (Ministry of Education and Human Resources Development, 2001).

To raise teaching qualifications and standards, the government has conducted a comprehensive evaluation of teachers' colleges within universities, colleges of education and graduate schools of education since 1998. The government determines the student quota and the financial subsidies for each teacher training institution, according to evaluation outcomes. Teachers are also allowed to participate selectively in various in-service programmes at their convenience. The accumulated training hours are used to qualify for promotion and performance-based payment.

Simultaneously, to enhance teachers' morale, the government has introduced a merit-based reward system as a new promotion scheme. Also the optimum class hours of teaching per week have been stipulated, to prevent teachers from being overloaded with classes. A new personnel system that prioritizes ability over seniority has been introduced (Ministry of Education and Human Resources Development, 2000). Teachers, however, have already noted the negative side of this new government policy, which seeks to create a new culture of education without substantial changes in the uniform educational infrastructure.

It must be asked now whether teachers have the ability, or the will, to create a new school culture fit for a learner-centred open education environment. In this regard, the government's intention was to reform teachers first, rather than to make them leaders who would practise open education in schools on their own initiative. Since 2000, there have been strong protests by teachers against the government's plan to expand the national curriculum, which started at the primary level and will be fully implemented by 2004.

The new curriculum was to provide a common national basic education up to the first year of high school, without the current division of grade-level distinctions of elementary, middle and high school. It was designed to diversify the learning process in terms of depth and phases, on the basis of the individual needs and ability of students (Ministry of Education and Human Resources Development, 2001).

However, it has been argued by the teachers' unions that the current education system is not ready to teach the new national curriculum designed for an 'open education' environment. With an average class size of 44 students in secondary schools, it seems improbable that teachers can bring students to the right level of individual attainment. Press reports showed that teachers claimed that, when the new curriculum is fully implemented, the current collapse of the classroom will become more visible.

In summary, there are growing concerns and reservations about the policy of transforming the national education system into a uniform 'open education system' in order to promote creativity. Unless the government diversifies the present standardized evaluation and selection mechanisms for school education, as well as for in-service and pre-service teacher education, the 'open education' policy may lead to a deterioration of educational standards.

New norms of conformity: globalization

In 1992, a civilian government took power and signalled the end of 30 years of military regimes. Since then, the government has consistently pursued strategies for internationalizing its domestic education. The government has stressed the need for a qualitative improvement in teacher education, so as to meet the new challenges of economic globalization, including the World Trade

Organization (WTO) agenda of liberalizing the international trades in educational and professional services. According to the official statement of the Ministry of Education, 'the goal of the 1995 Education Reform was to train excellent teachers who can meet the needs of the era of globalization and the information age, and the field of education' (MoE, 1998b). Ways to achieve international competitiveness in domestic teacher education were sought immediately. The Ministry of Education revised the education curriculum of teacher education institutions and strengthened the recruitment system for new teachers (The Presidential Commission on Education Reform, The Republic of Korea, 1997; MoE, 1999).

From 1995 to 1997, the Presidential Commission for Educational Reform issued at least five statements about official aims in preparing teachers for the 21st century. In South Korea, the prospects for the new century are now always associated with 'globalization', officially defined as characterizing the 'knowledge-intensive era' by the government (Chang, 1998). The educational reforms since the mid-1990s have focused on creating a new learner-centred creative educational environment in which teachers are to be equipped with new information and communication technology (ICT). During 1988–96, the number of teachers who received in-service training in ICT was 256,000 out of 300,000 (MoE, 1998a).

As expressed in the Education Reform Initiatives of 1995 and the Master Plan for the Information Infrastructure Project of 1997, the government aims to achieve a high level of ICT literacy. The ultimate goal is to create a new student-directed learning environment under which ICT is fully utilized in teaching and learning. Following the Master Plan, every teacher was to be provided with a PC for teaching preparation and administrative work by 2000, and every classroom has now been equipped with multimedia devices, such as PCs, OHPs, TVs and VCRs. The student–PC ratio will be down to five to one, and the network speed will be faster than at least 2 Mbps by 2005 (Ministry of Education and Human Resources Development, 2001).

The implementation of the government's Master Plan has made computer lessons mandatory for primary, secondary and upper secondary school students. Computer skills are evaluated in five categories, and students have to obtain a 'certificate of information knowledge' to advance their education. The grade level in these skills will be included in the official criteria for high school and university admissions. The Ministry of Education provides computer classes for school teachers, and plans to provide schools with full-time teachers who teach only computer classes (Ministry of Education and Korean Educational Development Institute, 2000). In implementing the Master Plan for the Information Infrastructure Project, the South Korean government is looking into the case of Singapore, which is managing and unifying information technology education in all school subjects at all levels of schooling under the slogans 'Thinking School' and 'Learning Nation' (The Presidential Commission on Education Reform, The Republic of Korea, 1997; World Bank, 2000).

To enhance the professionalization of teachers, whose role will be crucial in a global knowledge-based economy, several measures have been taken systematically since 1998. One measure was to lower the teachers' retirement age from 65 to 62, as announced by the Ministry of Education in the autumn of 1999. The aim was to speed up the influx of the new generation into the teaching profession, and to match the global knowledge-based economy with what can be taught by school teachers of the older generation.

The application of this new policy saw massive teacher retirements. An estimated 16,000 teachers had left the teaching profession and the vacancies had been filled with newly appointed teachers by 2000. As might be expected, the policy of lowering the official retirement age of school teachers aroused the strong resistance of teachers' unions such as the Korean Federation of Teachers' Associations (KFTA) and the National Educators' Labour Union (NELU), as well as public criticism of such drastic governmental measures. The largest and most powerful teachers' organization, the KFTA, was founded in 1947. It represents all kinds and levels of teachers, including university academics. In 1991, a special law was enacted to improve the socio-economic status of teachers. By the law, the KFTA has the official right of negotiation and consultation with the government over teachers' conditions of service. The KFTA demanded the resignation of the education minister immediately after the government announced the lowering of the teachers' retirement age in April 1999. The introduction of the early retirement policy and the subsequent voluntary retirement of teachers eventually resulted in a shortage of teachers, especially at primary schools. About 5,000 elementary school teachers under the mandatory age limit were reported to have requested to retire voluntarily in 2000.

Other measures taken by the South Korean government to enhance the quality of the school teachers required for the global knowledge-based economy were 1) the official requirement of a certificate of proficiency in English conversation skills introduced in the teacher education system, and 2) the requirement to teach English classes only in English at all levels of school education from 2001.

Accordingly, the teacher candidates who take the national teachers' qualification test will get extra points if they can demonstrate good proficiency in spoken English. In 2000 the Ministry of Education provided 300 million won (approximately equivalent to US $250,000 as of April 2001) and in 2001 1.5 billion won (approximately US $1.25 million) in grants for teachers to take language courses overseas, and to form research groups. Universities and colleges of education were advised to conduct lectures in English as part of their English teacher education courses. However, the financial crisis of 1997–98 made a great impact on the English language education policy. The number of native English teachers diminished from 600 to just 188 after the crisis. The Ministry of Education announced that it intended to increase this number (of 188) to 402 by 2001, and to provide, annually, intensive language training for 15,000 elementary school teachers from 2001.

For the overall improvement of quality in education, as Korea entered the 21st century, the Ministry of Education launched a reform project for higher education, called Brain Korea 21 (BK 21) in 1999. As an extensive government project investing $1.2 billion during the seven years starting from 1999, its ultimate mission is to normalize elementary and secondary education by reforming the university and college entrance system, as well as to extend the capacity of higher education institutions to create the knowledge and technology crucial for the future of South Korea in a globalized world (Ministry of Education and Human Resources Development, 2001).

As illustrated so far, since the civilian government took power in 1992 a 'globalization' policy has emerged, stressing new demands on every teacher and teacher candidate in South Korea. However, it can be argued that this new type of conformity may just reflect an Anglo-US norm (of globalization) legitimated by neo-liberal market ideology. The South Korean government has not sought alternative models of education that might be more valuable to survive the globalization era. The government's political rhetoric about globalization is closely associated with tightening management and control of in-service and pre-service teacher training programmes in the name of diversification and specialization of teaching and the encouragement of creativity in teaching and learning.

The themes of political subordination, tight socio-economic control by the government and a rigid culture of educational practice have continued since Japanese colonial times. The education system in South Korea has continued explicitly to serve the purpose of national economic development. Schools have produced the literate, skilled workforce that the state wanted for the national economy. Nevertheless, the university system as a whole has always been underfunded, though regulated by the government (KCUE, 1997). In that regard, South Korea has always kept the principle of cost-effectiveness of higher education. This seems congruent with the 'good value for money principle' of the neo-liberal market-oriented education system in England. Following this principle, the goals of teacher education continue to be strongly influenced by the state.

Philosophy behind the teacher education policy

Given the characteristics of the state-managed teacher education system in South Korea ever since the establishment of the modern formal education system, it is suggested that both the Confucian and the colonial cultural legacy are strong and visible in South Korean teacher education now. Entry to the teaching profession has always been regarded as an effective means for upward mobility, within the traditional aspiration to government service. Recruitment to teaching has been disconnected from social class background in recent history.

This characteristic may also be related to the shamanistic culture of Korea. According to In Whoe Kim, the indigenous value system of Korea can be traced in its long-surviving shamanistic culture. These Korean shamanistic values are identified with the commoners' culture as compared to the virtues of the high culture of the Confucian literati in Korea. The traditionally dominant cultural code of practice and the definition of excellence inherited by the Confucian literati class became absorbed in the newly legitimated, situation-oriented, opportunistic cultural code through the modern (colonial and post-colonial) state's social promotion system (Kim, 1988, 1993).

Given the situation-oriented culture in South Korea, teacher education and recruitment systems have been frequently changed on the basis of *ad hoc* educational policies. According to official government sources, the college entrance system has been changed more than 10 times since 1945 (Ministry of Education and Human Resources Development, 2000). This implies that South Korean educational reforms have mainly focused on immediate problems, for which short-term solutions were sought. Given these volatile circumstances, the best possible way for Koreans to climb up the social ladder officially was to attain a higher education diploma authorized by the state. This objective has been tightly linked to the government recruitment of teachers, and to the teacher education system *per se*.

Conclusion: retrospect and prospect

Looking back, South Korea has achieved spectacular growth in education as well as the economy. Enrolment is now universal in primary and secondary education, and the enrolment rate in higher education is among the highest in the world, even though colleges and universities in South Korea operate under strict enrolment limits. The enrolment rate of those graduating from academic high school to higher educational institutions in 2000 was 83.9 per cent whereas from vocational high school it was 41.9 per cent.

Overall, this chapter has illustrated four historical pressures for conformity that shaped teacher education in South Korea in the 20th century. The first is statism. There is a strongly surviving legacy from Confucian meritocratic principles and from the Japanese colonial government's recruitment of elites to teacher training and its reward system – upward social mobility. Second, another norm of conformity in South Korean society has been US world-views; liberal democracy and the ideology of a capitalist economy have been taught within a rather militaristic and autocratic schooling culture. Third, rigid conformity was maintained in South Korea because of its sensitive relationship with North Korea. However, the changing geopolitics around the Korean peninsula during and after the Cold War era, especially from 1998 onwards, have been creating a new dilemma: how to reconcile anti-communist nationalism with links with North Korea. A new revisionist approach is now being required, to redefine the national history curriculum for South Korea in the 21st century. The fourth theme of conformity is the economic-centred philosophy behind educational planning and policy making.

Formal education has always been managed under direct government control. This control may become even more intense now with the new Ministry of Education and Human Resources Development, which was launched in January 2001; its implications for teacher education will be interesting in the era of 'globalization'. Thus, the central dilemma of South Korean teacher education is the contradiction between, on the one hand, the new possibilities of educational globalization linked with a policy of educational internationalization and, on the other, the old politics of *dirigisme*. The future awaits construction.

References

Chang, Hyun (1998) Management implications of the ideological discourse of globalisation and re-engineering in South Korea, in *Perspectives on Korea*, ed Sang-Oak Lee and Duk-Soo Park, pp 1–15, University of Hawaii Press, Honolulu

Cole, D C and Lyman, P N (1971) *Korean Development*, Harvard University Press, Cambridge, MA

Kim, In Whoe (1988) *Hankook Moosock Sasang Yonku* (A Research on Shamanistic Ideology in Korea), Jipmoon-dang, Seoul

Kim, In Whoe (1993) *Hankook Kyoyook-eyu Yerksa-wa Moonje* (History of Korean Education and its Problems), Moon-eum Sa, Seoul

Kim, T (2001) *Forming the Academic Profession in East Asia: A comparative analysis of Korea, Malaysia and Singapore since colonial times*, Routledge, New York, London (forthcoming)

Korean Council for University Education (KCUE) (1997) *University Education Development Indicators*, ed Hyung-chung Lee and Young-hack Lee, KCUE, Seoul

Lee, Byung-Jin and Pang, Myung-suk (1998) Reform trends for teacher education in the Republic of Korea, Paper presented at AERA, 15 April

Mason, E S, Kim, M J and Cole, D C (1980) *The Economic and Social Modernization of the Republic of Korea*, Harvard University Press, Cambridge, MA

Ministry of Education (MoE) (1998a) *Education in Korea 1997–1998*, Ministry of Education, Seoul

Ministry of Education (1998b) *Republic of Korea: Fifty years of education*, Ministry of Education, Seoul

Ministry of Education (1998c) *The Vision for Education in 2002*, Ministry of Education, Seoul

Ministry of Education (1999) *A New Foundation for the Korean Economy*, Ministry of Education, Djnomics, Seoul

Ministry of Education and Human Resources Development (2000) *Education in Korea 2000*, Ministry of Education and Human Resources Development, Seoul

Ministry of Education and Human Resources Development (2001) *Education for the Future*, Ministry of Education and Human Resources Development, Seoul, http://www.moe.go.kr/eng/engmoebbs/view0010.htm

Ministry of Education and Korean Educational Development Institute (2000) *Brief Statistics on Korean Education 2000*, Ministry of Education and Korean Educational Development Institute, Seoul

The Presidential Commission on Education Reform, The Republic of Korea (1997) *Educational Reform for the 21st Century: To ensure leadership in the information and globalization era*, PCER Report, November, Seoul

World Bank (2000) *Global Education Reform: Singapore vision*, http://www1.worldbank.org/education/globaleducationreform/Singapore%20vision.htm

5. Greece: modernization and control in teacher education

Evie Zambeta

Introduction

Teacher education has always been a crucial and symbolically significant field of education policy. Historically speaking, the structure, context and content of teacher education mirror the political conditions prevailing in Greece in each particular period, and follow the turbulent political life of the country. In Greece there is a deep division between primary and secondary teachers' education. Secondary teachers' education was always provided at university level and it was discipline-oriented. As Cowen (2000) puts it, the university is based on the principles of academic autonomy and freedom; it could be argued that secondary teachers' education in Greece has been provided within a context of relative autonomy. The initial education and training of primary teachers, by contrast, has been a field of intense state control.

This chapter argues that the changing forms of governance in Greek primary teachers' education by no means imply that the state is abolishing the privilege of control over primary education. It rather suggests that the means and the processes of power reproduction are changing in view of the wider socio-economic and cultural changes that are taking place in Greece and in the global context. The change in the state's role on teacher education represents an attempt at modernization of Greek society and a restructuring of the dominant interests within the state and educational institutions. It will be further argued that teacher education is a particularly sensitive field of education policy that reflects dominant political ideologies regarding the relationship between education, society and the state. Furthermore, the wider transitions in the socio-economic sphere or in the terrain of political culture offer the contexts and framing of teacher education. The attempts at modernization, however, embody continuities with tradition. The chapter will first discuss three key areas in the context of the present *World Yearbook*, namely teacher identity and political surveillance, followed by an examination of the transition of state control to the steering state and, finally, the changing nature of Greek teacher education and its control with reference to globalization.

Teacher identity and political surveillance

The control of teacher identity has been a crucial component of state education building and a basic strategy for political surveillance. The development of the teacher has been the common project of teacher education on the one hand and of the construction of the profession on the other. First and foremost the profession has been constructed as a 'public service'. In spite of the fact that initially – according to the 1834 Education Act – primary schools were established at the local government level, the teachers were public servants supervised by state commissioners and subjected to the control of a structured bureaucratic hierarchy, which was accountable to the central state (Dimaras, 1987/88).

Gender is an important aspect of teacher education. Despite the legal provision regarding the education of female teachers, the first schools that educate teachers turn out to be exclusively male institutions. Till recently teacher education has been gendered. The prerequisites for entering these schools as well as the curricula differ by gender. Female teachers could enter the teacher training colleges at a younger age and with lower educational qualifications. They could even be shorter than their male colleagues, since height was one of the attributes considered as significant for those entering public service. Men were not allowed access to kindergarten teaching till 1982, when sex discrimination in teacher education was officially abolished. Gradually but steadily teacher education and the teaching profession itself follows a process of feminization in Greece. The situation, however, is not favourable to women regarding progression within the profession or the prospects for promotion to management posts (Kontogiannopoulou-Polydorides and Zambeta, 1997).

The regulation and control of teacher education is one of the first considerations of any new government as soon as it comes into power. Each time there has been a transition in terms of political power, a similar change takes place in the field of teacher education. It could be argued that teacher education is one of the most sensitive fields in education politics, which reflects the prevailing socio-economic and political conditions and the dominant ideologies regarding political surveillance. An indicative example is the teacher curriculum that was introduced by the fascist regime in 1937, which introduced military education in the pedagogical academies. Political surveillance, however, is not accomplished exclusively through teacher education. State control is exercised through central control of the curricula, textbooks, school inspection, and student and teacher assessment. Furthermore, discipline and order are maintained through the imposition of controls over the time and place of learning (Solomon, 1992) and through the codification, classification and framing of school knowledge.

Teacher education in late modernity: from state control to the steering state

The pedagogical academies were established as two-year post-secondary teacher training institutions. In 1933 they were perceived as an attempt at modernization and homogenization of teacher education. They were introduced after the recommendations of G Palaiologos, who had been influenced by the German model of teacher education. They represented a centralist, bureaucratic model of knowledge control, which could be seen to be highly contradictory. On the one hand they were based on classicism and encyclopaedism, while on the other they imparted a type of vocationalism that did not offer acquisition of scientific knowledge and research. The concepts of autonomy and academic freedom were alien to these institutions, with the Ministry of Education holding overall control of the organization, structures, appointment of teaching personnel, curriculum development and textbooks. In fact these schools have not witnessed any major restructuring since their foundation.

The only exception to that was the reform period of 1964, which was an attempt at modernization and upgrading of teacher education (Bouzakis, Tzikas and Anthopoulos, 1998). This reform, however, was suspended by the dictatorship, in 1967. The structure and content of the pedagogical academies was influenced mainly by the political culture of conservative and authoritarian regimes, and by the educational vision of romanticism and classicism. The pedagogical academies were favourable to linguistic purism, which was supported by the political right, and against any attempt at educational reform or resolution of the language question. After the restoration of parliamentary democracy in 1974 the debate regarding teacher education became intense. A committee appointed by the government to examine the educational system and submit a reform proposal plan came up with suggestions regarding the reorganization and upgrading of teacher education within the context of the pedagogical academies. In fact, the final proposal ignored other more radical suggestions regarding the organization of teacher education at the university level (Zambeta, 1994). It seems that the contradictions that were expressed in the 1974 educational committee represented the lack of consensus in Greek society regarding the ideal types of teacher and school. The political right that was then in power succeeded in resolving the language question that had been pending for decades, but in many cases did not manage to overcome tradition. The state control of teacher training was definitely one of these cases where tradition prevailed over modernization.

The decisive shift in teacher education took place in 1982 when the recently elected socialist government introduced an education law aiming at a major reform of university structures. Until 1981, Greek universities had a strict hierarchical structure based on the regime of the professorial chair. Whereas the university enjoyed 'self-management' and academic freedom, the crucial decisions regarding curriculum control and appointment of the academic staff rested with the powerful body of a limited number of professors. At the same time the overwhelming majority of the teaching staff was considered as assistant teaching personnel with limited responsibilities. The 1982 reform law abolished the regime of the chair and introduced a four-level academic staff hierarchy.

This policy was followed by the introduction of new modes of university management, which involved student participation and was based on the principles of academic autonomy and freedom. The key interests that gained access to the new institutions of university management were the student unions and the assistant teaching personnel. Both the students and the assistant teaching staff were more influenced then by the political left and contributed to a serious redefinition of power relationships within university institutions (Zambeta, 2000). The 1982 university reform law established university departments for teacher education. After a period of parallel coexistence the pedagogical academies and the schools for kindergarten teachers were eventually abolished in 1990. This was meant to be the end of direct state control over teacher education. It is worth wondering however why the state withdrew from this control and why it happened at this time.

The 1980s represented a transitional period in Greek society. The processes of transition were expressed in the political, socio-economic and cultural spheres, and had considerable impact on education. The change in political culture through modernization and democratization was related to the inclusion of Greece in the process of European integration. The process of modernization however involved contradictions and continuities with tradition (Zambeta, 2000). This period represented a transition from authoritarian state control to the steering state. The steering state here is perceived as a form of political governance that introduces new modes of surveillance and legitimization of power. In the case of the traditional authoritarian state, political surveillance is exercised through direct mechanisms of state intervention in educational institutions, eg appointment of teachers by the central state, administrative accountability and inspection, central curricular control, single textbooks, etc. In the case of the steering state, surveillance is exercised through forms of governance that involve devolution of power to other agents, defined as democratic or decentralized management, social participation of corporate interests, evaluation and assessment.

The steering state is by no means a less strong state. It might be an even stronger and more expanded state. It might also be a wiser state with wider deposits of legitimization and sophisticated technologies for mediating the global and the local, the social and the individual (Lindblad and Popkewitz, 2000). In other terms, part of state steering is the redefinition of the relationship between the state and civil society, and the introduction of new strategies for achieving social consensus and legitimating power. The technologies and strategies of political surveillance may change but not the object of surveillance *per se*. The transition from control to steering, however, should not be perceived as linear, universal or irreversible. It should rather be understood as a governance strategy that involves contradictions and continuities with tradition and the past.

The establishing of university departments for teacher education, within a context of wider democratization of education and the universities in particular, could be understood as a governance strategy on the part of the state. The change in the state's role on teacher education did not mean that the state abolished the privilege of control of teachers' identity or that it abandoned the object of political surveillance. It rather meant that the strategies of surveillance and the politics of identity differentiated, becoming more complex and less visible. The new strategies of surveillance involved the state steering through mediation of the group interests that formed the legitimating basis of the socialist government that came to power in 1981. The steering state did not exercise direct control on teacher education since the university was defined as autonomous from the state.

The new government, however, changed the balance of power within the university by empowering those group interests that were vital for its own power. Moreover, it developed new institutions of decision making, which were legitimized on the basis of the democratic principle of social participation (eg the department's general assembly, which is the main management institution of the university department, consists of all the academic staff and representatives from the student unions). Those group interests that acquired access to decision making, however, were not autonomous social actors. They also depended on the state through the various clientelist networks that contributed to the forming of social consensus (Charalambis, 1996; Mouzelis, 1993). In group clientelism, the mediation of interests forms a sort of political exchange and mutual dependence between the state and civil society. In this respect neither the state nor the group interests are autonomous from each other. This partly explains the contradictory character and the limitations of any attempt at reform. In this scheme no social actor is free fully to exercise its political will, and political surveillance is produced through mutual control.

This by no means implies that the potential influence of every social actor is the same. The steering state continues being a state where specific interests are dominant. It does imply, however, that the state functions by allowing certain group interests to satisfy their goals. For example, in making available university teacher education the state satisfies the interests of the primary teachers' unions and at the same time uses them as a legitimating agent of its educational, economic and social policy in general. A particularly indicative case is that of the automatic and unconditional payment of primary teachers that had graduated from the Pedagogical Academies to the university graduates. In a similar way the state uses the various new bodies of social participation that have been introduced in this period, for example the 'ESAP' (National Council of Higher Education) (Zambeta, 1994; Stamelos, 1999).

The new technologies of political surveillance are more sophisticated and smarter than those used by the traditional authoritarian state. Continuities with tradition, however, are also present and of vital importance for the sustaining of power. The case of the influence of the church in the early formation of teacher education departments offers an indicative example of this. It should be noted, however, that the state invents new forms of intervention in the field of teacher education, despite alleged university autonomy. The most important of them is the increasing importance attributed to school teaching experience of students in teacher education. In this respect the school itself and the school curriculum become an external governing mechanism that regulates the structure and the content of teacher education. This fact should not be considered a Greek peculiarity. The same seems to be the case in other countries too (for example, in England), which brings into serious question the limits of university autonomy as well as the professional status of teaching (Bash, 2000). In Greece, though, there is no uniformity in the curriculum between the various teacher education departments. It seems that in some particular cases the relative importance of school experience is exceptionally high, corresponding to a quarter of teacher training (Stamelos, 1999).

Teacher education in global perspective

It is widely acknowledged today that the dramatic changes taking place in the fields of biotechnology, as well as in information and communication technologies, exercise radical impacts on the structure of the world economy and tend to transform the relationship between education and society (Coulby, 2000). At the same time, international organizations such as the European Union, OECD, World Bank and UNESCO underline the need for modernization of educational systems so as to be able to respond to the demands of the new global knowledge society. Globalization is considered to be an unavoidable process, and the globalization of culture in particular is a central issue in the sociological debates of the last decade (Featherstone, 1990). Even when globalization is considered a contested concept, sociologists like Giddens (1998) speak about the softening of boundaries and the emergence of the 'cosmopolitan nation'. In the emerging knowledge economy, knowledge becomes a valuable trading commodity.

This is by no means a new situation. What is perhaps new is the means of control and diffusion of knowledge. Today schools and universities have stopped being the main institutions for transmission of knowledge and information. Many children know how to read and write on a computer before entering primary education. At the same time many others do not share this privilege: the sons and daughters of the poor, the economic immigrants or the indigenous minorities. Whereas the school insists on traditional knowledge, it expands the distance between the two categories and deepens the inequality. In other words, the school reproduces the interests of the ruling groups.

Some optimists like Porter (1999) speak about the perspective of the 'reflective school', which expresses in a concise way the contradictions that the school faces today: on one hand, the celebration of individualism as the main route to personal development and, on the other, the recognition of collectivism as a strategy for social cohesion and security. No matter how desirable this might be for some parts of society, the question is whether such a school could be possible today.

In a world of uncertainty and instability the school is asked to develop the illusionary concept of security and stability. Even if the school were able to accomplish this task, what else would this be if not what Coulby (2000) provocatively calls 'lies and nonsense'? The demand for 'reschooling' society, as a strategy towards reconstructing the prerequisites of social cohesion, implies a new ideological role for education towards imposing value systems and building imagined communities. If the school model as such is undergoing a crisis, this is not because of its failure to construct and generate value systems, but because of its inability to reveal the contradictory and selective character of its premises.

This said, it is not to assert arguments such as those of deschooling or deregulation of the public or individual choice. It rather suggests that, despite any sense of relative autonomy, school systems are state apparatuses that predominantly reproduce established power relationships. In doing so they stick to tradition, distance themselves from any sort of universalism and construct discrimination and prejudice. These attributes are intrinsic to state educational systems, and the perspective of change does not involve another kind of school, but another kind of state. The question is whether this type of state is visible in the forthcoming future. The above contradictions are evident in the field of teacher education in Greece. On one hand the strict state control seems to soften, whilst on the other state steering is ensured through new governance mechanisms in universities and what is called 'school teaching practice'.

State control in the field of primary education in general certainly remains untouched and it is exercised through central control of the curriculum and textbooks, and control of the teaching profession in terms of both recruitment and assessment of performance. The upgrading of teacher education at the university level broadens the legitimating basis of the government, and abolishes an outdated hierarchy within the teaching profession, since secondary education is by no means a privilege of the social elite any more. While abolishing a hierarchy within the teaching profession, the state establishes new forms of governance that generate new hierarchies of surveillance in education (such as the institutions of representation of the various group interests in decision making or the new mechanisms of education accountability and assessment). At the same time the policy of upgrading allows the state to develop many new university departments, a fact that serves the strategy of changing the old political order within the university institutions.

The discourse and political practices of international organizations have encouraged this strategy. The European Union in particular acts as a governance mechanism parallel to that of the state by setting and funding certain educational agendas. The European Community support frameworks have turned out to be a major source of funding for education and the universities in particular. The Greek state adjusts its education policy in order to fit these agendas and uses the European funds in order to reproduce clientelist networks and power relations. In the field of teacher education, for instance, the universities were obliged to undertake huge programmes of in-service teacher training that offered what has been called an 'academic equation' to the non-university graduates. This has been performed under the heading of teacher training in the 'European dimension of education' (Mavrogiorgos, 1994). In a context of restricted public funding, teacher education departments treated this opportunity as a means to get additional resources and develop the good will of the Ministry of Education.

Teacher education today is unavoidably subject to global impact coming either through funding mechanisms (such as those of the European funds) or through the public discourses of the international organizations, which tend to develop new ways of understanding and interpreting the contemporary world. On the other hand, the practice of the international organizations influences teacher education by setting standards and criteria of mutual recognition of qualifications. The standards for the qualified teacher's status or the Bologna Declaration on the development of a 'common higher education European space' unavoidably impose new thresholds, which the institutions of teacher education in Greece have not yet dealt with.

Teacher education is certainly also subject to the impact of society itself, which is undergoing dramatic changes, becoming more culturally diverse. The school has to deal with this diversity, and teacher education cannot avoid facing these new realities. However, ethnocentricity and cultural relativism are parallel forces in conflict, depicting the tensions between tradition and modernity in Greek education. These issues have begun to be discussed in universities and teacher education departments in particular, partly because they correspond to research and action projects funded by the European Union.

Their reception in schools is less favourable though. The interpretation of schools' resistance to change, however, also becomes part of teachers' education through the introduction of social sciences (Kontogiannopoulou-Polydorides, 1995), which is an almost totally new situation that takes place only in the context of university teacher education. Even when fears are expressed that the specific recontextualization of social sciences in teacher education constructs a theoretical 'bricolage' that does not form the basis for a critical understanding (Makrynioti and Solomon, 1991), it could still be argued that universities' academic autonomy should hold the keys of self-transformation.

Within a context of a changing global environment, Greek teacher education faces new dilemmas. As knowledge economies develop, teachers cannot cope with the amount of new knowledge produced. One of the main issues discussed during the past two decades was what has been called the 'scientific identity' of the teacher. Whilst in the past the most important aim of teacher education was the formation of a teacher's identity, today the concept of development of specific skills tends to become a crucial point in the teacher education political agenda. The multidisciplinary, encyclopaedic and rather descriptive approaches to knowledge are gradually becoming considered an inadequate way of preparing teachers, since they do not offer the scientific tools to knowledge acquisition and research. Traditional hierarchies within knowledge systems are being questioned. In the political debate the influence of the discourse of international organizations regarding the importance of new approaches to knowledge and the 'skills to learn how to learn' is fairly evident. At the same time the traditionalist discourse that advocates the 'preservation of Greek identity and the purity of its culture' is also present. The prospects for teacher education will probably reflect these conflicting discourses. The last two decades represent a transitional period in Greek teacher education, where intense state control has given place to rather indirect forms of state steering. Attempts at modernization are evident although they involve continuities with tradition.

References

Bash, L (2000) Regulation and autonomy in higher education: issues for teacher training in England and Wales, *Panepistemio*, **1**, pp 79–93 (in Greek)

Bouzakis, S, Tzikas, C and Anthopoulos, K (1998) *The Training of Primary and Kindergarten Teachers in Greece*, vol B, *The Period of the Pedagogical Academies and the Schools of Kindergarten Teachers*, Gutenberg, Athens (in Greek)

Charalambis, D (1996) Irrational contents of a typically rational system, in *Society and Politics: Aspects of the 3rd Greek Republic 1974–1994*, ed C Lyrintzis *et al*, Themelio, Athens (in Greek)

Coulby, D (2000) *Beyond the National Curriculum: Curricular centralism and cultural diversity in Europe and the USA*, Routledge, London

Cowen, R (2000) Academic freedom, universities and knowledge economies, *Panepistemio*, **2**, pp 3–23 (in Greek)

Dimaras, A (1987/88) The reform that never took place, *Ermes*, **I, II**, Athens (in Greek)

Featherstone, M (ed) (1990) *Global Culture: Nationalism, globalisation and modernity*, Sage, London

Giddens, A (1998) *The Third Way: The renewal of social democracy*, Polity Press, Cambridge

Kontogiannopoulou-Polydorides, G (1995) *Education, Politics and Practice: Sociological analysis*, Ellinika Grammata, Athens (in Greek)

Kontogiannopoulou-Polydorides, G and Zambeta, E (1997) Greece, in *Women in Educational Management*, ed M Wilson, Paul Chapman, London

Lindblad, S and Popkewitz, T S (eds) (2000) Public discourses on education governance and social integration and exclusion: analyses of policy texts in European contexts, *Uppsala Reports on Education*, **36**, Uppsala

Makrynioti, D and Solomon, J (1991) The introduction of social sciences in teacher education, in *The University in Greece Today: Economic, social and political dimensions*, ed S Karagiorgas Foundation, pp 399–413, S Karagiorgas Foundation, Athens (in Greek)

Mavrogiorgos, G (1994) Teachers' initial education and further training: aspects of isomorphism in the European dimension, in European Conference, *The Greek Teacher and its European Dimension*, pp 138–60, Lambrakis Studies Foundation and Kostea-Geitona Schools, Athens (in Greek)

Mouzelis, N (1993) The state in late development, *Greek Political Science Review*, **1**, pp 53–89 (in Greek)

Porter, J (1999) *Reschooling and the Global Future: Politics, economics and the English experience*, Symposium Books, Oxford

Solomon, J (1992) *Power and Order in the Modern Greek School*, Alexandria, Athens (in Greek)

Stamelos, G (1999) *The Teacher Education University Departments: Origins, present situation and perspectives*, Gutenberg, Athens (in Greek)

Zambeta, E (1994) *Education Politics in Primary Education (1974–1989)*, Themelio, Athens (in Greek)

Zambeta, E (2000) Greece: the lack of modernity and educational transitions, in *World Yearbook of Education 2000: Education in times of transition*, ed D Coulby, R Cowen and C Jones, pp 63–75, Kogan Page, London

Section II
Change and reform in teacher education

6. Teacher education in Malaysia: current issues and future prospects

Molly N N Lee

Introduction

The development of teacher education in Malaysia is closely related to the socio-economic and political development of the country as well as being influenced by the global trends on educational changes. With the advancement of information communication technology in the context of globalization, schools are only one of the many educational agencies in society. With the increase in sources of information and the rapid access to information, teachers have to cope with the problem of selection and prioritization of relevant information for themselves and their pupils (Thomas, 2000). In this chapter, an in-depth analysis of some Malaysian reforms and practices will show the influence of global trends on teacher education with reference to 1) the patterns and control of teacher education, 2) approaches to the curriculum of teacher education and 3) the preparation of teachers for a multicultural society.

Patterns and control of teacher education

As in most centralized education systems, teacher education is under the tight control of the state. The historical development of teacher education in Malaysia has resulted in a dual system of teacher training, involving two main types of institutions – one is administered by the Ministry of Education and the other by universities. The Ministry of Education is responsible for the training of non-graduate teachers, while the universities are responsible for the training of graduate teachers. There are 27 teacher training colleges throughout the country, preparing non-graduate teachers for both the primary and lower secondary schools. All these colleges follow a common curriculum, and all prospective teachers sit for a common examination, which is set by the Ministry of Education. The Ministry recruits all the students for these colleges, and the college lecturers are drawn from the rank and file of the graduate teaching force in the national school system. The core business of these training colleges is to offer initial teacher education programmes that are geared towards the professional, academic and personal development of prospective teachers. The national teacher education curriculum adopts a generalist approach for primary school teachers and subject specialization for teachers at the lower secondary level (Ministry of Education, 1991).

The public universities are responsible for the training of graduate teachers for secondary schools. Basically, there are two types of initial teacher education programmes, namely the consecutive programme and the concurrent programme. The consecutive programme is a one-year postgraduate diploma in education offered to students who have already obtained their first degree. This 'add-on' teacher education programme has both its advantages and disadvantages. This type of programme allows for quick responses to the changing demands of the labour market for teachers. Students who opt for the diploma of education programme do not have to make their career choice until they have completed their undergraduate education. However, the downside of this programme is that one year is too short a period for the students to be embedded in the ethos of the teaching profession.

To overcome this shortcoming, the universities have introduced the concurrent programme that takes in students for teacher education at the beginning of their undergraduate study. In the concurrent programme, the students do their education courses at the same time as they do their academic studies, thus extending the teacher education programme from one year to four years. Although these programmes are offered by the public universities, the Ministry of Education has a strong say in terms of types and length of programmes and student intakes for them.

The above analysis shows that teacher education is a shared responsibility between the teacher training colleges and the public universities. Such an institutional arrangement has both its advantages and disadvantages. Because the Ministry is directly responsible for teacher training, this makes it easier to control the demand and supply of teachers to some extent. The weakness lies in the fact that, unlike other countries, the teacher training colleges are not affiliated to any university and the award of the Malaysian diploma of teaching by the teacher training colleges is not validated by any professional body or university but by the Ministry itself. Hence, as far as non-graduate teachers are concerned, the Ministry of Education not only registers and employs them but also validates their awards. This practice is contrary to what is commonly found in other professions like doctors and engineers, where there is a deliberate effort to make a distinctive separation between the awarding body, the licensing body and the employing agency.

Therefore, if Malaysia is considering a move towards the professionalization of teachers to ensure that certain standards are maintained at the teacher training colleges, some radical changes will have to be made in this respect (Lee, 2000). In 1997, the Malaysia government established the National Accreditation Board to accredit courses offered by the private institutions of higher learning. There is a possibility that this mechanism of quality assurance will be extended to the public institutions of higher learning, such as the teacher training colleges, in the future.

In recent years, there has been a move towards more collaboration between teacher training colleges and universities in offering innovative teacher education programmes for practising teachers who wish to upgrade themselves. One such programme is a three-year twinning programme between a teacher training college and a local public university, which was launched in 1997, to upgrade non-graduate teachers to graduate teachers. In this programme, non-graduate teachers are required to undergo the first year of study in a designated teacher training college and then proceed to another two years of study in an affiliated university, specializing in secondary school subjects. On successful completion of the programme, they are awarded the Bachelor of Education (BEd) degree. A total of 14 teacher training colleges and seven local universities are currently involved in the running of this programme (Abdul Rafie, 1999).

Besides collaborative efforts among various institutions, there is also an 'academic drift' among the teacher education institutions in Malaysia. Since the mid-1980s, a number of the teacher training colleges have begun to offer programmes for the training of graduate teachers. This change has come about partly because an increasing number of college lecturers have pursued postgraduate studies and they are now in a position to take over some of the roles and responsibilities of the faculties of education in universities. In fact, it was recently announced that the universities will stop offering the postgraduate diploma of education starting from 2001. In line with this development, teacher educators in the universities are shifting their time, energy and resources to postgraduate programmes and educational research. In an attempt to consolidate resources, the Ministry of Education has upgraded a teacher training college to a university, University Perguruan Sultan Idris (UPSI), in 1997, and closed down three other colleges. It is likely that in time to come the universities will shed their responsibilities for the initial training of graduate teachers and focus their attention on providing postgraduate education for practising teachers and carrying out educational research.

One of the prevailing issues in teacher education is the recruitment of appropriate high-calibre candidates. The teaching profession does not attract the most talented young people (Lanier and Little, 1986). This is especially the case when it comes to attracting male teachers. The ratio of male to female students in a teacher training college in Penang in 1995 was as low as 1:4 (Lee, 2000). Teaching is not attractive, partly because of its low social status, and also because a teacher's job is complex and demanding. Therefore, it is imperative that the Ministry of Education continue to improve the working conditions of teachers and the quality of teacher education by initiating reforms like increasing teachers' salaries, lengthening teacher education programmes, raising admission requirements and improving the teaching career structures.

As in other countries, there is an upward trend in entrance and exit qualification, and a drift to longer and more advanced forms of teacher training
(Furlong, 1991).

The admission requirement to the teacher training colleges in Malaysia used
to be the equivalent of O level (that is, a Sijil Pelajaran Malaysia, obtained after
five years of secondary education), but now it is slowly being raised to the
equivalent of A level (that is, a Sijil Pelajaran Tinggi Malaysia, after seven
years of secondary education). Since 1996, the training period has been
lengthened from two and a half years to three years leading to a diploma in
teaching instead of a certificate of teaching, and the basic pay for college-
trained teachers has also been increased by 30 per cent (Lee, 2000). Similarly,
the career structure for graduate teachers has improved with the introduction
of new posts such as heads of subject departments in schools and master
teachers. Despite these policy initiatives, the teaching profession is always
experiencing a high rate of turnover, especially during economic boom times.
The problem of demand and supply of teachers continues to be one of the
main issues in teacher education in Malaysia.

Approaches to the curriculum of teacher education

The quality of teacher education does not depend only on the quality of the
student intakes and teacher educators but, more importantly, on the content
and methods of training. Many of the ideas, theories and approaches to
teacher education in Malaysia have been influenced by global trends in the
field. A brief review of the literature on teacher education shows that the theoretical perspective for teaching and learning has shifted from behavioural
approaches to cognitive constructivist approaches (Wittrock, 1986; Houston,
1990; Sikula *et al*, 1996). The behavioural approaches view teaching as a well-
defined, structured activity that can be taught as a set of skills, whereas the
constructivist approaches are based on the assumption that learning is fundamentally a socially mediated activity and teaching takes place in an ill-struc-
tured environment that is full of fuzzy problems for which there are no
prepared solutions (Willis and Mehlinger, 1996).

The technical-rational model is a behavioural approach to teacher education
that places great emphasis on the acquisition of teaching skills and competencies in order to become an effective teacher. On the other hand, the
reflective practitioner model is a constructivist approach to teacher education
that assumes that students cannot be told how to become an effective teacher.
They have to build or construct their own knowledge base and their own
professional skills, instead of being told by the 'experts'.

In the context of Malaysia, most of the teacher education programmes are
based on the technicist approach and a major portion of the time is devoted to the
acquisition of generic teaching skills such as preparing lesson plans, classroom

management skills, questioning techniques and assessment techniques. At the teacher training college level, a 'cook-recipe' (step-by-step) approach is often used. Training methods used to include teaching school curriculum subjects reflecting the emphasis of school examinations. However, at the tertiary level, there is a wider scope of coverage in the teacher education curriculum.

As in many other countries, the curriculum for initial teacher education comprises four components, namely academic subjects (major and minor), foundations of education, pedagogy and teaching practice (Houston, 1990). Some of the teacher education programmes, like those offered in the Universiti Sains Malaysia, Penang, are designed with a strong bias on developmental psychology. There is a heavy dosage of psychology courses including learning theories, the development of adolescents and student counselling. The developmental approach is also applied to the overall training of prospective teachers, particularly those who follow the four-year concurrent programmes.

The emphasis is on formative evaluation and block teaching practices, which attempt to help students to link theory and practice by drawing upon their experiences in schools. Most of the foundation courses are taught using a single-disciplinary approach, and only deliver 'facts and theories' about the philosophical, psychological, historical and sociological foundations of education. The content in these courses is usually presented in a neutral fashion lacking a critical perspective on both educational and social issues.

The future development of teacher education programmes in Malaysia should move away from the technicist approach to a reflective practitioner approach, and from a consensus approach to a critical approach. The purpose and content of the foundation courses should be changed to offer alternative perspectives on educational issues based on critical theory, postmodernism or deconstruction theory (McHoul and Luke, 1988). There should be a shift to a more controversial and contentious examination of ideological and political issues that frame education in the Malaysian society. Although there have been attempts to promote reflective teaching by teacher educators in Malaysia, many of the efforts have been focused on 'technical reflection' and not so much on 'practical reflection' and 'critical reflection' (Goodman, 1991).

Prospective teachers are asked to keep journals on what kinds of methods and techniques they used in their teaching practice and reflect on 'what works' and 'how to solve a given problem', like how to keep their pupils on task, how to diagnose pupils' weaknesses, how to obtain feedback from pupils and other problems (Lee, 1993). Reflection on technical questions is but a small step towards becoming a reflective practitioner. An important aspect of teacher education is to help teachers to realize and understand the values and beliefs that underlie their practices. Teachers need to be engaged in practical reflection on issues related to everyday school life such as student–teacher relationships, student–student relationships, curriculum choices, instructional or management decisions, and the social implications of particular educational practices. They should also be encouraged to reflect on the ethical and political concerns of education, to question the taken-for-granted assumptions about teaching and to understand the connection between classroom life and broader societal forces and structures.

As for teaching method courses, much of the content is based on the findings of process–product research on teacher effectiveness that identifies significant relations between student gain (product) and teacher performance (process) (Fenstermacher, 1978). The emphasis is on the acquisition of general pedagogical skills such as drills, practices, praises, time-on-task, respond time for questions and competence in subject matter. However, this approach to the teaching method courses has been heavily criticized for trivializing the teaching process. According to Shulman (1987: 6), 'Critical features of teaching, such as the subject matter being taught, the classroom context, the physical and psychological characteristics of the students, or the accomplishment of purposes not readily assessed on standardised tests, are typically ignored in the quest for general principles of effective teaching'. Instead of generic skills, Shulman advocates the development of a 'pedagogical content knowledge' base that aims at blending content and pedagogy into an understanding of how particular topics, problems or issues are organized, represented and adapted to the diverse interests and abilities of learners. Teacher educators in Malaysia are quite aware of this current trend in teacher education but not much has been done to adopt this approach in their programmes, partly because of a lack of research appropriate to the local context.

Although there has been an ideological shift towards school-based teacher education, especially in the United Kingdom, based on a rhetoric of the superiority of 'practice' to 'theory' (McBride, 1996), the involvement of schools in teacher education in Malaysia is based more on practical reasons than on ideological. The current British debate is on 'Who should be the teacher educator?' and 'What roles should higher education and schools play in teacher education?' Since the 1980s, the responsibility for teacher education has been more classroom-based relating to the notion of 'relevance' (Furlong *et al*, 1996). Universities are to form partnerships with schools, so that teachers can take up joint responsibility for the supervision and assessment of students on school experience and be involved in other dimensions of training such as subject studies, curriculum courses and professional studies.

However, the partnership between universities and schools in teacher education in Malaysia has been limited and has been developed only recently. The schools have always been involved in teaching practice, but not the teachers. In the past, trainee teachers were sent to schools to do their teaching practice and it was the university or college lecturers who supervised and assessed them. But in recent years, because of the large number of students involved, many universities are encountering logistic problems in placing their students in schools as well as supervising them during their teaching practice.

To overcome these problems, cooperating teachers from the schools are recruited to help in the supervision of trainee teachers. Unfortunately, there are many practical constraints in building a viable partnership between universities and schools. Because of heavy workload, large course size and the problem of physical distance, the cooperating teachers scheme encountered practical problems pertaining to coordination, resources, coherence and communication. Often cooperating teachers participating in the scheme do not quite know what their roles are and what they are expected to do. For such a scheme to work, it is imperative that university staff should maintain close communication and establish routine forms of collaboration with cooperating teachers.

One strategy would be to structure more school-based assignments involving investigations of schools or classroom practices on some issues in the courses offered by the universities. The design and assessment of this school-based work could be done by the university staff in collaboration with the cooperating teachers. Cooperating teachers would need to be given proper briefing and training so that they could play their role as mentors to trainee teachers more effectively.

Teachers for cultural diversity

Malaysia is a multi-ethnic society, comprising Malays, Chinese, Indians and other indigenous ethnic groups. Cultural diversity in Malaysia is related not only to ethnicity but also includes religion, language, social class and regional differences. In many multicultural societies, the prevailing issue is how to strike a balance between maintaining social cohesion and celebrating diversity. As asked by Craft (1990), when does the acculturation necessary for full participation in society become repressive assimilation, especially in a culturally hegemonic society; and when does the celebration of cultural diversity cease to enrich and become a source of social instability, especially in a society that values cultural pluralism? The paramount challenge is how to develop an educational system to meet the diverse and competing demands of different interest groups and how to prepare teachers to teach culturally diverse students.

Governments in pluralistic societies tend to see education as an important means of promoting national unity among the culturally diverse groups within the country. The educational response in Malaysia is to develop a centralized national education system, with a common language of instruction in secondary and tertiary education, common curricula and common examinations in the school system. However, the minority groups were able to negotiate for the provision of primary education in Chinese and Tamil. Although there is structural diversity in the national educational system, what goes on in school is tightly controlled by the Malaysian government. Similarly, teacher training institutions are also centrally controlled. The dilemma for teacher educators in Malaysia is how to train teachers from diverse cultural backgrounds to teach a national curriculum to diverse learners.

In view of the overriding educational goal of national unity, the initial teacher education curriculum contains both 'cultural-specific' and 'cultural-general' socialization strategies (Zeichner and Hoeft, 1996). In the cultural-specific approach, Chinese and Indians are trained in the teacher training colleges to teach specifically in the Chinese and Tamil primary schools. On the other hand, the cultural-general approach is concerned with the preparation of all prospective teachers to teach culturally diverse students. The Ministry of Education stated explicitly that all Malaysian teachers should 'know something of the religious customs, cultures and traditions of the various people in the country' (Ministry of Education, 1991: 73). To sensitize prospective teachers to the socio-cultural context of Malaysian society, they are required to take core subjects such as Islamic religious knowledge (for Muslim students only), moral education (for non-Muslim students), Malaysian society and Islamic civilization.

The purposes of these courses are to socialize teachers to the religious and cultural susceptibilities of all Malaysians, to break down prejudices and ignorance among their pupils and to foster an understanding and acceptance of different religious and cultural practices (Lee, 1996). It is interesting to note that, apart from these specific courses, there is little about cultural diversity infused in the other courses in the teacher education programmes. At best these specific courses may help prospective teachers to gain some knowledge about other cultures and avoid stereotyping 'the other', but more needs to be done if the quality of intercultural teacher education is to be improved. The intercultural role of a teacher includes sharing with class members the values and beliefs of all individuals, acquiring cultural sensitivity in teaching subjects like history and language, and making use of the cross-cultural interfaces in a multicultural classroom to widen pupils' perspectives to a particular issue (Thomas, 2000).

It is not adequate for prospective teachers to be sensitive to the cultural background of their pupils, but they should be able to cope with the particular needs of certain groups of children, such as those from rural regions, estates, lower social class and new immigrant groups. Teacher educators in Malaysia need to develop a 'cultural-sensitive pedagogy' that is more sensitive to the cultural needs of both the teachers and learners (Thomas, 1997). A cultural-sensitive pedagogy is also one that 'can accommodate both global ideas and is yet sensitive to contextual needs (ie cultural needs) of both learners and teachers' (Thomas 1997: 25). One of the effects of globalization is the interaction of global culture with local culture.

This interaction is usually mediated by the nation-states. Individual nation-states may attempt to promote, channel or block the global flow of people, technology, finance, media images, information and ideas, with varying degrees of success depending upon the power of resources they possess (Appaduria, 1990). At the school level, teachers would have to learn how to mediate between the global and local, and to develop a critical attitude towards the impact of the global culture on the young students under their care. As society changes, the social demand on the role of teachers also changes. Therefore, the challenge in teacher education is how to provide continuing education and training for the professional development of teachers.

Conclusion

In this chapter, I have given an overview of teacher education in Malaysia and highlighted some of the current issues and future prospects that arise from three key areas, namely 1) the changing patterns of teacher education and control by the state, 2) approaches to the teacher education curriculum and 3) the preparation of teachers for cultural diversity. My analysis shows that teacher education is a shared responsibility between the teaching training colleges and the public universities, with the schools playing a minimal role in helping to supervise trainee teachers during their practice. The state has a strong control of teacher education, in particular the training of non-graduate teachers. The Ministry of Education trains all the non-graduate teachers, validates their awards, registers them and employs them in the national school system. Some radical changes would have to be made if the awarding body, licensing body and employing agency for non-graduate teachers were to be separated in the future, as found in other professions. There is also a need to think of alternative routes to teacher education if the problem of demand and supply of teachers is to be overcome.

Much needs to be done in revamping the curriculum of teacher education. There should be a shift from a technical-rational approach to a reflective practitioner model of teacher education, with more emphasis on the development of multiple perspectives among prospective teachers on educational and social issues, and a better understanding of the relationship between education and society. Teaching methods should stress the importance of pedagogical content knowledge, and the values and beliefs that underlie teaching practices. School teachers have to be more involved with teacher education by playing the mentor role to trainee teachers during their practice in schools.

The practice of a 'one-size-fits-all' approach has to make way for a more culturally sensitive approach to teacher education. Teachers from different cultural backgrounds have to be prepared to teach a national curriculum to diverse learners. Therefore teacher education programmes should include both 'cultural-specific' and 'cultural-general' socialization strategies as well as 'culturally sensitive pedagogy'. The future development of teacher education should take into account the changing role of teachers as Malaysian society changes with the effects of globalization, in particular the impact of information communication technology.

References

Abdul Rafie, B M (1999) Improving teacher effectiveness through certification, Paper presented in the APEID International Seminar on Innovation and Reform in Teacher Education for the 21st Century in the Asia Pacific Region, 14–22 October, Kigashi-Hiroshima City, Japan

Appaduria, A (1990) Disjuncture and difference in global cultural economy, in *Global Culture*, ed M Featherstone, pp 295–310, Sage, London

Craft, M (1990) Teacher education in multicultural Britain, in *British Universities and Teacher Education: A century of change*, ed J B Thomas, Falmer Press, London

Fenstermacher, G D (1978) A philosophical consideration of recent research on teacher effectiveness, *Review of Research in Education*, **6**, pp 157–85

Furlong, J (1991) The future of initial teacher education: lessons from British experience, Paper presented at the Regional Seminar on Teacher Education: Challenges in the 21st Century, 18–20 November, Penang

Furlong, J *et al* (1996) From integration to partnership: changing structures in initial teacher education, in *Teacher Education Policy*, ed R McBride, pp 22–35, Falmer Press, London

Goodman, J (1991) Using a methods course to promote reflection and inquiry among preservice teachers, in *Issues and Practices in Inquiry-oriented Teacher Education*, ed T Tabachnick, B Robert and K Zeichner, pp 56–76, Falmer Press, London

Houston, W R (ed) (1990) *Handbook of Research on Teacher Education*, Macmillan, New York

Lanier, J E and Little, J W (1986) Research on teacher education, in *Handbook of Research on Teaching*, 3rd edn, ed M C Wittrock, pp 527–69, Macmillan, New York

Lee, M N N (1993) Value clarification through reflective teaching, in *Teacher Education from the Perspectives of Reflective Teaching*, ed P L Kim *et al*, School of Educational Studies, Universiti Sains Malaysia, Penang

Lee, M N N (1996) Unity in diversity: teacher education in multicultural Malaysia, in *Teacher Education in Plural Societies*, ed M Craft, pp 72–81, Falmer Press, London

Lee, M N N (2000) The development of teacher education in Malaysia: problems and challenges, *Asia Pacific Journal of Teacher Education and Development*, **3** (2), pp 1–16

McBride, R (ed) (1996) *Teacher Education Policy*, Falmer Press, London

McHoul, A and Luke, A (1988) Epistemological groundings of educational studies: a critique, *Journal of Educational Thought*, **22** (3), pp 178–89

Ministry of Education (1991) Teacher education: practices and prospects, Paper presented at the Regional Seminar on Teacher Education: Challenges in the 21st Century, 18–20 November, Penang

Shulman, L (1987) Knowledge and teaching: foundations for a new reform, *Harvard Educational Review*, **57** (1), pp 1–22

Sikula, J *et al* (eds) (1996) *Handbook of Research on Teacher Education*, 2nd edn, Macmillan, New York

Thomas, E (1997) Developing a cultural-sensitive pedagogy: tackling a problem of melding 'global culture' within existing cultural contexts, *International Journal of Educational Development*, **17** (1), pp 13–26

Thomas, E (2000) *Culture and Schooling: Building bridges between research, praxis and professionalism*, John Wiley & Sons, Chichester

Willis, J W and Mehlinger, H D (1996) Information technology and teacher education, in *Handbook of Research on Teacher Education*, 2nd edn, ed J Sikula, T J Buttery and E Guyton, pp 978–1029, Macmillan, New York

Wittrock, M C (ed) (1986) *Handbook of Research on Teaching*, 3rd edn, Macmillan, New York

Zeichner, K M and Hoeft, K (1996) Teacher socialization for cultural diversity, in *Handbook of Research on Teacher Education*, 2nd edn, ed J Sikula *et al*, pp 525–47, Macmillan, New York

7. Strategic choices for teacher development in South Africa: enabling effective transformation in education

Relebohile Moletsane

Introduction

Demands for the transformation of the education system in general, and that of higher education institutions in particular, have been numerous in post-apartheid South Africa. In particular, the transition to democracy and the perceived prestige of formerly white institutions have led to 'the influx' of black students to these establishments. In turn, to reflect and respond to the changed characteristics of students they now enrol, for these institutions, an organizational and individual commitment to overhaul policies and teaching programmes has become imperative. In the present chapter the socio-political context of teacher education will be discussed as a background to the transformation process followed by a detailed examination of the approaches to curriculum transformation. The penultimate section of the chapter will discuss the frameworks for transformation, followed by a concluding analysis of the dilemmas and prospects of teacher education in South Africa in the light of transformation issues.

The socio-political context of teacher education

Among the many policy frameworks that have been developed in the recent past is the revised *Norms and Standards for Educators* (Department of Education, 1998) document, which alerts us to the perceived role and expectations for schools, teachers and teacher education in our relatively new democracy. The document identifies the aim of teacher education as educating teachers to teach effectively within the complexity of the South African context. High among the priorities for transformation is the eradication of social inequities, the transition to democratic, inclusive and equitable systems in all sectors of society. Implicit in this is the need for teachers to be empowered to become change agents in their schools and communities.

Within this context, efforts to produce effective teachers for our schools involve not only systemic reforms, but institutional and personal change as well. This suggests a transformative role of education and especially of teacher education in society. In essence, teacher education institutions are expected to produce teachers who are able to respond to this task in the context of the changing characteristics and needs of the students they teach, as well as the volatile nature of the society and the world they live in.

In the context of the socio-political changes of the past six years, institutions have committed themselves to increasing access to tertiary education for historically excluded racial communities. Ironically, from this commitment and the policies and practices that have emerged from it, racial integration on the one hand, and white flight on the other, have resulted. According to Glen (2000), generally, white student numbers had decreased from 222,049 in 1993 to about 163,780 in 1999. The flight of white students is said to result from perceptions of drops in educational standards at these institutions. Also institutions have committed themselves to increasing access for geographically isolated students.

Another dimension to increasing access to the university for previously excluded groups is the integration of the teaching and support staff in various structures of the institution. To use the University of Natal, Durban as an illustration, the teacher education programme employs 12 teaching staff and four support staff members. Of these, six are black (four black African and two Indian) and the rest are white. In terms of gender, seven are male and nine female. The inequalities are also skewed against blacks in terms of academic staffing levels. For instance, at the University of Natal teacher education programme, of the four professors and six senior lecturers in the programme, only two are black (one Indian and the other black African and both are at senior lecturer level). The inequalities, not only in terms of numbers but also in the levels of qualifications and experience between the different racial groups, have implications for curriculum transformation and implementation in the programmes. To address this, mentorships, as well as training and development for new staff, have been identified in the school's equity plan to reduce tension.

It is this tension between the call to provide quality and the need to overhaul programmes to meet the changing needs of students that informs recent curriculum development efforts in many institutions. Should institutions and programmes in post-apartheid South Africa aim to 'maintain standards' set for and originally conceptualized for a racially segregated system, or should they aim to reconceptualize their curricula to reflect a different purpose and ethos for education? Already, many advocates and critics of educational transformation in higher education institutions charge that current change efforts tend to fall short in their attempts to provide access, equality and quality for all students, as mandated by national policies and social changes in the country. Instead, a tension seems to exist, in which most institutions seem to have succeeded in providing access to a wider group of people than before, but in which quality in the content and processes of their programmes continues to be elusive.

Such critics also charge that most institutional efforts focus on restructuring existing curricula and programmes rather than on reconceptualizing them

(Grimmett, 1995; Elliot, 1993). However, providing access to tertiary education to masses of previously excluded students is not enough; a real difference in the students' lives needs to be made. This requires purposeful reconceptualization of the teacher education curriculum (Dzvimbo and van der Westhuizen, 1997) rather than the current adaptation, reform and restructuring. This can only be achieved through the development of transformative teacher education programmes and imaginative approaches to curriculum transformation.

Approaches to curriculum transformation

In this section two key questions will be addressed. 1) What approaches to curriculum transformation have been adopted in teacher education programmes at various institutions in South Africa? 2) To what extent are such curriculum change efforts not only restructured to provide quality, but also reconceptualized to strive for the social reconstruction of teacher education in post-apartheid South Africa? This section will examine five areas that help to respond to the two key questions above.

1 The policy approach to change

New demands on teachers and teacher education have influenced the nature and extent of curriculum transformation at various institutions. Such demands originate from the educational policy context, the changing social context, and the historical function and context of the university. For example, in recognizing the need for a transformative approach to curriculum change in teacher education, the University of Natal (1997) identifies the overall aim of teacher education as to 'produce reflective, capable and flexible teachers who are committed to meeting the needs of the changing educational context of a democratic South Africa'.

In the past six years South Africa has seen a plethora of national and local policy frameworks to guide curriculum transformation in the education system in general, and in teacher education in particular, eg the National Qualifications Framework (NQF); Norms and Standards for Educators (Department of Education, 1998); South African Schools Act (Department of Education, 1996). But, as Dzvimbo and van der Westhuizen (1997) rightly point out, teacher education policies seem to be skewed in favour of restructuring rather than reconceptualization. These workers argue that while such restructuring may lead to change, real improvement that results from reconceptualization of the programmes is not achieved.

2 Economic approach to change

A second approach most favoured by teacher education programmes in South Africa is the economic approach to curriculum change. This approach stems from the ways in which curriculum change initiatives have recognized and responded to the historical function of the institution. One of the legacies we inherited from the apartheid system is the categorization of teacher education into college, technikon and university education and the lack of articulation among the three sectors. Colleges of education, by and large, were regarded as an extension of schooling. Thus, while university faculties were concerned mainly with teaching, research and development, colleges were designed to train teachers in the implementation of the school syllabi (Lubisi, 1999).

As the rationalization of the training colleges and their articulation with other sectors became necessary, the number of institutions is currently being reduced significantly. The national subsidy and university funding policies and practices have also contributed to the adoption of an economic approach to curriculum change in teacher education. The new university funding system of full-time equivalence (FTE) has meant that, in order to be financially viable, schools and departments have had to recruit more students than ever before. With the general fall in student numbers in tertiary institutions, this has meant that recruitment and acceptance criteria are often not strictly followed, justifying perceptions that educational standards in these institutions have fallen. Such economic approaches to curriculum change favour discourses and practices of restructuring, resulting in superficial change, rather than reconceptualization and genuine transformation for a new context.

3 The need for liberatory paradigms of education

Transformation in teacher education programmes is also hampered because teaching and learning have had to overcome impacts of years of traditional paradigms of education in schools and undergraduate programmes (Shor, 1987). After all, students in such programmes do not enter teacher education as blank slates. Rather, they have all served a long apprenticeship of observation in schools and undergraduate programmes that do not develop or encourage critical thought among learners (Lortie, 1975). When they enter teacher education programmes, they tend to prefer those same models of teaching and learning and, in turn, teach their learners (eg during teaching practice and after) the way they were taught.

In addition, there is a common belief among educators and others that it was mainly through the education system, especially the education of teachers, that apartheid South Africa was able to maintain its authoritarian socio-political system. Through an authoritarian system of government, racial segregation of all social systems, including education, was justified and legitimized. In particular, teachers were not educated to examine possible educational alternatives, or their role in the transformation of society in general, and that of education in particular. Teacher education did not offer the language to critique or develop social and educational alternatives (Giroux and Simon, 1984).

As stated previously, democracy requires citizens who can critically reflect on the paradigms that inform their education system and programmes. In order to prepare teachers for such a role, one of the goals of teacher education programmes needs to be to 'decolonize' students' minds by translating their political freedom into psychological liberation (Ngugi wa Thiongo, cited in Jansen, 1990).

For this to occur, paradigms of education that provide critical theoretical orientations to educational policy and practice should be adopted. These should, among other things, produce teachers who are able to develop curricula, around forms of culture and school knowledge, that empower students who traditionally have been excluded from the benefits of a critical education, especially at the tertiary level. Experience suggests that increasing access to tertiary education for previously excluded groups is not enough. The quality of the experiences and processes they are engaged in during their tenure in the institution has to make a difference to their lives. But how can institutions couple equitable admission policies with quality-curricula programmes for all?

4 Responding to the socio-political context

Socio-political factors such as racial violence, crime, drug and alcohol abuse, sexual and other forms of violence against women and children, HIV / AIDS and poverty are just a few of the many challenges that have come to define post-apartheid South Africa. In response, teacher education programmes have developed and implemented individual modules and projects that examine issues ranging across gender and violence in schools, HIV / AIDS, education for social justice, barriers to learning and others. Such offerings aim to provide students with knowledge, managerial and transformational skills necessary to function within and outside the school context. The problem again often lies in the lack of holistic and integrated responses to these socio-political factors as they impact on education.

As Dzvimbo and van der Westhuizen concluded (1997), curriculum change initiatives such as these tend to put emphasis on adapting existing offerings and methodologies, attaining particular goals, such as addressing policy requirements, and maintaining patterns that are regarded as of high standards. Instead of engaging in transformative curriculum development for post-apartheid teacher education, what drives individual and programme change is mostly policy mandates and economic considerations, resulting in adaptation rather than reconceptualization.

5 Quality with equity and the politics of maintenance

Reflected in the above discussion is the recognition that the educational context in which institutions find themselves has changed significantly. For

example, the societal mandate for racial integration, the fall in student enrolments and the need for economic survival by departments and individuals in
the institutions have often led to a relaxation of student recruitment and
selection procedures. This change in the profile of students who are admitted
to the programmes tends to limit efforts effectively to transform practice. In
the corridors as well as in staff meetings, colleagues have often complained
that the change in student profile has meant that they scale down both the
quantity and the quality of their courses to reach the new students.

Such sentiments and practices imply that, while diversity is a necessary and
inevitable element of change in post-apartheid South Africa, the varied social
and academic backgrounds from which these students originate require extra
effort if teacher education programmes are to respond effectively to their
needs, especially those of African students from disadvantaged rural and
township schools. In order to provide access and equity in teacher education,
quality gets sacrificed. Could this be an excuse for maintaining the status quo?
Should we use the standards of a past era and context to judge curricular
quality, or should new criteria be developed for judging the effectiveness of
the curriculum in educating for a different purpose in a changing context?
Identifying and developing prospects for effective teacher education in South
Africa that will address the above challenges requires relevant frameworks to
inform the policies, curriculum development and practice in the various institutions and programmes. The next section explores a few such frameworks.

Frameworks for curriculum transformation

Several frameworks relevant to a liberatory approach to transformation
emerge from available literature. A *first framework* would be one that enabled
teacher education institutions to redefine their purpose and ethos within the
context of post-apartheid South Africa. To this effect, one framework comes
from Fullan's (1999) notion of the moral purpose to educational reform, which
addresses notions of vision and purpose of curriculum transformation. Citing
Oakes *et al* (1998), Fullan perceives a moral purpose in educational change as
seeking to achieve parity in opportunity and achievement across diverse
groups of students. This for him means that, in addition to improving
students' academic achievement through curriculum change efforts, institutions need to identify ways of motivating all students to learn, particularly
those diverse others who may be alienated by the new environment in which
they suddenly find themselves. Thus, this chapter explores the different ways
in which the vision, content and processes in teacher education programmes
can reflect a commitment to redress the imbalances of the past and make a
difference in students' lives.

Fullan's (1999) recognition of the link between curriculum change and
power offers another useful framework for transformative teacher education

programmes. Fullan's theory suggests that the moral purpose of educational transformation involves altering the power structure. To illustrate, it is likely that, most often, efforts to adopt this approach to curriculum change will be met with opposition from powerful individuals (eg academics, management, students and parents), who charge that such an approach tends to lower the quality of education in the institution. For these powerful members of the university community, curriculum change should ensure increased academic achievement among students and account to internal and external policy mandates and criteria. However, as Fullan concludes, 'the greater the emphasis on academic achievement through high stakes accountability, the greater the gap becomes between the advantaged and disadvantaged students' (p 19). To bridge this gap, both academic and social integration and support for all students become equally important. To do this, the unequal power structure of the institution has to be altered, and the new students (in many cases, black African students from educationally disadvantaged backgrounds) need to be integrated into both the academic and the social environments of the organization.

A *second framework* would be one in which all student teachers need to be able to participate fully in both the academic and social lives of the institutions they are enrolled in. Reviews of literature suggest a growing need for holistic approaches to the education of disadvantaged students (eg African students at historically white universities), in which both their academic and non-academic concerns are addressed (Hofmeyer and Spence, 1989).

Miller, Leinhardt and Zigmond (1988) and Damico and Roth (1993) also wrote on the importance of integration and engagement for the success of educationally disadvantaged students in educational institutions. On the one hand, academic engagement is defined as the ways in which students respond to the formal curriculum, ie the content, academic standards and learning tasks (Miller, Leinhardt and Zigmond, 1988; Wehlage *et al*, cited by Damico and Roth, 1993). Social engagement, on the other hand, is defined as interpersonal relationships and participation in the life of the institution, ie its extra-curricular and co-curricular activities (Miller, Leinhardt and Zigmond, 1988). These authors suggest that it is important to understand both the academic and social features of the institution in order to explain how students become integrated and successful, or alienated and unsuccessful in their educational endeavours. They suggest that integration into the life of an institution on one end of a continuum may result from engagement, while alienation may result from disengagement (Fine, 1985; Miller, Leinhardt and Zigmond, 1988; Newmann, 1981).

While curriculum change efforts in many of the teacher education institutions show evidence of striving to recognize and address the needs of the diverse students they enrol, for many, particularly the in-service students, social integration is not easy. Reasons for this include their part-time status as students and their non-residency at the institutions that enrol them, as well as lack of concerted efforts by the institutions to institute policies and practices that promote the social integration of all students. The dilemma facing institutions and programmes is the demand for transformation from previously excluded students on the one hand and, on the other, the perceptions of white students and parents that, by accommodating the needs of these students, standards are often compromised.

Prospects for addressing the above may lie in a *third framework* that comes from Dzvimbo and van der Westhuizen's (1997) call for a paradigm shift from restructuring to purposeful reconceptualization of teacher education programmes. In purposeful reconceptualization, civil society, ideology, histories and voices of previously excluded groups form the focus of transformation of teacher education programmes. This leads to the uncovering of new languages that help teachers and teacher educators to acknowledge the multiple experiences and perspectives students and others bring to the teaching and learning situation because of their location in different social, cultural and economic backgrounds.

Recognizing the disempowering effects of current mainstream discourses in teacher education for students from diverse backgrounds, this framework calls for a return to authentic local discourses and identities in informing the curriculum. The framework recognizes the important role of students' backgrounds, as well as that of local communities in informing and resourcing the reconceptualization of teacher education programmes.

Dilemmas revisited and the prospects

This chapter has identified several dilemmas facing teacher education institutions and programmes in their quest for real transformation in the education system of the newly democratic South Africa. Let us examine some of these dilemmas further.

The context and moral purpose of teacher education programmes

Teacher education programmes and teaching in general suggest a need for a moral purpose for the education system in order to redress the imbalances of the past, and to make a difference in students' lives. To illustrate, on a personal or individual level, racial desegregation and studying at previously white institutions should make a difference to black students' lives. Their confidence in and the prestige in which they hold programmes and instructors at these institutions should lead to beliefs that they are getting their money's worth and that the programmes are going to impact on their lives positively. While one would expect that these students would be motivated to learn because of their perceptions of the university and their instructors, the views of the latter often speak differently. The students' backgrounds and prior learning are often seen as a barrier to effective learning in an environment that imposes different expectations to those they normally experience. Such a perception is problematic for two obvious reasons. First, the deficit view of learners' background and their ability to learn effectively may lead to lower expectations of their performance, and the absence of strategies that could motivate them to learn, particularly those who may be alienated by the new environment in which they suddenly find themselves (Fullan, 1999). Second, such low expectations may contribute to the actual scaling down of not only the quantity but the quality of the teacher education programmes as well, thus justifying the view that standards are dropping in the programmes.

Provision of equity, and support for social and academic integration

A second dilemma involves the institutions' commitment to provide equity, and support for the social and academic integration of the diverse students enrolled in teacher education programmes across the country. While policy makers, academics, educators and the general public in South Africa agree that a complete reconceptualization of teacher education programmes is needed if effective implementation of the new policies is to become a reality at school level, the approaches adopted by various institutions act as barriers to real transformation. For real transformation to occur, a recognition of the differential power relations between students and instructors, and between the previously privileged and those who were marginalized by different forms of oppression is necessary. As Christie (1993) and Fullan (1999) state, there is a significant link between curriculum change and power.

A programme's commitment to defending and sustaining transformative curriculum development initiatives in the face of opposition, from economically and socially powerful students and parents who charge that such an approach tends to lower the quality of education in the institution, depends on the views and values held by staff towards the students they serve. The instructors' negative views about the diverse students' academic and social backgrounds may mean that they also are not convinced of the possible success of truly transformative programmes.

The prospects for the success of transformative programmes may lie in the selection and ordering of curriculum knowledge, pedagogy and assessment procedures that are not skewed in favour of those with the social power and control in the institution. To start with, changes in admission policies and practices regarding those students who are labelled 'less able' in 'high status' or 'difficult' courses are necessary. Continuing to exclude them, as is currently the practice in some courses, is tantamount to maintaining the status quo and contradictory to transformative curriculum development. A critical examination of social inequalities and the ways in which education functions to reproduce and legitimate them (Giroux and McLaren, 1986) should form part of the content of teacher education programmes. In addition, to respond to criticism regarding relevance in the curriculum and students' inability to engage in critical analysis, Giroux and McLaren (1986) suggest making knowledge meaningful to students before making it critical.

Practices and discourses in teacher education

Lastly, the discussion in this chapter indicates that practices and discourses in teacher education still favour adaptation, reform and restructuring rather than purposeful reconceptualization of the teacher education curriculum as discussed by Dzvimbo and van der Westhuizen (1997). Providing access to tertiary education to masses of previously excluded students is not enough. To make a real difference in their lives, purposeful effort should be made to uncover their previously silenced voices in significant ways in the teaching and learning environment of teacher education. The multiple experiences and perspectives the students and others bring to the teaching and learning situation need to be acknowledged and utilized to inform curriculum transformation in teacher education.

On the one hand it is undeniable that, in their quest for the transformation of teacher education programmes, institutions are faced with several dilemmas regarding the purpose and focus of change. On the other, within these dilemmas lie several prospects for effective curriculum development and change in teacher education. A comprehensive and careful analysis of the academic and socio-political context within which education occurs may result in strategic choices for the country's teacher education and development.

References

Christie, P (1993) School desegregation and curriculum in South Africa: a case study, in *Inventing Knowledge: Contests in curriculum construction*, ed N Taylor, Maskew Miller, Cape Town

Damico, S B and Roth, J (1993) A different kind of responsibility: social and academic engagement of general track high school students, in *At Risk Students: Portraits, policies, programmes, and practices*, ed R Donmoyer and R Kos, University of New York Press, NY

Department of Education (1996) *South African Schools Act* (No. 84 OF 1996), Ministry of Education, Pretoria

Department of Education (1998) *Norms and Standards for Educators*, COTEP, Pretoria

Dzvimbo, K P and van der Westhuizen, G (1997) Shifting paradigms in the discourse of teacher education in southern Africa, Paper presented at the Annual Conference of the Kenton Education Association, 31 October – 2 November, Hermanus, South Africa

Elliot, J (1993) *Reconstructing Teacher Education: Teacher development*, Falmer Press, London

Fine, M (1985) Dropping out of high school: an inside look, *Social Policy*, **16**, pp 43–50

Fullan, M (1999) *Change Forces: The sequel*, Falmer Press, London

Giroux, H A and McLaren, P (1986) Teacher education and the politics of engagement: the case for democratic schooling, *Harvard Educational Review*, **56** (3), pp 5–30

Giroux, H A and Simon, R (1984) Curriculum study and cultural politics, *Journal of Education*, **166**, pp 226–38

Glen, I (2000) The learning curve, *The Money Standard*, **2** (2), pp 42–45

Grimmett, P P (1995) Reconceptualising teacher education: preparing teachers for revitalized schools, in *Changing Times in Teacher Education: Restructuring or reconceptualisation?*, ed M F Wideen and P P Grimmett, Falmer Press, London

Hofmeyer, J and Spence, R (1989) Bridges to the future, *Optima*, **37**, pp 37–48

Jansen, J (1990) Curriculum in post-apartheid dispensation, in *Pedagogy of Domination: Toward a democratic education in South Africa*, ed M Nkomo, Africa World Press, Inc, Trenton, NJ

Lortie, D C (1975) *School Teacher: A sociological study*, University of Chicago Press, Chicago

Lubisi, R C (1999) Teacher education in South African universities: a few points to ponder, Address to CCERSA Teacher Education Summit, 11 November, Pretoria

Miller, S E, Leinhardt, G and Zigmond, N (1988) Influencing engagement through accommodation: an ethnographic study of at-risk students, *American Educational Research Journal*, **25**, pp 465–87

Newmann, F M (1981) Reducing student alienation in high schools: implications of theory, *Harvard Educational Review*, **51**, pp 546–64

Oakes, J et al (1998) Norm politics of equity minded change, in *International Handbook of Educational Change*, ed A Hargreaves *et al*, Kluver Arens, Dordrecht

Shor, I (1987) Equality is excellence: transforming teacher education and the learning process, *Harvard Educational Review*, **56** (4), pp 406–26

University of Natal (1997) *Teaching Practice Guidelines*, School of Education, University of Natal, Durban

University of Natal (1999) *Strategic Initiatives for the University of Natal*, University of Natal, Durban

8. Contemporary problems in teacher education in Brazil

Luciola L Santos

Introduction

This chapter provides a discussion of teacher training in Brazil raising some of the principal issues in the field. The chapter will examine an outline of the history of Brazilian teacher training, followed by an analysis of the current problems to be faced in teacher education. The role played by the World Bank in the context of Brazilian education will also be discussed, together with current research into teacher education. The problems and future prospects facing teacher education in Brazil will conclude the chapter.

The historical context

The Brazilian education system in the 20th century

According to Prado (1976), Brazil at the beginning of the 20th century could be characterized as a typically agrarian country. Many considered education to be a fundamental component of the social agenda, since the Brazilian educational system only reached a minority of its population. At the beginning of the last century no more than 9 per cent of the population aged 5 to 19 were registered in primary or secondary education (Romanelli, 1988). From the second decade of the 20th century, and particularly during the 1930s, new ideas on education began to circulate in the country, influenced by European and US literature in the field, and encouraged by the prevailing climate of change. Teacher training courses for primary education were created in the 1830s, but the training of secondary school teachers only appeared in 1934 at the recently created University of São Paulo (USP).

Castro (1984) made a survey of the articles published in the very important Brazilian Journal of Education (*Revista Brasileira de Educação*). According to Castro, the articles referring to teaching, written in the 40s, appeared to subscribe to the ideas of the New School Movement. Castro states that some articles call for a more practical approach, particularly in the teaching of the natural sciences and mathematics and emphasizing the need to use students' own experience. According to Nunes (1985), the number of teacher training colleges (*escolas normais*) increased greatly after 1930, and this increase grew stronger up until the 50s and 60s, when these schools began to proliferate in the small towns of the country.

According to Romanelli (1988), the beginning of the military regime saw a great educational crisis. She describes this crisis as resulting from an increase in the level of demand for education, which had already been intensifying for some time. To overcome the educational problems, the military regime undertook a number of reforms at all levels of education. The Educational Technology (ET) Movement offered the Brazilian education system an opportunity to make education available to more students. The attempts that were made to integrate ET into the teaching system took the form of projects implemented by government educational bodies, the creation of areas of specialization in postgraduate courses and the integration of ET, and finally concepts and proposals into the pedagogical curriculum of the teacher training courses. However, after some years, the use of the principles of ET began to be questioned in teacher training courses, but ET had a strong influence on educational practice.

The failure of the technicist approach is probably due to three factors. Firstly, its practice had demonstrated that it was unable to resolve the problems in the field of education, specifically in the training of teachers. Secondly, this model was unable to generate the enthusiasm of the older generation of teachers trained in a liberal tradition. Thirdly, with the failure of the technocratic policies of the military government, ET was as heavily criticized as the social and political model adopted by the regime.

Teacher training in the 1980s

Within the pedagogical field, the critique of the technicist approach formed part of a wider debate about the function and the political nature of education. With the increasing freedom of academic debate, this discussion flourished, particularly in the social sciences. The 'return to democracy' undoubtedly made the academic debate possible and, at the same time, that debate contributed to the opening of the regime itself, and focused questions directly related to the quality of state education and training of teachers. Within the field of education, the need to improve the professional training offered to teachers and educational specialists arose, from an awareness of the low success rate experienced by the Brazilian school system, which had extremely high repeat (retake) and drop-out levels.

The discussion on reforming teacher training courses, as part of a concern with improving primary and secondary education, emphasized the need to change the curriculum of these courses. Throughout this entire period, the issues of the training given to teachers and the structure and the quality of the teacher training courses were analysed and discussed. The courses in pedagogy, intended for graduate educational specialists, began to be reformulated so as to include the objective of producing teachers for the first years of primary education. The structure of university courses for secondary teachers (*licenciatura*), which prepared them to teach a variety of subjects, was also strongly criticized. Such courses were organized in a way that combined pedagogical instruction with subject content.

The debate on the reformulation of training courses for teachers has been coordinated on a national basis by an organization known as the National Movement for the Reformulation of Training Courses for Educators. At its second national meeting in 1986, the issue of reformulation of training courses for teachers in universities, among others, was debated in conjunction with the process of restructuring universities themselves. At the beginning of the 80s, when discussing teacher education, two points were taken as fundamental: the political nature of pedagogical activities and the commitment of educators to the poorer classes. It was held that improvements in courses for teachers and specialists did not depend solely on changes in the organization of such courses. At this stage, it was felt to be more important to define the nature of the teaching profession and the role of the teacher, and use this as the basic guideline for the reform of teacher training.

The changing concept of the teacher's role

Academic work has aimed at the study of the processes by which the practical training of teachers develops while carrying out their professional activities. In this field, studies of teacher knowledge deserve special mention. These studies explore how teachers acquire knowledge about their profession during the daily routine of the school and their activities. Analysis of the construction of this knowledge includes studies of school culture and its everyday routines.

At the present time, it is also important to consider the growing use of the so-called post-structuralist and postmodern theories in education. The greater part of this literature seems to contain ideas that are extremely productive for the study of education. Their great contribution lies, above all, in the establishment of the relationship between power and knowledge. It is also the case that, in the greater part of this literature, discourse has central importance, not only as the representation of reality but also in the way that it constitutes it. In this way, the conception of the teacher found in pedagogical theories comes to be seen as an essential factor in the construction of teacher identity. In the same way, the analysis of power brings into question the different types of existing educational organization in schools, and attempts to identify which interests are served and which are ignored. On this basis, as regards the education of teachers, it is possible to raise the question of power relationships that influence the practices of teachers as both academics and reflective professionals. This type of analysis problematizes some of the assumptions that have formed the basis of discussions about the education of teachers in the previous and present decade. However, it is necessary to use these ideas with a certain degree of care, since their uncritical use may conceal, rather than reveal, the meaning of pedagogical practice within social reality.

Current problems and dilemmas in Brazilian teacher education

At the present time, there has been discussion of a series of proposals and regulations for teacher education made by the federal government and, at the same time, an enormous range of proposals have been made regarding pre- and in-service teacher training courses.

First of all, it is important to emphasize that, in accordance with the Law of Educational Regulations and Principles, which became law in 1996, the education of teachers for the first stages of basic education must be at higher educational institutions. To make this possible, it proposes the establishment of a higher teacher training course (*escolas normais superiores*). The courses in pedagogy intended for educational specialists (supervisors, administrators, inspectors, etc) began to be taken by teachers for the first stages of primary education from the 80s onwards. The proposal to set up a higher teacher training course has been opposed by critical educators, since these courses are designed to impart teaching techniques rather than knowledge of educational theories and research. Higher teacher training colleges can be set up that do not necessarily have any involvement with research. In addition to this, the pedagogical courses associated with universities include educational research, and are based on the belief that the activities of teaching and research should go together in institutions of teacher education.

Secondly, the structure of the teacher training courses as regards the various subjects in the more advanced stages of basic education has been heavily criti- cized. Despite the criticisms about the separation of subject-based education from the pedagogical education at the end of the course, little change has been made. The literature in this area (Pereira, 2000; Brzezinski, 1996) recommends that the pedagogic education of teachers should begin at the start of the course as should familiarization with work by means of practical activities and periods of classroom training. Another aspect discussed has been the need for subject-related education to be linked to teacher training, since the depart- ments and faculties of biology, history, geography, mathematics, etc have shown a complete lack of interest in teacher training issues.

Thirdly, the spread of higher education courses for untrained working teachers deserves special mention. These courses have been given in different higher education institutions during the teachers' vacations, and complemented by distance learning activities. At present, projects containing proposals for distance learning courses for teacher training are beginning to be developed. For example, the state of Minas Gerais is planning a distance learning course for 12,000 teachers in primary education who do not have a higher degree.

Fourthly, a large increase in projects for in-service teacher training, with the objective of updating and improving teacher performance, is taking place. These courses deal with specific teaching content as well as a wide variety of pedagogical problems and such issues as violence, sex and drugs in schools. These courses are offered by the state ministries of education, in partnership with different universities and educational organizations. The in-service training projects take the form of distance learning courses or those requiring attendance at the institution. Many of these projects, which have reached a large number of teachers, have been financed by the World Bank (WB). For this reason, the role of the WB's policies in the direction taken by teacher training in Brazil has been the subject of debate, and this will be discussed in the next section.

Brazil and the World Bank policy on teacher training

As was noted above, the WB has financed large-scale educational projects at the federal and state levels. Some of these projects are directed at untrained teachers as in the case of the pro-training programme (*Proformação*), which reaches 32,000 teachers at federal level. In the same way, the states have worked to improve the performance of teachers with in-service training such as the continuing education programme, developed by the state ministry of the state of São Paulo, which has involved 84,000 teachers, and the *Procap* programme, implemented by the state ministry of education of the state of Minas Gerais, which has reached 100,000 teachers. Many of these programmes were developed by different Brazilian states through direct negotiations between the state ministries of education and the WB.

It is important to highlight, however, that in Brazil the concept of equal rights used by the WB has been the target of critical analysis in some public policy studies (Oliveira, 1999; Paiva and Warde, 1994). For the WB, equal rights will be attained by ensuring universal access to basic education. As regards the economy, this will lead to a more qualified workforce and an excess of labour supply over demand, resulting in lower wages. In addition to the priority given to basic education for economic development, the WB also argues for the need to improve the quality of this level of education. According to Torres (1996), as far as the WB is concerned, the quality of teaching is related to the existence of certain determining factors resulting from a more effective learning process. The WB gives priority to three of these factors: an increase in the length of education, improvements in educational books and in-service teacher training.

To begin with, it is worth mentioning the fact that the WB gives priority to in-service training over pre-service training (Torres, 1996; Lauglo, 1997). As was highlighted by Santos (1998), this emphasis on in-service training is a result of an analysis that holds economic factors to be the most important and is based on cost–benefit analysis, in which teacher training is conceived of in terms of the best method of producing a technically competent professional. Thus, in-service training is seen to be the cheapest and most efficient way of producing education professionals.

In addition to this, within in-service education the WB prioritizes subject knowledge, alleging that this has more influence on the students' results than any pedagogical knowledge that teachers might have. The Bank also recommends using distance learning, bearing in mind that its cost is lower than that of methods that require attendance at an institution. However, educational research has shown that, in teaching, it is not possible to separate content from the forms in which it is studied, and that it is vitally important in this process to consider the influence of educators' values and moral commitment and the culture of the school. In relation to distance learning, it can be argued that there is, at present, little evidence based on research that would allow reliable statements about the use of this method of teaching in the process of in-service teacher training.

On the question of the efficiency of courses that seek to modify teaching practice, it is important to present some observations. The literature on in-service training emphasizes the need to work with teachers in schools as a whole, in order to bring about a general change in their methods of work, since carrying it out with only part of the teaching staff can create difficulties. These difficulties arise because of failure to change the system in operation in the institution and by the activities of teachers who have not been convinced of the need for the changes. It has also been pointed out in the literature that the types of in-service training that concentrate on day-to-day problems faced by teachers, where theory is used as a tool to understand such problems, are more effective than those that end up dealing with theoretical aspects that have little connection with the day-to-day reality of schools. So, this being the case, training programmes should be a continuous process of activities rather than sporadically provided ones.

Research into teacher training

Research on teacher training in Brazil now includes questions to do with trainees' class, gender and race. It is within this framework that discussions take place regarding the tension to which this occupational group is subjected as they struggle between the processes of proletarianization and professionalization. The range of analyses of teachers' work has widened with the appearance of work on the occupational diseases to which they are subject. Another collection of research is directed at discussions of the processes of teacher training. On the one hand, curriculum structure and the type of orientation it provides is analysed, while, on the other hand, in-service training is investigated in an attempt to understand how teacher knowledge is created within the institution of the school, under the influence of culture, values, school routines and relationships with colleagues. In general, one can say that these have been the lines of investigation of the greatest number of studies on teacher training in Brazil. The content and direction of these studies have had repercussions on the restructuring of the actual courses and subjects of faculties and departments of education.

In this context it may be noted that the studies carried out by Donald Schön (1983, 1987) have created great interest in research on the analysis of the nature of professional activities, and on academic education in different fields of activity. Based on his work, a vast literature has been produced on teaching practices. Schön's ideas about the reflective practitioner became known in Brazil in the 90s, in particular by means of articles written by the Portuguese author Novoa (1992, 1995), the Spanish author Péres (1992) and also by the US author Zeichner (1992, 1993). As well as these, the work done on teacher training and activity by Perrenoud (1993) and Tardif (1991) has also had repercussions on the nature of teaching.

The literature on the proletarianization of the teaching force and on the feminization of the teaching profession has been widely discussed on the basis of work of British and US writers at the end of the 80s and the beginning of the 90s. Nevertheless, research on teacher training has faced great challenges. It can be said that, on the one hand, there are some intellectuals who, with great clarity and brilliance, produce first-class work, which can be considered excellent summaries of the available international literature. In an elegant and clear-sighted manner, they deal with the problems in education, raising stimulating issues that encourage debate on the issues. On the other hand, we have a group of researchers who seek to ponder over educational reality and investigate it in all its dynamism, but who often do not get very far owing to lack of theoretical sophistication.

Thus, the great challenge to be faced, at the present time, consists of combining the brilliance of the first type of work with the content of the second, in order to produce quality research. Another great challenge lies in allying the utopias of critical theory, which put forward a project for education as liberation, with the contributions deriving from other approaches that capture in richer detail the daily routine of the school and its culture.

The prospects

The drop-out and repeat rates, as well as the illiteracy statistics and low level of schooling of the Brazilian population, have led to the establishment of various educational projects and programmes designed to serve the needs of the poorer classes and to make it possible to retain them in school. On the basis of an analysis of how the educational system works, transforming social and cultural differences into educational inequalities, the way in which schools operate in the process of educational exclusion has already been discussed above. There has been an investigation of how schools facilitate or restrict the development of critical thinking and pupils' interest in the different aspects of our culture, and how schools develop specific forms of thinking to the detriment of others, in sum, how schools form or limit a person's way of being and acting through the schooling process.

In this context, alternative curriculum proposals are sought that will allow the incorporation of pupils into the school system. The debate about the development of a curriculum proposal that will make the school truly democratic by offering quality learning has come up against various difficulties among which we may highlight teacher training.

There is a series of problems arising from this situation that will influence the prospects for improving the teacher education system for the future in Brazil. These problems include linking improved performance to better salaries, reducing educational inequalities between rural and urban regions (by implementing experimental projects that combine work and study) and also making use of distance learning. Changing the structure of university courses for teacher training, even if this requires changing the structure of the university itself, is another problem. Establishing educational policies that are orientated more towards practical necessities, without losing sight of political, social and cultural questions, is yet another issue. Finally, establishing a more productive partnership between educational theories, university research and the practical realities of teaching is also a key problem that needs solving. These are some of the challenges and prospects faced in teacher education in Brazil, which, despite the fact that they occur with great intensity and frequency here, are also part of the educational reality of most countries in the world.

References

Brzezinski, I (1996) *Formação de Professores: Um desafio*, UCG, Goiânia

Castro, R (1984) A didática na revista brasileira de estudos pedagógicos: um percurso de quatro décadas, *Revista Brasileira de Estudos Pedagógicos*

Lauglo, J (1997) Críticas às prioridades e estratégias do Banco Mundial para a educação, *Cadernos de Pesquisa*, 10 March

Novoa, A (ed) (1992) *Os Professores e a sua Formação*, Dom Quixote, Lisboa

Novoa, A (1995) *Profissão Professor*, Porto Editora, Lisboa

Nunes, C (1985) A sina desvendada, *Educação em Revista*

Oliveira, D A (1999) As reformas em curso nos sistemas públicos de educação básica: empregabilidade e equidade social, in *Política e Trabalho na Escola*, ed A Oliveira and M R T Duarte, Autêntica, Belo Horizonte

Paiva, V and Warde, M J (1994) Novo paradigma de desenvolvimento e centralidade do ensino básico, in *Transformação Produtiva e Equidade: A questão do ensino básico*, ed V Paiva, Papirus, Campinas

Pereira, J (2000) E. *Formação de Professores: Pesquisas, representaçòCes e poder*, Autêntica, Belo Horizonte

Péres, G (1992) O pensamento prático do professor: a formação do professor como profissional reflexivo, in *Os Professores e a sua Formação*, ed A Novoa, Dom Quixote, Lisboa

Perrenoud, P (1993) *Práticas Pedagógicas, Profissão Docente e Formação: Novas perspectivas*, Dom Quixote, Lisboa

Prado, J C (1976) *História Econômica do Brasil*, Brasiliense, São Paulo

Romanelli, R (1988) *História da Educação no Brasil (1930/73)*, Vozes, Petrópolis

Santos, L (1998) De C P Dimensò Ces pedagógicas e políticas da formação continua, in *Caminhos da Profissionalização do Magistério*, ed A Ilma Passos, VEIGA, Papirus, Campinas

Schön, D A (1983) *The Reflective Practitioner: How professionals think in action*, Basic Books, New York

Schön, D A (1987) *Educating the Reflective Practitioner*, Jossey-Bass, London, San Francisco

Tardif, M et al (1991) Os professores face ao saber: esboço de uma problemática do saber docente, *Teoria e Educação*, **4**

Torres, R M (1996) Melhorar a qualidade da educação básica? As estratégias do Banco Mundial, in *O Banco Mundial e as Políticas Educacionais*, ed L de Tomasi et al, Cortez/PUC-SP, São Paulo

Zeichner, K M (1992) Formar professores como profissionais reflexivos, in *Os Professores e a sua Formação*, ed A Novoa, Dom Quixote, Lisboa

Zeichner, K M (1993) *Formação Reflexiva de Professores: Idéias e práticas*, EDUCA, Lisboa

9. Policies and new schemes of teacher education and training: some Japanese issues

Shin'ichi Suzuki

Introduction

In the 1990s, the central government invited several advisory councils to assist in introducing new policies for Japanese education to adapt to global standards in economic and political terms. The Ministry of Education (MoE) also invited the Central Council for Education (CCE). Each council deliberated on the relevance of school curricula, the efficiency of school management, and efficient strategies for the improvement and enhancement of the teaching force. Lifelong learning schemes were to be developed as part of a national network, and new standardized courses of study introduced to all schools from primary to secondary levels. Against strong criticism from the teaching force, MoE decided to introduce new criteria. Requirements for teaching certificates were increased, as is described later in this chapter. The teaching force was to be developed as a strong foundation to the education system. We will examine in this chapter two key aspects of policy and change affecting teacher education: firstly, the main education policies underlying teacher education and secondly, innovation in teacher education past and present.

Main currents in educational policies

In this part of the chapter we will discuss five key areas of educational policy as they relate to future prospects for Japanese teacher education.

1 The core issue of national identity

The general aims of education are often described in terms of 'the spiritual, moral, mental and physical development of pupils'. Such examples can be found internationally in many UNESCO sources. Governmental documents and leading industrialists noted that schools in Japan based the mental and physical development of pupils on the principle of an egalitarian ethos of equal opportunity when the pupil population is not homogeneous. This deprives pupils of alternative paths for their individual development (Ohta *et al*, 1978). Learning attainment and school curricula have their roots in the political, economic and socio-cultural foundations of Japanese society. The emergence of nuclear families deprived young families of aged wisdom in nurturing their offspring. This was accompanied by a decline in the transmission of traditional, ethical and cultural values to the younger generation. Parents have come to realize that their children are in need of personal development and that the moral and spiritual development of pupils should be re-emphasized.

2 Children's positive commitment to life

Children should be guided to full cultivation of their abilities and capabilities to prepare them for performing their roles in adult life and to equip them with enough knowledge and skills to carry out their responsibilities as mature citizens. In this sense, the spiritual and moral development of children must be accompanied by their mental, cultural and physical development. This means children need opportunities at school to develop themselves in the full sense of the word. In 1998, the CCE proposed a new course of studies. The proposals included more flexible school curricula, with more free time for children to enrich their school lives. School education law was revised in 1998 and 1999, and a new course of studies was ordered by the Minister (MoE, 2001). In 2002 the revised codes will come into full effect. New textbooks are now in preparation. A new type of cross-curricular activity is described as 'integrated learning'. In the primary schools, an integrated scheme of 'life study' has been introduced to the lower classes from first to third grades, and there are a few trials at the secondary school level.

The new school curriculum is conceived and organized to encourage children as individuals and as part of a group to develop their own courses of study, and to relate them to their own lives. School curricula should be consistent with children's ways of feeling, reasoning, judging, selecting and committing. It is probably too early at this stage to say whether children will be motivated to a greater extent by the new measures outlined above.

3 A new hierarchy of higher learning and common culture

Deregulation was one of the leading themes of the National Council on Educational Reform (NCER) when it started its deliberation on education for the 21st century. This idea was implemented in many ways. The independent University Council (UC) established in 1987 is an example. The UC issued a succession of proposals regarding higher education. Accepting the recommendations issued by the UC, the MoE has revised the code for the awarding of degrees, abolished the old regulations on university management and introduced new criteria for university and college assessment. Offering more flexible opportunities for adult learners to enter higher education was also proposed.

The Lifelong Learning Council (LLC), established in 1990, replaced the Council for Social Education. In 1991 it announced several strategies for promoting lifelong learning that should be relevant to the various needs of society in the 21st century. It proposed reorganizing the structure of schooling from pre-primary to post-tertiary level. Universities and junior colleges were to play important roles in teacher education and training, with all teachers being recruited at first-degree level. With the restructuring of the tertiary educational system, universities have come to be extremely heterogeneous in their education mission. There is often a mismatch between the aims of higher education and the professional expectations of teachers.

4 IT and the intellectualization of learning systems

The Final Report of the NCER (1987) stressed the urgency of educational adaptation to the information age. In 1984 when NCER was launched, nearly 80 per cent of state senior high schools were already provided with computers (Muta, 1990). MoE planned in 1985 to grant more than 2 billion yen to local state schools to assist them to purchase computers for pupils and teachers. In 1988 the earmarked budget for school computers was increased to 2.9 billion yen, and in 1989 to 3.4 billion yen (Sakamoto and Stern, 1989). Other government ministries, the Ministry of Post and Telecommunications and the Ministry of International Trade and Industry, were anxious to update the communication networks and eager to introduce new schemes to educational institutions. They collaborated with MoE to provide the educational sector with opportunities to develop software for computer-assisted learning. Information technologies are widely used individually and collectively in all fields of education. It is common for pupils, students, adult learners and researchers to use so-called intelligent rooms and buildings when they study or learn. Personal computers are commonly used to access information networks in all educational and research institutions.

5 Issues of childhood: identity problems and the high crime rate

Maladjustment of children is commonplace nowadays. Japan is perplexed by a succession of crimes committed by adolescents aged between 14 and 17. Under the former juvenile law, boys and girls under the age of 14 could not be prosecuted for a crime but were sent to a juvenile offenders institution. Victims often wished that the offending child could be punished, as with an adult offender. Some citizens felt that the juvenile courts should be stricter, and that the age of prosecution should be lowered to 14. This has now been done. The path of juvenile law reform from educative principles to retributive punishment may show complex social changes. At the same time, it indicates how hard it is now for children to establish a moral identity.

Schooling does not help children find their cultural or vocational identities. They are at a loss in finding their own ways towards their own future. Sato (1998) described this kind of situation as 'bright bewilderment'. People born in Japan in the 1970s and 1980s are now in schools, universities and colleges, in a world that is quite different from that of preceding generations. The society in which they were brought up was an affluent one, and the society they are living in now is characterized by acquisition and possessiveness (Suzuki, 1998). This may distance them from natural and social reality.

Teacher education innovation: past and present

It is now apparent that Japanese school teachers have to cope with typical issues of present-day civilization. They are expected to have the ability as professionals to deal with everyday educational matters and socio-educational issues. It is therefore imperative for the teaching force to equip itself with new knowledge, new skills and a new mission. However, there are several factors that are relevant in assessing teachers' professional ethos and teacher education institutions. These are discussed below.

Institutional improvement of teacher education

Institutional improvement of teacher education and training did not necessarily satisfy the needs of schools where teachers were forced to tackle the new problems of difficult classes. Teachers could not control pupils' behaviour because pupils did not follow directions and advice. Such situations varied from school to school and from region to region. It was not easy for the affected schools to establish a useful relationship with parents and others who could join in solving the problems of their children.

Besides, the rapid decrease in the school population affected the number of school teachers. Older teachers found it more difficult to cope effectively with intricate problems of class management. From 1995 to 1997, the central government reduced the number of civil servants. This forced all national universities to rationalize and reorganize themselves, and this applied also to national universities for teacher education.

MoE had already decided that all national universities for teacher education should establish graduate schools of education to provide courses for MEd degrees for school teachers. In the year when MoE invited the Council for Teacher Training (CTT) to consider the most relevant schemes of teacher education and teaching qualifications, a national network of graduate schools of education had already been established.

Enactment of CTT recommendations

CTT produced key recommendations in 1997, 1998 and 1999. A supplementary recommendation was submitted in 2000. As a result, MoE introduced a new bill on teacher education and teaching qualifications in 1999, and in the same year it was enacted as a revised law of teacher education and teaching certificates. The Minister revised the regulations to require all intending teachers to practise both in special schools and in hospitals or welfare institutions before serving in schools.

Under the old scheme of teacher education for primary to senior secondary levels, students studied subject disciplines, professional studies, teaching practice and optional subjects. The credits for each subject varied according to the level of teaching, eg primary or secondary. The number of credits for subject disciplines was high compared to those for professional training and optional subjects.

The new scheme for the basic course increased professional training substantially for most trainees, especially at the secondary level, and there was an increase in credits for optional subjects as well. The new scheme for professional subjects included subjects such as introduction to the teaching profession, foundations of education, curriculum studies, career guidance, professional seminars and teaching practice. The new scheme is further elaborated upon in the Appendix to this chapter.

Newly revised interpretations of teachers' certificates

The philosophy of course restructuring cannot be isolated from issues of school education. Some points need to be made about secondary education and its relationship to primary schooling. The average enrolment ratio for compulsory secondary schooling is nearly 100 per cent at each age level. Most students (97 per cent) completing junior secondary school education continue their schooling to the age of 18 (MoE, 1999). However, underlying these figures are issues of longer absenteeism from schools and insufficient vocational guidance in schools.

The annual statistics of school education published by MoE show a gradual increase in longer absenteeism at all levels of schooling. The 1999 statistics indicate that 82,807 primary schoolchildren were absent from school in 1998, of whom 26,017 were so-called *futoko-ji* (school-phobic). The statistics also show that there were 145,184 junior secondary absentees, among whom 101,675 were classified as school-phobic. Sociological, psychological and medical understanding of these cases is indispensable. School teachers are asked to acquire more basic knowledge and techniques, and so counselling is required for all teachers.

Vocational guidance is given to pupils in junior secondary schools. On the whole, however, school teachers guide their pupils and students in such a way as to encourage them to select general and liberal education courses. Statistics show that fewer students attend vocational colleges (MoE, 1999). Job selection is a key factor in self-identification for students whose social participation depends on it. If teachers and the schooling system are not successful in helping students to select jobs, the total system of schooling cannot be said to be functioning as well as expected. In this sense, teacher education should be centred around vocational and career guidance.

Graduate schools and their roles in teacher education and training

As mentioned above, a national network of graduate schools of education today offers opportunities in education, training and retraining to both new and senior teachers. Other universities and junior colleges also provide teachers with opportunities in education and training. However, most universities do not have graduate schools of education. MoE has decided to run a type of federal graduate course for a PhD in education, by way of amalgamating several local universities. This course will be developed and maintained by the MoE. Hence, there has emerged a national network of teacher education and training, which consists solely of national tertiary institutions. In spite of the administrative agreement to preserve an open-entry system in teacher education, the structure of teacher education in present-day Japan has turned out to be strictly bilateral: the national graduate universities of education, and the rest. Structural changes of this sort in teacher education are exactly in line with the proposals made earlier by the report from CCE in 1971. What role the educational sciences will play in the development of teacher education remains a key issue.

Future issues and prospects

A great deal of university reform has taken place in Japan since the mid-1990s. For example, a legal instrument of school administration has been implemented, by which the principle of free school choice may be introduced in any school district. Every school is to have a school board for its efficient management, whose membership is open to parents and members of the community. The principles of personnel management of teachers are to change in line with participatory planning and open competition. New issues for the teaching profession, beside the matters of basic qualifications, may arise here.

What are these new issues? They may be teacher assessment schemes and implementation of teacher training programmes based on teachers' needs. Pilot teacher assessment schemes have been launched in several places like Tokyo and Osaka, but the core issue of achieving fairness in assessment has not been resolved yet. Assessment should be made and developed communally among teachers first and secondly among all those concerned with schooling. Participatory assessment schemes could be launched, cultivated and developed.

Teachers have organized self-supporting networks for retraining themselves. However, their activities are not as yet organized by a general teaching council. That might be one reason why Japanese teachers cannot enjoy such high professional status as medical doctors or lawyers. In this global world, school teachers are apt to deal with many international issues in their classes, such as language teaching for immigrant children and teaching traditional cultures. All teachers must teach democracy, tolerance and peace to their pupils in international contexts.

All of these require that intending teachers are educated and trained as critical intellectuals. They should be intellectuals because they need to be able to help children to overcome the contradictions in the processes of learning and living (Suzuki, 1992). If necessary, teachers have to create new principles. However, Japanese school teachers have little say in creating and establishing their own professional creeds and job standards. As Hargreaves says, 'Just when the very most is expected of them, teachers appear to be given less support, less respect, and less opportunity to be creative, flexible and innovative than before' (Hargreaves and Leslie, 2000: 151).

A possible proposal for enhancing teachers' status would be to create a regional network for teacher education and training, whose membership should be open to teachers themselves, educational administrators, university and college academic staff, university and college students, parents or carers, and representatives from communities. University teachers and non-teaching staff should cooperate to establish and run such schemes.

If we are successful in organizing such a forum not only nationally but internationally, teacher education and training should be more effective and fruitful in coping with the tasks of education. It could be possible for us to organize several 'teachers' groups', teaching anywhere as and when required. The school curriculum should also be developed through international collaboration, making it possible for us to have textbooks of common history, common geography, common literature, common fine arts and others.

Appendix

The new scheme of teacher education includes the following subjects:

- *Professional seminar*: newly introduced. The topics of the seminar should be related to general objectives of culture and civilization, with tasks of the teaching profession. Seminar instructors should be invited from wider ranges of disciplines including education.
- *Curriculum studies*: integration of related fields. The topics should cover areas such as curriculum development, subject teaching methods, moral education,

methods of extra-curricular activities and computer-assisted learning. Broader assessment techniques should be included.

- *Career and vocational guidance*: reclaim of pupil and student guidance. The topics should cover theories and methods of pupil and student guidance, counselling, and theories and methods of career guidance.
- *Teaching practice*. The length of teaching practice should be extended to at least five weeks for primary school teachers and to three weeks for junior secondary school teachers.
- *Foundations of education*: theoretical aspects of related professional practice. The topics should be related to historical and philosophical aspects of educational ideas, cover school management and school administration, and include the socio-economic functions of the schooling system as a modern societal institution. In addition, psychological development of schoolchildren and processes of learning should be put into course programmes.

References

Hargreaves, A and Leslie, L (2000) The paradoxical profession, *Prospects*, **114** (30), 2 June, UNESCO, Paris

MoE (1999) *Statistics of School Education*, (Gyousei), MoE, Tokyo

MoE (2001) Law of education, No. 127 (on national flag and national anthem), in *Laws of Education*, ed A Kita *et al*, MoE, Tokyo

Muta, Hiromitsu (1990) Innovation of class teaching methods assisted with computer, in Innovation of teaching: contents and methods, *Education in Japan*, vol 6, ed R Kuroha *et al*, pp 229–64, Kyoiku Kaihatsu Kenkyusho

National Council on Educational Reform (NCER) (1987) Fourth report on educational reforms (Ministry of Education), in *Laws of Education*, 2001, ed A Kita *et al*, pp 917–31, Sanseido, Tokyo

Ohta, T *et al* (1978) *History of Modern Education in Japan: Post war era*, Chapters 1, 2, Iwanami, Tokyo

Sakamoto, T and Stern, S (1989) Educational computing in Japan, *Educational Technology Research*, **11**, pp 1–9

Sato, Manabu (1998) Children running away from learning, *SEKAI*, **644**, pp 63–72, January, Iwanami, Tokyo

Suzuki, Shin'ichi (ed) (1992) *History of Teacher Education Innovation: Ten years of the Japan Association of Private Universities for Teacher Education*, vol 2, pp 602–03, JAPUTE (Japanese version)

Suzuki, Shin'ichi (ed) (1998) *Teacher Education: Issues and prospects*, pp 165–66, Gakubunsha, Tokyo (Japanese version)

10. Teacher education in Poland: reform and reassessment

Janusz Tomiak

Introduction

In modern pedagogical theory, the key significance of teacher education for ensuring effective learning in educational establishments of all kinds and at all levels of education is now universally recognized. However, we should be aware of the fact that the writings of Western thinkers were not at all easily available for proper consideration as a foundation of modern educational theory in the countries of Central Eastern and Eastern Europe, which for nearly half a century following World War Two were, against the wishes of an overwhelming majority of their populations, forced to accept the domination of Marxism-Leninism as an ever-present ideology. This forms a backdrop to the present account.

In this chapter Polish teacher education will be examined within the underlying theme of reform and reassessment. A brief background to Polish education reform will be followed by a discussion of teacher education theories and ideologies in communist and post-communist Poland. The reform of initial and in-service teacher education will then be examined. Sections on teacher supply, teacher responsibilities and Polish teachers as professionals will be discussed in the context of reform and change. The role of research into teacher education in Poland, and the future prospects for teachers and their training will conclude the chapter.

The background

Following the end of World War Two, the communist government in Poland attempted to reduce what was considered useful knowledge to polytechnical experience and technical and vocational training, promoting Marxist ideology and a secular value system. Its efforts proved largely futile, as the teachers as a body adhered strongly to the traditional national system of values incorporating, it must be stressed, radical elements inherited from the past. They generally refrained from open atheistic agitation and education in

the collectives advocated by such people as the well-known Soviet peda-
gogue, Makarenko (Tomiak, 1997).

This was one of the main reasons why the transition to an open and liberally
oriented democratic society in the 1990s, though far from easy and fraught
with problems and dilemmas of several kinds, could proceed along peaceful
and not openly confrontational ideological lines. The points of conflict came to
be located much more in the difficulties associated with the speeding up of the
process of educational modernization, teachers' remuneration and in-service
education programmes, the question of the division of responsibility for the
different kinds of schools between the central, regional and local authorities,
and the actual costing of educational reforms. These were, however, no trivial
matters that could be easily resolved by whatever government was in power,
and were bound to create lasting tensions and severe difficulties that could not
be quickly resolved.

That requires a more detailed examination of all the factors involved in the
ensuing disputes, which, instead of gradually getting less and less heated,
became more and more bitter and protracted. Naturally, major educational
reforms are never easy and, inevitably, require a well-thought-out strategy,
time and adequate financial provision. However, a reform of teacher
education connected with a full-scale transition from a command to a free
market economy, and from a centralized one-party state to a truly democratic
society presents a real challenge to the nation (Tomiak, 2000a, 2000b).

Theories and ideologies in teacher education

There was a significant difference between the model of the teacher in the Soviet
Union, where teachers were explicitly required to be active participants in the
process of communist construction with all the ideological rigours that went
with it, and the Polish People's Republic, particularly in the 1970s and 1980s,
where socialism was defined as a system being built by the people for the people
(Komitet Ekspertow, 1973). It is also worth noting that the principal educational
reform proposals in the 1970s and 1980s focused not upon radical ideological
imperatives, but upon making the educational process more relevant to national
economic needs, the equalization of educational opportunity, the development
of character and personality and trying to devise ways and means for
continuous education (Komitet Ekspertow, 1989). Nevertheless, the difference
between particularly Poland and the Soviet Union should not be overlooked.
With the collapse of communism, an opportunity potentially appeared for a
complete reorganization of the system of education in the country and a redefinition of the teacher's role in a society freed from politically induced constraints.
That potential was, however, seriously curtailed by several factors.

First, there ought to have been a clear vision of what the new open and
democratic society was to strive for in the long run. Yet the energies of the

people seemed to have largely spent themselves in trying to remove all the features of the old and, now, discredited system rather than elaborating a clear vision of the future. Prolonged debates along these lines produced wide-ranging and largely confusing opinions as to what of the old order could be retained and what was to be eradicated. Teacher education was, naturally, very much one of the problems that came under consideration.

Second, modern Western theories of teacher education, previously constantly criticized and condemned as serving the needs of capitalism, were largely unknown in the Polish People's Republic and could not pave the way towards a new concept of the role of the teacher. In consequence, the tendency manifested itself simply to turn to ideas of formerly promoted values that were grounded in materialistic philosophy. Inadequate efforts were made to focus attention upon the role that teachers were to play in establishing a genuinely free and open society and, particularly, moral and civic education. Insufficient emphasis was placed upon respecting the right, and at the same time the duty, of all persons to accept the responsibility for deciding what values to pursue and being ready to offer a rational justification for doing so. This was regrettable, as it would have helped greatly to formulate with much greater clarity a new concept of the role of the teacher, leading to the formulation of a theory of teacher education in post-communist society. The lack of a wider recognition of the crucial significance of civic education in a democratic society created another lacuna in the essential movement towards ensuring that all young people could gain, through school, a working knowledge of the techniques of social participation, in order to play in adulthood their proper role as active, and not passive, citizens. Yet this is what every teacher educator and hence every teacher must be fully aware of.

A centre for citizenship education came into existence in Warsaw at the beginning of the 1990s and it offered advice on civic education to teachers working at all levels of education. Quite apart from this, a collaborative project, The School in a Democratic Society, was started in 1992 between the Citizenship Development for a Global Age Program at Ohio State University, and the Polish Ministry of National Education, with the aim of contributing to the development of a democratic civic culture in Poland (Hamot, 1998). These are useful initiatives, which should pave the way towards the formulation of the key ingredients in a theory of teacher education corresponding to the requirements of a democratic society.

Reforming initial teacher education

Initial teacher education has been the subject of attention in Poland for many years in respect of both its organization and content of studies. As early as 1973, the Committee of Experts criticized the binary system of teacher training in their *Raport o Stanie Oswiaty w Polskiei Republice Ludowej* (Report on the Condition of Education in the Polish People's Republic). Under this system teachers in the kindergarten and lower grades of the then existing basic schools were trained in *studia nauczycielskie* (teachers' studies), and those in the upper grades of the basic schools and the *livea* (*lycées*) were educated in *wyzsze szkoly pedagogiczne* (higher pedagogical schools) and universities (Komitet Ekspertow, 1973).

Another important report, *Edukacia Narodowym Priorytetem* (Education: A national priority) of 1989, by another Committee of Experts, did the same. It drew attention to a relatively short period of training in *studia nauczy-cielskie*, lasting two years, and an inadequate pedagogical preparation for teaching by students in universities, whose attention was concentrated primarily upon their main field of specialization (Komitet Ekspertow, 1989). This document also stated that, in the initial as well as in the in-service education of teachers, much greater stress was being put on the transmission of theoretical knowledge than upon its application in practice. That, obviously, was a very serious weakness, which required immediate and determined correction.

The most devastating comment, however, seems to have been that trainee teachers attached particular importance to passive memorization of knowledge, in order to reproduce it in the examinations, and followed this pattern later in their own pedagogical activity. Homework set in schools largely involved memorizing particular sections of the school textbooks. In secondary education, discussions on any subject frequently turned into pseudo-discussions, as teachers tended to direct those discussions towards what they themselves considered acceptable. In lessons in schools one could seldom come across polemical statements, divergent opinions and, espe-cially, views expressed that did not agree with those presented by the teachers (Komitet Ekspertow, 1989). This required change and it was the teacher educators who could bring it about. The report appeared, however, at a time when everybody's attention was concentrated upon the most exciting political changes, and so its contents and recommendations were soon forgotten. Today, there is a growing awareness everywhere that great importance must be attached to teacher education, as improvement in the quality of life of the people can be achieved only through, not in spite of, teachers (OECD, 1990).

Reforming in-service teacher education

The educational reforms introduced in the late 1990s, in addition to changing the structure of primary and secondary education, included the reform of teacher in-service education. The whole teaching body was to be categorized into four different levels, reflecting professional expertise. This was directly linked to a successful completion of professional part-time courses, pursued concurrently with working in schools. The four categories were specified as follows:

1. *stazysta* – assistant teacher;
2. *nauczyciel kontraktowy* – contract teacher;
3. *nauczyciel mianowany* – nominated teacher;
4. *nauczyciel dyplomowany* – (advanced) diploma teacher.

According to the rules proposed in the amended *Karta Nauczyciela* (Teacher's Charter), assistant teachers would be promoted to the grade of contract teacher by the head of the school; from this grade to that of nominated teacher by the body administering the school; and from the grade of nominated teacher to that of diploma teacher by the inspectorate, ie the qualifying commission. Moving up the scale was conditional upon successfully completing the appropriate professional course, satisfactorily fulfilling all the assignments and passing an examination. Courses were to be offered in pedagogical institutes in large cities, so that, in practice, attendance was often complicated by the fact that teachers had to travel from their place of residence to a particular city, which was often situated a long distance away from where they lived and worked, and the process was therefore arduous and time-consuming (Ministerstwo Oswiaty Narodwej, 2000).

The point was that moving up the scale was associated with an increase in teachers' salaries. These were not negligible. For this very reason the teachers themselves favoured the reform measures. According to governmental proposals, in 2002 contract teachers would receive 125 per cent, nominated teachers 175 per cent and diploma teachers 225 per cent of assistant teachers' pay. In fact, the Ministry of National Education allocated considerable amounts of money for this purpose for the school year 1999/2000 and subsequent years. The problem was that, according to the parallel administrative reforms, it was the local authorities that were responsible for most teachers' salaries, although the Ministry's subsidies were to be forthcoming (Ministerstwo Oswiaty Narodwej, 2000).

The actual popularity of in-service teacher education courses and the unexpectedly high amounts of money needed for the increases, coupled with growing expenditure by local authorities in general, quickly led to sizeable deficits in finances. In fact, the problem was so acute that the Minister of Education, Professor Miroslaw Handke, who was very much the main source of the initiative in this reform, accepted full responsibility for the Ministry's failure to make adequate financial provision for the additional funds. He resigned in the summer of 2000. His place was taken by Professor Edmund Wittbrodt who succeeded in obtaining the assurances of the Prime Minister, Jerzy Buzek, that the required amount of money would be secured from the budgetary reserve. This ended the crisis for the time being, but in the longer term the problem remains.

The crux of the matter is that the whole programme of several major concurrent social and economic reforms of the present government is producing an unacceptably high level of budgetary deficit. The general elections due in the autumn of 2001 are very likely to lead to a change of government but the difficulties remain. The country's predicament is of the greatest political significance, especially at the present time, when Poland is firmly set to become a member of the European Union in the near future, and there are very strict preconditions that must be met in order to make accession possible.

Teacher supply and teacher shortage

Despite the strenuous efforts by the educational authorities to ensure adequate numbers of teachers for all subjects, real problems developed in respect of the teaching of modern Western languages and information technology. Enthusiastic students desiring to become teachers of these subjects found private business, including foreign enterprises, paid higher salaries and so tempted them to choose a better-paid and more promising career in business instead. The exodus continued unabated and resulted in a serious shortage of teachers of these subjects in many schools. The arrival of a number of US volunteers, enthusiastic but not qualified, made little impact. In 1990 the first education volunteers began work in foreign language teacher training establishments in Poland. They were recruited by the London-based East European Partnership, which was sponsored jointly by the British Council, the British Know How Fund, the British Red Cross, the European Union, Oxfam, CAFOD, the Sainsbury Trust and other organizations. Similar help came from France and Germany, but the demand for qualified teachers of Western languages continues.

In so far as the teaching of information technology and the use of computers was concerned, similar problems were experienced. Despite a marked increase in the number of computers in schools, acquired with the help of the Ministry of National Education, there was a shortage of well-qualified teachers to ensure their effective use. This caused a slowdown in the acquisition of an indispensable modern skill by many pupils, which still continues (*Glos Nauczycielski*, 2000). On the other hand, large numbers of younger and liberally minded teachers quickly exploited the new opportunities to choose new syllabuses and textbooks free from the previous political bias. Here was another problem, as some teachers of literature and history appeared to move too far in the opposite direction. Condemning the past, they wanted to propagate an unreserved and wholehearted enthusiasm for private enterprise and a market economy. Efforts, however, have been made to identify the aims of teaching history and literature as means of providing food for thought, supplying knowledge concerning alternative value systems and encouraging pupils to make their own choice and to be able to justify it on rational grounds (Tomiak, 2001).

Increasing teachers' responsibilities

The mass media and, especially, the teachers' periodicals repeatedly draw attention to the fact that teaching in schools, particularly teaching adolescents, provides nowadays a real challenge to teachers. All teachers, young as well as old, often face large classes of urban youth who generally lack respect for those who are supposed to be in charge of them, and possess a genuine desire to help them in their studies. Young teachers frequently become discouraged very quickly in trying to do their best under difficult circumstances. This leads to stress, frustration, loss of confidence in their ability to cope and sometimes to a prolonged absence from school by the members of staff. Some teachers, discouraged by slack discipline and violent behaviour on the part of a growing number of older pupils, retire prematurely on health grounds.

As in many other countries, the more relaxed and permissive social climate has led, unfortunately, to an evident abuse of the liberalization of the former rules of behaviour, and the lessening of personal responsibility for conduct among some individuals. The use of drugs, widespread smoking and also alcoholism have been reported from many schools and clearly documented (*Glos Nauczycielski*, 2000). Fortunately, there are still many schools in the country in which good discipline prevails, where breaking the school code of conduct is an exception and the teachers' tasks are manageable. There are in fact some excellent educational establishments where the problems indicated above are never experienced at all and the teachers' lives are happier.

Tragically, Polish children are not immune to infection by the HIV virus and the spread of AIDS. Records show that the first HIV infection in Poland was reported in 1985 and the first AIDS victim was identified a year later. By October 2000 there were 6,023 persons registered as infected with HIV and 826 as suffering from AIDS. Apparently, some 10 per cent of those infected were young people under 20 years of age. Particularly affected were youth from the capital, Warsaw, and Upper and Lower Silesia (*Glos Nauczycielski*, 2000). The pupils' knowledge of the dangers of HIV and AIDS seems to be patchy and generally inadequate, considering the real threat HIV and AIDS constitute to the health and, indeed, the life of an individual. Comparisons with other countries reveal that, in so far as school programmes devised to learn about the dangers of HIV and AIDS are concerned, Poland lags very much behind not only such countries as Australia, Britain and the United States, but also even Slovakia. There are, however, now opportunities in postgraduate pedagogical courses in cities such as Warsaw and Zielona Gora for preparing teachers of sex education in schools, which stress the importance of awareness of sexually transmitted diseases (*Glos Nauczycielski*, 2000).

All this may serve as an indication of the additional responsibilities of teachers and teacher educators alike. Acting *in loco parentis*, they have a duty to protect the children and the young people they teach from the new dangers that can no longer be ignored.

Polish teachers as a profession

After the disaster of the Second World War, which wiped out an over-whelming majority of the Polish intelligentsia, teachers came to be recruited from the ranks of the urban and rural working class whose education had in many cases been interrupted by the war. High proportions of them were women who had to be rushed through short emergency training schemes. They considered it their primary patriotic duty to devote all their energies to the education of the younger generation, making up for the time lost during the years of the occupation; despite serious gaps in their own education, they accepted the heavy burden of their daily work willingly. They deferred the struggle for a more tangible recognition of their efforts for future professional recompense. On the other hand, the unified state school system after 1945 made the profession itself united and strong, while the dirigistic form of government precluded open conflict over pay and conditions of work.

The end of communist rule brought about certain changes in the situation. The non-state sector of education came into existence with a great degree of independence from the state, including pay and conditions of employment for the teachers working within it. For the rest of the teaching profession, little has changed in terms of remuneration, working conditions and initial education of teachers. The changing economic climate produced new trends, however. Businesspeople and entrepreneurs took advantage of the liberalization of regulations in respect of production and trade. But the economic shock therapy introduced by the liberal reformer, Leszek Balcerowicz, began to bite. Inflation targets failed to be reached and the general level of prices began to rise. Those who worked in the social service sector of the economy, particu-larly, experienced a decline in the purchasing power of their salaries.

The teachers demanded an increase in their pay, which the government could not meet. Wider ranks of teachers began to show their dissatisfaction by organized protests and threatened strike action. The Polish Teachers' Union was unable to force the government to accept the Union's postulates and had to submit to the government's plans to offer higher pay only on the condition that professional competence was enhanced by successful completion of in-service courses. That in itself had obvious advantages, but at the same time it was a clear indication that the bargaining power of the teaching profession concerning its members' pay and conditions of work was limited.

Research in teacher education

A number of publications of recent origin have stressed the crucial importance of a more penetrating analysis in research concerning teacher education for all reforms in the field (Tisher and Wideen, 1990). A critical assessment of what actually constitutes the real weaknesses in the education of teachers in a country is, however, rendered difficult by the fact that deeper insights into the matter can only be fully developed by properly organized teams of researchers and institutions influencing and supporting one another. Only then can a valid, reliable and comprehensive picture of the existing set-up emerge. That requires a lot from the individual researchers and research establishments, which suffer from inadequate financial support and are only too often deeply involved in the process of teaching. They may also be cut off from scholars pursuing similar inquiries in other languages in other countries.

In the case of the countries formerly constituting the communist bloc, the latter consideration was of great consequence. Education, according to the principles of Marxism-Leninism, was an area where eternal vigilance against hostile bourgeois influence was of paramount importance. Contacts with pedagogical thought in the West and active cooperation with Western scholars were not only discouraged, but also rendered difficult and limited to strictly supervised channels, to reduce the unwelcome foreign influences to the minimum. Some contacts with Western scholars, particularly in the case of Polish educators, were none the less made and maintained despite the difficulties.

The situation changed radically in the 1990s. Important contributions to research in teacher education were then made in Poland that indicated considerable interest in Western research in the field, and the growing familiarity of Polish educators with the ongoing research in Western Europe and the United States. Some recent examples of that tendency can be identified. What is relevant here is not so much the numerous articles regretting an inadequate number of home studies concerning research on teacher education (Kupisiewicz, 1995), stressing repeatedly the shortcomings of the existing cadres (Szymanski, 1995) or concerning the difficulties connected with transformation of the mentality of practising teachers (Turnowiecki, 1995). What really counts is a number of contributions that come from scholars who are quite familiar with current research on teacher education in the English-speaking countries and other countries in Western Europe.

Here belongs the work of Professor Krzysztof Polak, which analyses the role of the teacher as an innovator, referring to teachers' expectations and their realization in practice, and the development of innovative attitudes, and creative and coherent critical thinking, which could all lead towards an authentic educational transformation in the country. Having surveyed the work of some 350 teachers, Polak defines his multidimensional model of an innovative syndrome, which ought to help future teachers play a much more progressive role in the teaching process (Polak, 1995).

Another writer, Boguslawa Matwijow, develops in her writings the concept of effective transition from authoritarianism to pedagogical democracy, drawing upon a new notion of an integrated pedagogical system, postulated by Professor Stanislaw Palka. This encompasses a broad range of pedagogical research associated with self-education, self-realization and creativity of the learner throughout his or her lifetime. Matwijow refers to the writings of John White, William Perdue and Z D Gordon in considering the preparation of teachers for an open society (Matwijow, 1995). In her book *Sarnoksztaltowanie sie Czlowieka* (Creativity of Man), Matwijow draws upon several US and British pedagogues and psychologists, linking her own analysis of the process of individual creativity with the concept of life-span developmental psychology (Matwijow, 1994). Research in teacher education can be greatly enhanced by the translation of the writings of well-known Western educationists into Polish, thereby reaching much wider ranks of teachers and teacher educators. Basil Bernstein's analysis of the socio-linguistic aspects of learning, including his notion of the relationship between social class and restricted and elaborated language codes, selection and control, visible and invisible pedagogies, the classification and framing of knowledge and related issues, is now available in an excellent Polish translation and easily accessible in a volume entitled *Odtwarzanie Kultury* (The Reproduction of Culture) (1990).

Future prospects

It is clear from the evidence provided that reforming teacher education in Poland still presents a challenge. Therefore it is all the more important to promote international cooperation in the field. Significantly, in the 1990s repeated pleas were made in several international conferences and symposia to formulate programmes for promoting joint action in order to improve the quality, dimensions and cross-country dissemination of the results of research in teacher education, so far largely pursued by individuals or research teams in particular countries (OECD, 1990).

Earlier, in 1987, the American Educational Research Association at their annual meeting proposed concrete action to establish and develop collaborative teams and networks of researchers in the field (Tisher and Wideen, 1990). It was stressed that the papers presented in the meeting in the shape of 'descriptions, analyses, comparisons and contrasts about research in teacher education in different cultural contexts have created an awareness of successes and deficiencies in teacher education, lacunae in our understanding of the process, strengths and limitations of the research' (Tisher and Wideen, 1990: 121).

This multiple kind of awareness is, clearly, the first necessary move in the right direction and can, in time, produce tangible results in research in teacher education from which all countries could gain important comparative and analytical insights. For the decision makers responsible for actual improvement in teacher training everywhere in the world this would provide a valid and reliable stimulus for action. The envisaged expansion of the European Union eastwards could also prove beneficial in this respect. Teacher educators in Western European countries could then reach directly their counterparts in

Central Eastern Europe, share with them the results of their own labour, establish permanent links with them and create joint research networks. The sporadic and limited contacts that already exist would thus become regular channels that would benefit all the people concerned.

References

Bernstein, B (1990) *Odtwarzanie Kultury* (The Reproduction of Culture), PIW, Warsaw

Glos Nauczycielski (The Teachers' Voice) (2000) 1, p 8, 6, p 6, Warsaw

Hamot, G E (1998) A case of teacher education reform in Poland's transitional democracy, *European Education, Uniformity Amid Diversity: Uniting teacher education in Europe*, Part 2, pp 5–24, Sharpe, New York

Komitet Ekspertow (Committee of Experts) (1973) *Raport o Stanie Oswiaty w Polskiei Republice Ludowej* (Report on the Condition of Education in the Polish People's Republic), PWN, Warsaw

Komitet Ekspertow (Committee of Experts) (1989) *Edukacia Narodowym Priorytetem* (Education: A national priority), PWN, Warsaw

Kupisiewicz, C (1995) Szkolnictwo polskie: demokratyzacja i przetrwanie jako cel reformy (Polish school system: democratization and survival as the aim of the reform), in *Szkola i Pedagogika w Dobie Przelomu* (School and Pedagogy in the Period of Upheaval), ed T Lewowicki *et al*, pp 140–51, Zak, Warsaw

Matwijow, B (1994) *Sarnoksztaltowanie sie Czlowieka* (Creativity of Man), UJ, Cracow

Matwijow, B (1995) From authoritarianism to pedagogical democracy, in *Modernization Crisis: The transformation of Poland*, ed W D Perdue, pp 191–201, Praeger, Westport, CT, London

Ministerstwo Oswiaty Narodwej (Ministry of National Education) (2000) *List do Pracownikow Ohwiaty* (A Letter to Workers in Education), MEN, Warsaw

OECD (1990) *The Teacher Today*, OECD, Paris

Polak, K (1995) Pedagogical innovation and the new role of the teacher, in *Modernization Crisis: The transformation of Poland*, ed W D Perdue, pp 179–90, Praeger, Westport, CT, London

Szymanski, M S (1995) Polskie spoleczenstwo i szkola w dobie przelomu (Polish society and school in the period of upheaval), in *Szkola i Pedagogika w Dobie Przelomu* (School and Pedagogy in the Period of Upheaval), ed T Lewowicki *et al*, pp 214–27, Zak, Warsaw

Tisher, R P and Wideen, M F (1990) *Research in Teacher Education: International perspectives*, Falmer Press, London

Tomiak, J (1997) Looking back, looking forward: education in Central-Eastern Europe on the eve of the XXIst century, in *Vergleichende Erziehungswissenschaft: Herausforderung, Vermittlung, Praxis – Festschrift für Wolfgang Mitter zum 70. Geburtstag*, vol 1, ed C Kodron *et al*, pp 426–35, Bohlau, Köln

Tomiak, J (2000a) Polish education facing the twenty-first century: dilemmas and difficulties, *Comparative Education*, **36** (2), pp 177–86

Tomiak, J (2000b) Poland in transition, in *World Yearbook of Education 2000: Education in times of transition*, ed D Coulby, R Cowen and C Jones, pp 133–44, Kogan Page, London

Tomiak, J (2001) Changing cultures and schools in Poland, in *World Yearbook of Education 2001: Values, culture and education*, ed J Cairns, D Lawton and R Gardner, pp 258–67, Kogan Page, London

Turnowiecki, W (1995) Edukacja a proces transformacji w Polsce u progu lat Dziewiecdziesiatych (Education and the process of transformation in Poland at the beginning of the 1990s), in *Szkola i Pedagogika w Dobie Przelomu* (School and Pedagogy in the Period of Upheaval), ed T Lewowicki *et al*, pp 200–06, Zak, Warsaw

11. International teacher education: from dilemmas to principles of action

Marvin Wideen, Peter Grimmett and Ian Andrews

Introduction

Many authors have questioned why teacher education has not achieved its rightful place in the broad scheme of education (Sheehan and Fullan, 1995; Howey, 1995; Tyson, 1994; Grimmett, 1995; Wideen, 1995; Wideen and Grimmett, 1997). Like the economic trend toward globalization and a free market, the restructuring of teacher education appears to have an irrepressible momentum. How, then, do teacher educators create a constructive counterpoint? We believe such hopeful action is more necessary today than ever. Not to think so equates to folding one's tent. We firmly believe that both effective practice and inquiry in teacher education can play significant roles in changing perceptions about schooling, and in contributing to more effective teaching and learning at all levels in society. But we also recognize that such a belief has to find expression within a changed context, one that emphasizes and encourages government intervention. In this chapter, then, we attempt to illustrate this sense of possibility, of working within government-led restructuring, by examining two international cases of curriculum reform that had clear implications for the restructuring of schools and teacher preparation in Jamaica, and Trinidad and Tobago.

The two cases we describe involve initiatives to reform the education of youth, at both primary and secondary levels of schooling. The teacher education focus took on considerable significance in each country's reform, where we worked as consultants in teacher education and professional development. In this chapter, we share what we learnt from that experience. We identify dilemmas, offer a conceptual framework and set out principles for working toward the improvement of teacher education in international settings. We believe that what we learnt can shed light on problematic features of teacher education in a variety of settings.

Cases in point

The government of Jamaica, supported by the Inter-American Development Bank (IADB), plans to implement a newly developed primary curriculum into the schools of Jamaica, which focuses on an inte-gration and child-centred learning. Though Jamaica has achieved universal primary education, the quality of that education varies greatly across geographical and socio-economic groups, and reports show low quality of achievement among primary children. Teacher education, both at the pre-service and in-service levels, became an important facet of the change that planners sought in the country. At the pre-service level, the 12 teachers colleges would also require changes in their curriculum and the methods by which instructors taught that curriculum. At the in-service level of teacher education, planners would face similar challenges. The new integrated curriculum and the notion of child-centred learning would involve a paradigm shift in thinking among most of the primary teachers in the country. While improving support through facilities and learning materials, qualitative change will primarily come from better-qualified teachers. Thus, the reform revolved around teacher education, both initial teacher preparation and the ongoing professional development of teachers.

In the context of achieving equity, Romain (1997) describes the situation in his country, Trinidad and Tobago, as far from ideal. He argues that the system that had served the country well in terms of providing upward mobility for its citizens had now become a problem in reinforcing the status quo. He finds the places in the secondary system as badly skewed, with the poor having low participation rates. The argument of equity in Trinidad and Tobago then became a matter of increasing the opportunities for all children to achieve to the best of their ability. The twin goals of equality of educational opportunity and modernizing teaching and learning would pose new problems for teachers and principals. A major change would be required to make it possible for all children to learn to the best of their ability, the intent of the new reform. This intent would shift teaching from a didactic approach to instruction, to one that involved active learning with greater student participation. As in the case of Jamaica, this reform would provide a major challenge for teacher education at all levels. For example, a programme of in-service teacher education would be required to equip a large number of beginning teachers in the country who had no pedagogical training whatsoever.

Both countries would face a number of issues in implementing these reforms. Changing the way both teachers and the general population think about teaching and learning would be central among them. Both countries had considerable success in an educational system based on a colonial model that saw the imposition of European cultural views on curriculum and teaching. But that system has now outlived its usefulness. The strengths of that colonial system would now be a limiting factor to change and innovation. Teacher education at both the pre-service and in-service levels would be central in effecting this change.

Dilemmas

In our own work and in observing the work of other consultants in these two settings, we became aware of certain dilemmas that limited the effectiveness of teacher education as a vehicle for reform:

- *Contextual relevance vs outsider imposition.* Planners choose consultants because they have expertise to assist those in the local setting to improve education. But problems arise with transporting innovative teaching ideas across the hall of a school, or from school to school in the same district. Typically, innovative ideas do not travel well. International work involves ideas travelling from one country to another. It can become a matter of outsider's imposition and insider's reality. For example, we saw consultants proposing state-of-the-art computer systems for schools having only a single telephone and limited expertise. Thus, as consultants, we faced the age-old dilemma of gauging the technical and pedagogical relevance when moving from one context to another.
- *Detached planning vs cultural sensitivity.* External consultants have the luxury of detached planning based on the cultural experience they bring to the local context. Obviously, a certain amount of detachment in such planning brings huge advantages to most local situations. The dilemma arises when detached planning lacks cultural sensitivity. Further, when the detached plan begins to 'overtake' the local context, a further related issue arises where both external consultant and local participants become dependent on the 'plan', forgoing the need to seek independence. Fidelity to the newly developed plan moves to the forefront at the expense of encouraging an independent stance on the part of the local participants.
- *The colonial template vs post-colonial engagement.* Both nations had experienced European colonialism. As Romain (1997) noted, colonial times carried the benefit of upward social mobility for those surviving the elitist educational system. Planners, teachers and others had risen to their current level or station because of their colonial education. What planners now proposed involved a type of post-colonial engagement in which many of the old values would be called into question. The dilemma in this case involved embracing the complexity, ambiguity and diversity typical of post-colonial engagement.
- *Collegiality vs individualism.* Consistency in approach became one of the features central to the professional development plans put together to support the reforms in both countries. Clearly, such consistency would involve a collaborative approach among key players, a common proposal in the current research and professional literature. The dilemma one faces in attempting to work toward a consistent approach through collaboration arises from the fact that most consultants and participants take a highly individualistic stance to their work. The individual and institutional norms in both countries, as in most parts of the Western world, revolve around

individualism, not collaboration. Rewards typically favour individual people who survive through competition. The dilemma runs deep. In this context, do universities with their deep traditions of individualism offer the best place for teacher preparation? Meanwhile, the rhetoric of collaboration continues, high on form but low on substance.

- *The quick fix vs sustainability.* A tendency in both countries among consultants and planners alike involved finding the quick fix or the 'magic bullet'. An infusion of money, a well-timed workshop or the key policy decision might provide the quick fix. A few months down the line, however, it became clear that without a plan for sustainability such 'silver bullets' would do little in terms of long-range improvement in the schools. Thus, we found ourselves contemplating benchmarks and ongoing funding that would keep things alive once planners had moved on to other issues and the consultants had gone home.

Moving from dilemmas to principles of action: a framework

These dilemmas faced us as consultants on a daily basis. We recognized the dilemmas in our own work and observed them in the work of others. We spent at least part of our consultancy struggling with the process in which we found ourselves. We watched as consultants failed at the 'white knight' role in which they sought to cure or solve the local problem with one sweep of an overhead or an imported idea. We did not wish a similar fate on anyone. To avoid this trap, we set about taking a thoughtful analysis of the task we had been set. This led us to develop a conceptual framework (see Table 11.1) that would guide our work and provide a heuristic in working with the educators in both countries. We summarize this framework before identifying the principles and prospects to guide action. The framework focuses upon curriculum because that provided the focus of our work in both countries.

Ways of understanding change

Chinn and Benne (1976) have summarized three general change strategies: power coercive, rational empirical and normative re-educative. Power coercion (used in a positive not a pejorative light) involves the use of sanctions, legislative mandates, rewards and any other means of social power to effect change. Rational empirical strategies rely primarily on the use of knowledge and its power to bring about change. Where participants see the value of a certain practice based on the presentation of knowledge about it, they will act upon that knowledge. Normative re-educative strategies focus on individuals and groups and assume that they are inherently active, seeking satisfaction from their work. Change occurs as group norms change.

Table 11.1 Framework for professional development and teacher preparation rationalization in the Jamaica Primary Education Support Project (PESP)

Change Paradigms	Power Coercive	Rational Empirical	Normative Re-educative
Conceptions of Curriculum	*transmissive –* curriculum as product	*transactional –* curriculum as practice	*transformational –* curriculum as praxis
Approaches to Curriculum Implementation	fidelity	mutual adaptation	curriculum enactment
Strands of Professional Development	knowledge transfer and skill development	reflective practice	socio-political-cultural focus
Conceptions of Teacher Education Rationalization	rationalization without reconceptualization	rationalization in advance of reconceptualization	rationalization emerging out of reconceptualized practice

Conceptions of curriculum

Grundy (1987) characterized curriculum as product, as practice and as praxis. Miller and Seller (1990) named these three perspectives transmissive, transactional and transformational. When curriculum is viewed as *product*, the function of education is to transmit facts, skills and values to students. Specifically, this perspective stresses mastery of traditional school subjects through traditional teaching methods, particularly using textbook learning and a subject orientation. The movement is unidirectional from teacher to student (as *tabula rasa*).

When curriculum is viewed as *practice*, the function of education is to engender a dialogue between students, assumed to be capable of rational problem solving, and the curriculum. The purpose of this dialogue is to provide opportunities for students to construct knowledge by transacting with the curriculum and others. Specifically, this perspective stresses cognitive development and a sharpening of the intellect. Dialogue is, by definition, reciprocal.

When curriculum is viewed as *praxis*, education enables students to become critically aware of how they perceive the world and their acting in it. The purpose is to emancipate them from the ideological distortions (eg the premise that some groups in society should be privileged over others) that might disempower or bias their minds toward an unreflective way of thinking. This is done by helping them experience how humans construct the world in which they live. These three perspectives parallel different approaches to curriculum implementation.

Approaches to curriculum implementation

Curriculum changes inevitably imply change of the role and responsibilities of the teachers who carry out the implementation. Thus, how we implement curriculum change becomes as significant to outcomes as its content (Snyder, Bolin and Zumwalt, 1992). An assumption that actual use of a planned innovation will correspond to planned or intended use (the *fidelity* approach) usually guarantees that most planned education change will fail.

On the other hand, the *mutual adaptation* perspective acknowledges that during implementation teachers make adaptations of the innovation to their own programme, which to some extent alters the theoretical assumptions of the original design.

The *curriculum enactment* perspective extends the mutual adaptation approach to acknowledge that teachers not only adapt the curriculum but actually shape it during implementation according to their own theoretical constructs.

In reality, some teachers perceive their role as acquiring and mastering the best techniques of instruction as efficiently as possible, which leads to an *instrumental* approach. Other teachers understand their role as engaging in continual inquiry into persistent perplexities of pedagogy. This understanding leads to an *exploratory* approach. However, most teachers function *pragmatically* between these two points and adapt the curriculum in ways that fit with the practicalities of their classrooms. These three different approaches are largely determined by how the individual teacher views the knowledge content and instructional processes of the planned curriculum.

The role of teachers in curriculum implementation

Teachers subscribing to the instrumental approach look for prescriptions for practice. They respond positively to hard, top-down *fidelity* approaches to curriculum implementation. They see their role as one of installing what experts have deemed appropriate, and expect curriculum developers to provide detailed teaching guides with accompanying materials and training in their use.

Teachers adhering to a *pragmatic* approach look less for prescriptions and more for adaptations that work for them and their students in specific classroom contexts. They also expect an array of materials, activities and strategies, but choose to use whatever works for them regardless of whether or not it coincides with the goals of the planned curriculum. They respond more positively to an approach that encourages them to adjust the curriculum to the learning needs of their students and the variations of their context.

Teachers who take an *exploratory* approach favour practices that emerge from their own classroom explorations. For them, the starting point of curriculum implementation lies in their students' learning needs and the specific context in which they teach. They see themselves enacting the curriculum according to the deeply held theoretical constructs that guide their interpretation of students and context.

Conceptions of professional development

We conceive of professional development in three different ways. The first, the *knowledge transfer and skill development* perspective, revolves around training teachers to use externally developed programmes or around the updating of teachers in the latest research-based knowledge in the content areas. This approach makes teachers into passive recipients and leaves them little room for reflection on classroom context and its inherent problematic features.

The second, the *reflective practice* perspective, involves changing the teacher's beliefs, values and classroom behaviour. It uses classroom action research to examine how teachers' values and beliefs affect what they do with students and honours the knowledge teachers construct when reflecting in and on teaching.

The third, the *socio-political-cultural* change perspective, focuses on the social context of teaching as a condition for development. Teachers examine the political, moral and social constraints that impede student learning.

Ways of understanding teacher education rationalization

Rationalizing teacher education can also be understood in three ways. The first perspective, *rationalization without reconceptualization*, is top-down, often politically motivated and harsh in its effect. Teacher educators are only involved in a passive and reactive role.

A second perspective assumes that some rationalization must be imposed, but that its purpose is to provide opportunities for subsequent reconceptualization of programme and practice. This *rationalization in advance of reconceptualization* perspective is consultative, inviting teacher educators' participation as a way of creating understandings about how the reconceptualization will unfold.

A third perspective, *rationalization emerging out of reconceptualized practice*, is a collaborative, bottom-up approach, structured to strengthen and reinforce practices that have issued from reconceptualization.

The heuristic framework

The framework builds on an examination of change paradigms, conceptions of curriculum and different approaches to curriculum implementation. The knowledge transfer and skill development approach to professional development contrasts with other perspectives, which emphasize reflective practice and socio-political-cultural change. Approaches to rationalization are framed around the extent to which reconceptualization is absent or present in the purposes and actual enactment of restructuring.

Policy makers who view teachers' role in curriculum implementation instrumentally tend to favour the fidelity approach because they want to ensure that the new curriculum is installed without variation. They lean toward the knowledge transfer and skill development approach to professional development and tend to enact a harsh, top-down form of rationalization that is devoid of reconceptualization.

Policy makers who view teachers' role in curriculum implementation pragmatically tend to favour the mutual adaptation approach, and concern themselves with determining how much variation should be permitted. They lean toward a reflective practice approach to professional development and see programme rationalization as a catalyst for bringing about subsequent reconceptualization of practice.

Policy makers who view teachers as exploratory and responsible professionals in curriculum implementation tend to favour the enactment approach, which leads them inevitably to grapple with the question of whether, how and to what extent teachers and students can be trusted and empowered to produce socially desirable outcomes. They view professional development as providing opportunities for teachers to examine the social, cultural and political factors in the context of schools that facilitate or impede students' learning, and use the rationalization process in teacher education to strengthen and reinforce those practices that have emerged from reconceptualization.

Our recommended *modus operandi* depended on several premises:

- The curriculum reform initiative in both countries represented a movement away from a transmissive curriculum.
- Research had found that the fidelity approach to curriculum implementation does not work.
- The effectiveness of the knowledge transfer and skill development approach to professional development is unproven.
- Jurisdictions practising a harsh form of top-down political rationalization have had to undo some of the damage their action unwittingly created.

Thus, we proposed that the first set of approaches would not work well in the Caribbean education reform. At the same time, we believed that many Caribbean teachers might not yet be equipped for the exploratory role that accompanies the curriculum enactment approach in curriculum implementation, and the corresponding socio-cultural-political approach to professional development. We also believed that the teacher educators might not be ready for entering responsively and responsibly into a collaborative approach to rationalization. Thus, we came out in favour of an implementation approach along *mutual adaptation* lines, an approach to professional development framed around *reflective practice*, and a *consultative and participatory* approach to the rationalization of teacher education in advance of reconceptualization. In doing so, we realized that the framework contained within it certain principles of action. Because we believe these principles hold implications for teacher education in international and other settings, they merit closer scrutiny.

Principles of action and prospects for reform

One afternoon, the senior author watched an engineer guide a group of local construction workers in the dismantling of a crane standing beside the hotel where he was staying. The engineer had obviously been brought in to advise on the project, as a consultant. His approach to the assembled crew was impressive. He told them exactly what to do, piece by piece, as the crane came down over three days. There could be no ambiguity here nor any slip-ups for that matter. The dismantling process required a clear sequence of events to occur to avoid the crane toppling on to the hotel or the workers below. The author watched in fascination. He envied someone whose work was so technically clear that it did not need to take account of differences in cultural understandings. To act like that in the education realm would be to invite disaster. The task of a teacher educator consultant is quite different from that of a crane-dismantling consultant. Ambiguity replaces clarity, negotiation replaces direction and mutual adaptation replaces outsider imposition. In reflecting on the work of the education consultants in the two reform settings, it occurred to us that certain principles that could improve the prospects for reform by engaging local people could be identified:

- *Implementation: learning the new curriculum in context.* Mutual adaptation acknowledges that during implementation teachers typically make adaptations of the innovation to their own programme, which to some extent alters the theoretical assumptions of the original design. Thus, teachers begin to learn the new curriculum in the context of their classroom settings. Closely related to this principle is the notion of situated learning. Situated learning occurs on the job in social settings where individuals view their work in terms of group norms, and ideas brought into their workplace become springboards to improving practice. Learning in such situations provides the basis on which teachers learn to adapt the curriculum to their own needs. The most productive stance for consultants in this setting would be a 'working with' approach rather than 'working on' or 'directing'.
- *Engaging participants in reflection.* The value of the framework as a heuristic device required participants to engage in a process of reflection. We found three techniques productive in Trinidad and Tobago, and Jamaica, which appeared to work at all levels of the educational system: interviewing and study process, the use of process groups, and progressive focusing. Interviews and the study of reports represent the stock in trade of external consultants. The more people who can be interviewed and the more reports

that can be read, the more comprehensive the study. When local people became an integral part of these interviews and study, the process prospects for reform improved. Process groups, which are modified focus groups, provided some of the most powerful data we collected. This technique, which built upon the concept of situated learning, produced insights that carried well beyond those that would have emanated from the same individuals interviewed separately. Typically, such groups focused on a limited number of questions or problems to be solved. Progressive focusing involved the gradual shaping and reshaping of courses of action over the length of a consultancy. To engage in such a process, consultants must circulate emerging ideas early in the process such that participants can examine and critique prospects, and see their own role in implementation. Thus, courses of action are shaped over time as opposed to appearing suddenly in the final report. The final report then contains few surprises.

- *Identifying perspectives.* As consultants, we believe that part of our role involves identifying and bringing to the level of discussion the various perspectives at play in a given situation. We make the assumption that in a social system different perspectives drive the thinking and actions of the groups involved. In order to arrive at courses of action that have sustainability, such perspectives must be identified and discussed. This does not rule out concerted action. Rather, it becomes a prerequisite for it. To achieve this goal we found the conceptual framework particularly useful. By presenting it to individuals and groups it legitimized the notion that the change proposed would be perspectives-driven. In short, the framework legitimized flexibility.

- *An inquiry orientation.* Central to these principles lies the notion of learning from inquiry and research. At a fundamental level, consultancy should be about inquiry into the social condition with the aim to improve it. While certainty can be assumed in some areas, it remains elusive in most others. Such learning is not just learning about the people and the country that provide the focus of a particular consultancy. Rather, it also includes inquiry into the process of consultancy itself. Reflection and recording play an important part in inquiry and research. As consultants, we would encourage those in the national situation to reflect on the processes in which they have been engaged.

- *Avoiding templates.* Consultants frequently enter new situations with a template into which the local problems must fit. Whether the situation involves institutional strengthening, curriculum change or professional development, the problems of the country in which the consultation occurs must be shaped to fit the solution that worked 'back home' or in some other jurisdiction. While no consultant can appear with a clean slate, we believe that a country has its own unique problems requiring unique solutions. As consultants, we enter wishing to respect the local conditions and seek solutions that work locally.

Summary and conclusion

Teacher preparation has received much criticism over the years. Many contend that it has not found its place in education, particularly where reform has been the agenda. The authors of this chapter draw on their experience in international education to examine the dilemmas that confront us as we attempt to make teacher education a more viable force in education, and improve the prospects of success. We draw on two Caribbean countries where the role of teacher education became a central part of educational reform. In the case of Jamaica, the reform involved implementing a newly developed primary programme that would move the primary schools from a traditional curriculum to a student-centred curriculum based on integrated subject matter. The Trinidad and Tobago reform involved a modernization of the secondary school curriculum and teaching approaches. Teacher education, both pre-service and in-service, played a central role in both countries.

The five dilemmas we identify began as working problems in these two countries. But their examination and analysis convinced us that these dilemmas may well apply in any situation where pre-service and in-service education become vehicles for educational reform. The first two dilemmas – contextual relevance vs outsider imposition, and detached planning vs cultural sensitivity – revolve around maintaining sensitivity to local culture. The third and fourth dilemmas involve the relationship between dependency and independence. Gaining independence from the outside consultant or from traditional colonial practices created dilemmas for local participants. How does one break away from practices that have served one well in the past? To work through these dilemmas, we used a broad-based framework that outlined three paradigms – transmissive, transactional and transformational. This framework provided a heuristic approach to deal with the dilemmas. The principles on which our work was based grew out of this framework.

The dilemmas of international teacher education are stressful for consultants. We suggest they are underridden by an omni-dilemma: by temporarily taking control away from indigenous educators, consultants are supposed to prepare those educators to take control of their own work. Thus, at the heart of the work of international consultants lies an implicit conflict: between the consultants' responsibility for providing expert input and their responsibility for helping indigenous educators to learn how to make their own important contribution to the education reform. The one treats indigenous people as passive recipients and the other treats them as active participants. We believe that the framework we developed and the principles of action embedded within it go a long way toward addressing the implicit conflict created by this omni-dilemma. Indeed, we would add that our work has provided us with an omni-principle of action that seemed to override all the others, that of *the need for contextual relevance and cultural sensitivity*. Disasters in international teacher education occur when indigenous educators and policy makers regard the work of consultants as lacking in cultural sensitivity. Typically, their recommendations are deemed unworkable in the local context. Based on our experience in two Caribbean countries, we submit that this principle of contextual relevance and cultural sensitivity is critical to work in international teacher education.

References

Chinn, R and Benne, K D (1976) General change strategies for effecting change in human systems, in *The Planning of Change*, ed W C Bennis *et al*, Holt, Rinehart and Winston, New York

Grimmett, P P (1995) Reconceptualising teacher education: preparing teachers for revitalised schools, in *Changing Times in Teacher Education: Restructuring or reconceptualizing?*, ed M F Wideen and P P Grimmett, pp 202–25, Falmer Press, London

Grundy, S (1987) *Curriculum: Product or praxis?*, Falmer Press, London

Howey, K (1995) The United States: the context for the restructuring and reconceptualisation of teacher preparation, in *Changing Times in Teacher Education: Restructuring or reconceptualizing?*, ed M F Wideen and P P Grimmett, Falmer Press, London

Miller, J P and Seller, W (1990) *Curriculum: Perspectives and practice*, Copp Clark Pitman Ltd, Toronto

Romain, R (1997) Trinidad and Tobago post primary education, A study conducted for the Caribbean Development Bank and the Ministry of Education

Sheehan, N and Fullan, M (1995) Teacher education in Canada: a case study of British Columbia and Ontario, in *Changing Times in Teacher Education: Restructuring or reconceptualizing?*, ed M F Wideen and P P Grimmett, pp 89–102, Falmer Press, London

Snyder, J, Bolin, F and Zumwalt, K (1992) Curriculum implementation, in *The Handbook of Research on Curriculum*, ed P W Jackson, pp 402–35, Macmillan, New York

Tyson, H (1994) *Who Will Teach the Children?*, Jossey-Bass, San Francisco

Wideen, M F (1995) Teacher education at the crossroads, in *Changing Times in Teacher Education: Restructuring or reconceptualizing?*, ed M F Wideen and P P Grimmett, pp 1–16, Falmer Press, London

Wideen, M F and Grimmett, P P (1997) Exploring futures in initial teacher education: the landscape and the quest, in *Exploring Futures in Initial Teacher Education*, ed A S Hudson and D Lambert, pp 3–42, London University Institute of Education Press, London

Section III
Cultural perspectives and the education of teachers

12. Educating immigrant schoolchildren: cultural dilemmas and prospects for teacher education in Spain

Felix Etxeberria

Introduction

In this chapter the situation of immigrant pupils in schools within the Spanish state will be analysed. Furthermore, the challenges facing teachers involved in intercultural education and the issue of institutional support will be tackled. The different models for schooling with immigrants in Spain will be examined with the related issue of resources. It will also be underlined that it should not only be public-sector centres that take on the education of immigrants. We will analyse the beliefs, attitudes and strategies of teaching personnel, their training and the institutional support in Spain for the teaching of immigrant children. Finally, there will be a discussion of the problems and prospects facing teacher training and education, together with a discussion of proposals for teacher training in the context of a global future in which it will be demonstrated that there is sufficient knowledge and resources to carry out meaningful intercultural programmes.

Immigrant pupils in Spain

Not all immigrants have the same cultural and economic situation, and the problems arising in the classroom may be different according to the country of origin and the socio-economic situation of the family. In this first part of this chapter, we set out to analyse how many immigrants there are, their countries of origin, where they are receiving schooling and what school programmes they can expect.

Immigrant distribution

How many immigrants are there and who are they? When talking about immigrants or the children of immigrants in our classrooms, it is necessary to make a preliminary assessment of the extent of the phenomenon, to find out which are the main groups of immigrants and to see if they have characteristics in common or, if different, whether that indicates a non-uniform educational approach. It must be pointed out that the proportion of immigrant pupils in Spain does not exceed 2 per cent of the school rolls. The corresponding figures in other countries are considerably higher, eg France has 7 per cent and Germany 9 per cent. To get an idea of the number of immigrant pupils receiving schooling within the ambit of the Ministry of Education and Science (MEC), in the Basque Country Autonomous Community (CAPV) and in Catalonia, see Table 12.1.

The numerical distribution in our educational systems leads us to the conclusion that the principal groups of immigrant pupils are the Maghrebians, Latin Americans, Asians, EU citizens and other Europeans. It is for these pupils that we have to develop our strategies, which will have to be diversified.

Diversity of educational challenges

Linking the socio-economic and cultural aspects of the groups of immigrants, we can see from Table 12.2 the various types of situations and challenges there are in educating immigrant groups.

There are four principal groups of immigrants, according to linguistic origin and/or socio-economic situation of the families, and with language difficulties in ascending order 1–4.

Socio-economic and cultural diversity of pupils and centres

In Spain, amongst immigrant children, or children of immigrant origin, we have to distinguish between those who, from an educational perspective, belong to different pupil categories and have specific educational needs. Generally speaking, the difficulty of schooling children who speak Berber at home will not be the same as that of teaching those who speak the Spanish

Table 12.1 Numbers of immigrant schoolchildren in Spain

Immigration Students' Country of Origin	Spain (1996–97)	CPAV (2000)	Catalonia (1999)
Maghrebians (Morocco, Algeria and Tunis)	17,076	568	7,151
Hispanic	14,699	488	3,463
Portuguese		491	
Asians	5,417	285	1,112
European Union	19,176	279	2,105
Rest of Europe	4,811	169	958
Total	61,179	2,280	14,789
% of total school population of the area	1	1	1.6

Source: Gobierno (2000); Generalitat de Catalunya (1999); Ministerio de Educación y Ciencias (1998)

Table 12.2   Linguistic origin of immigrant schoolchildren

Socio-economic Level	Linguistic Origin	
	Latin American Hispanic Countries	Other languages Arabic, Portuguese, Chinese, French, German, etc
High	1 Groups of Latin American origin, with a good economic level, which are not going to have problems adapting to the centre.	2 Immigrants from Europe or the USA with a good economic level.
Low	3 Hispanic immigrants with a low socio-economic level.	4 Groups of diverse linguistic origin, such as Arab, Chinese, Portuguese, etc.

spoken in Colombia; nor between those who speak English at home and those who speak Portuguese. Moreover, to each one of these languages, a differing socio-economic level may be applicable (see Table 12.3). In the case of the Basque country, four out of five immigrant pupils can be considered as being from low socio-economic levels or belonging to the 'Third World'. Similar proportions are registered in the Spanish state as a whole, although autonomous communities that receive more Third World immigrants are Catalonia and Madrid (Carbonell, 1995).

It should not be forgotten that the situation is different for those groups that have some form of institutional support from their country of origin, as in the case of Portuguese pupils or, to a lesser extent, Moroccan pupils (Etxeberria, 2000). In brief, there are pupils who have exclusively linguistic problems, others who have exclusively socio-economic problems, others who belong to cultures distant from a European one and still others who have all these problems at the same time.

The pupils of immigrant origin who are schooled at private centres are mostly European and US. So we can state that the immigrant population distributes itself in a selective way in the schools: those with a higher socio-economic and cultural level attend private centres, including schools that

Table 12.3   Socio-economic categories of immigrant schoolchildren by country of origin

Category	Country of Origin	Percentage
High socio-economic level	Europe, USA	21%
Low socio-economic level and Spanish-speaking	Hispano-American countries	22%
Low socio-economic level and speaking other than Spanish	Morocco, Portugal, Brazil, Asia, Africa	57%
Total		100%

cater for their particular linguistic and cultural identity (English, German or French schools), while the government-run schools receive the majority of immigrant pupils in the lowest socio-economic groups (Maghrebians, Portuguese, Brazilians, Hispanics, Asians and Africans).

Moreover, the immigrant pupils in private schools mostly come from families from the European Union or the United States, that is, pupils who have a high socio-economic level. On the other hand, pupils of more humble origins are found in greater proportions in publicly accountable schools. So, these data indicate that it is the public educational centres that take in foreign pupils to a greater extent, particularly those who have a less advantaged socio-economic level.

Teaching immigrants

Some members of the teaching profession, in dealing with multiculturalism, find themselves in a cloud of misconceptions and beliefs that limit their ability to work in a comprehensive and harmonious manner. For a number of teachers, intercultural education has a lesser importance than other issues, such as special education (Generalitat de Catalunya, 1996). There are teachers who subscribe to the view that everything represented within each culture is good in itself, demonstrating a kind of non-critical cultural relativism whereby there is nothing to discuss or argue about in our culture or in others (Jordán, 1998).

Other teachers see an exclusively problematic panorama in the multicultural reality, viewing the presence of different cultures as an inevitably conflicting and complicated situation (Jordán, 1994). The survey carried out by the Basque government in 1992 brings to light the difference in perceptions between, on one hand, primary school teachers, who are favourable towards diversity and, on the other hand, secondary school teachers, who think it impossible to be all-embracing (Gobierno, 1992). We also find a high percentage of indifference towards minority groups: Gypsies, 49 per cent; Arabs, 41 per cent; black Africans, 30 per cent; Jews, 21 per cent (Calvo, 1990), which would indicate that the teaching profession reflects society in this way, demonstrating a higher rate of indifference than their pupils.

Institutional support for intercultural education

In general terms, our schools continue to be places where pupils are treated as a homogeneous block, as though there are few children who are not 'the average' and do not conform with the basic uniformity of that average. This is despite the fact that the average pupil is less and less a reality, as socio-cultural differences become more and more diverse. There is, however, sufficient legal and institutional support to plan strategies for diversity projects in education in Spain as a whole (Colectivo IOE, 1995; Aguado, 1996). It is possible to summarize the fundamental tenets of education for diversity in Spain as follows:

- the right to a quality education for all pupils;
- education in democratic and intercultural values for all pupils including human rights;
- rejection of discrimination and inequalities;
- a system of compulsory education that embraces these principles.

Thus, the transparency of ideas of the educational establishment and what they mean for a global educational project become important, as does the drawing up of strategies and materials for putting intercultural education into practice.

Models for schooling with immigrants in Spain

The main source of disagreement on planning school programmes for minority groups usually stems from the current dilemma between supporting the culture and language of origin of the pupil, and attempting to insert her or him as rapidly as possible into the host culture, with the aim of promoting school and social success. In general, the educational establishment wishes to integrate foreign students in the best way possible, but discrepancies arise when it comes to establishing a strategy to that end (Colectivo IOE, 1996). The false dilemma is based on a perceived obligation to choose between socio-economic and socio-cultural integration when, in reality, they are both sides of the same coin and are inseparable. If we are only looking to economic integration, we may be leaving out important aspects in the development of the pupils. However, if we concentrate solely on cultural integration to the detriment of an academic education, we may be inviting the pupils into a vicious circle of school failure and social marginalization or even exclusion.

There are a number of perspectives that aim at integration although they may produce different results because of the strategies employed. Three such perspectives to integration in schooling are discussed below.

The monocultural or assimilationist perspective

This perspective is an attempt to get pupils of immigrant origin to 'integrate' as fast as possible into the host educational system and society. To this end, they are frequently encouraged to learn the host tongue as quickly as possible in order to facilitate their progress in adapting. This is the most common practice in our educational establishments. Defence of the culture of origin and cultivation of the family cultural identity are seen by the educators, with the best of intentions, as a policy that ends up being prejudicial to the pupil, because they are a waste of time – time that could be better used for academic learning – and also because this preservation of identity could result in pupils continuing to bear the stigma of being immigrants.

The monocultural model may be accompanied by measures of help and support in order to compensate for any difficulties encountered in the acquisition of the host language, in academic achievement or in any social aspect. It is still the case that many of the institutions responsible for the education of immigrant children depend on the compensatory education units of the Basque government education department, the Generalitat de Catalunya or the Spanish Ministerio de Educación y Ciencia. In the pupils' enrolment bulletin for schools in Catalonia, immigrant children are told that they have a series of teachers and social assistants forming part of the compensatory education programme. This bulletin is published in six languages: Catalan, Spanish, French, English, Chinese and Arabic. Moreover, it states that immigrant pupils have at their disposal courses and workshops to help them acquire the host language.

This compensatory factor, although not enough in itself, has to be taken into account, as we have seen that nearly 80 per cent of the immigrant-origin pupils are in a disadvantaged socio-economic situation and a significant percentage of them do not know the language(s) of the host country. In any case, whatever the perspectives adopted with immigrant pupils (monocultural, bicultural or intercultural), compensatory measures are necessary.

This approach to the social integration of the pupil, often well intentioned, nevertheless has the disadvantage that it does not take into account the cultural roots and identity of children of immigrant origin. In fact, although it may favour their school and social integration, it requires their families to relinquish the maintenance of their culture, traditions and language, which in some cases is a high price to pay, and a subsequent source of contradiction and discontent. The syndrome of the foreigner who is not accepted as indigenous but who does not have his or her own identity can trigger anxiety and a cultural anomie, as has been described for Maghrebian and Latin American groups in Spain (Colectivo IOE, 1996; Páez, 2000).

The bicultural or multicultural perspective

This perspective to schooling involves an advance, and a recognition of the value and dignity of the minority culture. This relative advance with respect to the previous monocultural perspective is a reality in some of our schools, where classes are organized in Arabic, Portuguese and Chinese. These classes are aimed directly at the pupils in question and, at times, are scheduled outside the school timetable, in premises apart from the school buildings themselves. Thus, we have Arabic classes for certain communities and Chinese for others.

Otherwise they are given as part of the school timetable, as exemplified by a number of activities undertaken by the Portuguese Language and Culture in

Spain Programme (Etxeberria, 2000) or certain programmes in the Arab language in Madrid and Barcelona (Colectivo IOE, 1996). However, this approach may lead to a certain segregation or ghettoization of pupils who participate. If the majority group does not come to appreciate the value of that culture, and find it worth knowing and cultivating, the final result may be that the prejudices and negative attitudes to minority groups predominate over respect and solidarity. In this case we are 'saving' the culture of origin but within a multicultural context.

The intercultural perspective

This perspective tries to achieve a climate of dialogue between cultures, with the aim of improving the self-esteem of immigrants by overcoming certain prejudices of the majority-group pupils. In our country there are few examples of this, the most exemplary being the Portuguese Language and Culture in Spain Programme (PLCP) (Etxeberria, 2000), which is carried out in options of various intensity, from multicultural forms to intercultural ones. In the same vein are the initiatives that insert the minority culture into the classroom, either symbolically or in a fully integrated way within the school curriculum. But the fundamental difference with this strategy is not whether there is more or less time given to the minority language and culture, but rather the way in which this integration is carried out, eg dialogue, communication or interaction. In intercultural programmes such as the PLCP, the important thing is the attempt to achieve a harmonious multilingual interaction within the classroom.

Resources in intercultural education

It is true that there has not been a coherent or homogeneous response from those responsible for education regarding schooling for immigrant children, and neither are there clear procedures backed up by adequate resources and support. This is the reality. It becomes more serious with the knowledge that basic teacher training programmes do not have specific subjects or courses on the theme of intercultural education, and that in-service training is still wanting, depending, as it often does, on the good will of the teacher in question. It will be argued here that we have sufficient knowledge and experience to put into place in our schools intercultural education projects that can respond well to the challenges of education with minorities. It should be clear from this that the training of teachers in intercultural education is essential. It should be understood that we have adequate programmes and experience, and a sound approach, given that the proportion (less than 2 per cent) of foreign pupils does not constitute a major demographic challenge. Above all we wish to show through our work that intercultural education is not qualitatively different from other education provision, with or without the presence of immigrant pupils.

Problems and prospects

We have already touched on the situation regarding teaching staff and their main difficulties in respect of intercultural education. In general, there is ample unanimity, in official reports, scientific studies, the conclusions of experts and the impressions gained by teachers and professional teams in their day-to-day work. The main problems and prospects facing the teachers trying to manage intercultural education include bewilderment, anxiety, confusion and uncertainty. Ethnocentrism and relativism, with a tendency to homogeneity in the classroom and a rejection of promoting diversity (Jordán, 1998), are also challenges. Given this panorama, it would seem evident that one of the keys to real success in intercultural education in our schools lies in the optimum preparation of our teachers, both at the initial stages of teacher training and in the in-service aspects. Nevertheless, the situation in which teachers in the Spanish state find themselves is far from this ideal, as is discussed below.

Initial training

Initial teacher training does not include material related to positive attitudes to diversity and intercultural education. In the case of training for the secondary level of education, the existence of pedagogic adaptation courses is not a viable option, given the future responsibilities of secondary teachers without previous qualifications. The deficiencies of this system have been made manifestly clear elsewhere (Esteve, 1997).

In-service training

In-service teacher training has many real possibilities for improving and updating, offering courses and projects within the centre, but it lacks the global strategy that is urgently needed, particularly in the secondary education sector where teachers have a degree in their specialist subject but nothing else. In the Basque country, there is the teacher training Garatu Plan (Gobierno, 2000), which addresses in an elementary way the demands of teaching staff in this matter. Similarly, the Generalitat de Catalunya (1999) has courses in place for the training of teachers in intercultural education, as well as link-up programmes with SOS Racism and with the Instituto Catalán del Mediterráneo. The University of the Basque Country has, since 1993, offered a postgraduate degree in intercultural studies that permits a more serious approach to the in-service training of teachers and other professionals. The University of Barcelona and other universities in Spain offer training courses in intercultural education. However, neither in the autonomous communities of the Basque country and Catalonia nor in the rest of the Spanish state are there really adequate initial or in-service teacher training programmes in intercultural education (Aguado, 1996).

Conversion or retraining of teaching staff

Given the lack of teacher training programmes for intercultural education, a number of educational authorities have focused training in a way that it is more like an invitation to spiritual exercises, a true 'conversion', instead of a scientific preparation to meet educational problems. Both in Catalonia and in the Spanish MEC (Ministry of Education and Science), but also in the Basque country, we have detected an individualistic approach, a personal retraining in intercultural education, as if training in this comes via some species of reflection or illumination. It is necessary, however, to be aware of the obstacles and risks of intercultural education and the change in the global (hidden) curriculum. Nevertheless, it is also necessary to call attention to actual training plans to prepare teachers for the challenges of intercultural education, as Carbonell (1995) points out.

The failure of the training courses

The conclusion that we can draw from the training courses that we are familiar with, and that of Jordán (1994) regarding in-service courses, is quite discouraging. In general, teachers taking part in such programmes evaluated that, instead of changing their attitudes and beliefs in a positive way, the participants come out 'vaccinated' against the education of different groups in the same classroom. Those who participate in these courses often claim that the training is impractical and unrealistic and that it does not identify with what actually happens in the classroom. There is too much of an ideological slant from the teacher trainers, and the programmes are seen as boring.

There are those who think that teachers resistant to dealing with diversity in the classroom always find fault with all kinds of intercultural education programmes when they attend the training sessions. They make a point of emphasizing supposed contradictions between practice and theory, arguing that the theoretical part is 'divorced from reality', and that the practical part may be valid for some educational establishments but not for theirs. Generally, the discourse derives from the school's specific problem for which there is 'no solution' apart from increasing resources and employing an extra support teacher to take on the work. In this way, intercultural education will always be the task of the 'other' teacher, not the tutor, as often happens when dealing with education with Gypsies (Enguita, 1999).

Nevertheless, the majority of educators involved in training programmes of this nature sincerely want to have the practical wherewithal available for use in their classrooms. This is why it is important to give these courses the right balance of theory and praxis, to achieve reflection and change in attitudes of the teachers and, at the same time, to provide the necessary guidelines for facing the needs of the classroom.

Proposals for teacher training

Conscious that the teaching staff is the key element in improving education, the author believes that it is fundamental that a series of clear guidelines be laid down, which can channel the worries of educators through training programmes. The following proposals reflect a basis for such training, as reflected in the work of Gagliardi (1995), Aguado (1996), Carbonell (1995), Muñoz (1997) and Jordán (1998). A number of separate areas have been identified:

- *The global perspective.* The problems facing multicultural education are not resolved by adopting isolated measures. An awareness is needed that the responses require teamwork from the teaching staff, participation of the family, local groups and the media, and involvement of the centre's global curriculum and the legislation regarding foreigners. It is important to be aware of this complexity in order to place teacher training in its correct context. The general design of the training course should take into account that excessively theoretical or 'pie-in-the-sky' approaches may provoke the 'vaccination' effect, whereby teachers have their prejudices about intercultural education reinforced, and results contrary to the desired ones are achieved. Although a global vision of the subject is necessary, with special attention given to the environmental or hidden curriculum, it is wise to make gradual proposals, avoiding a too-complex approach that can be carried out only with difficulty. Starting with one day, one subject, one week or one smaller project, it is possible to provide an experience that can subsequently be generalized to the rest of the curriculum.
- *Concrete proposals adapted to the centre.* The course should offer answers to the specific problems indicated without falling into the stereotype recipes that offer nothing. It should also provide a critical review of the problems and possibilities of adapting what the training offers. It is important to start with real problems and look for genuine and solid solutions, instead of starting with a theoretical approach and then finishing with practical proposals that arise from those problems. This inductive focus encourages starting from the problems actually experienced and ending up with a more theoretical and wider consideration.
- *Quality and utility.* Intercultural education must be, and must be seen to be, linked to a genuine quality education in which harmonious living together, respect and school success for all pupils are actively encouraged. The real possibilities offered by the centre's global curriculum and classroom programmes and the conventional methodological resources need to be demonstrated. Pedagogical problems have to be de-dramatized, and those activities actually being carried out analysed, in order to take full advantage of them within the project. Intercultural education must be seen as having relevance and utility.

- *Theoretical and practical training.* Training should provide a solid theoretical basis and reliable equipment, balanced to face the problems confronting intercultural education. It is also necessary to facilitate access to basic knowledge about minority cultures, and the consequences that these have on schooling such as, for example, differences in values, customs, time-frames, educational systems in the countries of origin and the role of the family in education. Pedagogic and professional suitability should be taken into account, so that contrasted educational strategies may be employed. The teacher must be provided with good working practices to learn by immersion the necessary skills in centres developing positive experiences.

Conclusion

Teacher training is one of the key elements in the proper functioning of intercultural education, and thus the efforts of the whole community should address this challenge if we want efficacy in the integration of immigrants in our schools, resulting in improved social harmony and enrichment through cultural diversity. Some teachers view the changes taking place in their schools with trepidation, but wish to respond efficiently to the new challenges. This is why they are asking for more and better training. If we can manage to convince educators to see teaching immigrants as just another pedagogical and enriching experience, and not as a threat, we will have advanced greatly along the road to the integration of minorities. It will be necessary, therefore, to establish training programmes that take on board the real needs of each centre and respond to the demands of the teaching staff.

References

Aguado, M T (1996) *Educación Multicultural: Su teoría y su práctica*, Cuadernos de UNED, Madrid

Calvo, T (1990) *El Racismo que Viene*, Editorial Tecnos, Madrid

Carbonell i Paris, F (1995) *Inmigración: Diversidad cultural, desigualdad social y educación*, MEC, Madrid

Colectivo IOE (1995) *Presencia del Sur: Marroquíes en Cataluña*, Generalitat de Catalunya, Institut Catala d'Estudis Mediterranis, Barcelona

Colectivo IOE (1996) *La Educación Intercultural a Prueba: Hijos de inmigrantes marroquíes en la escuela*, MEC, Madrid

Enguita, F M (1999) *Alumnos Gitanos en la Escuela Paya*, Ariel, Barcelona

Esteve, J M (1997) *La Formación Inicial de los Profesores de Secundaria*, Editorial Ariel, Barcelona

Etxeberria, F (2000) *Políticas Educativas Europeas (especialmente el capítulo sobre educación intercultural y el programa de lengua y cultura portuguesa)*, Editorial Ariel, Barcelona

Gagliardi, Raul (1995) *Teacher Training and Multiculturalism*, UNESCO Publication, Paris

Generalitat de Catalunya (1996) *Educació Intercultural*, Departament d'Ensenyament, Barcelona

Generalitat de Catalunya (1999) *Escolaritzacio d'Alumnat fill de Families Immingrantes*, Departament d'Ensenyament, Barcelona

Gobierno, V (1992) *Debate Social sobre el Diseño Curricular base de la Comunidad Autónoma Vasca*, Departamento de Educación, Vitoria-Gasteiz

Gobierno, Vasco (2000) *Plan Garatu Formacion del Profesorado*, Departamento de Educacion, Vitoria-Gasteiz

Jordán, J A (1994) *La Escuela Multicultural*, Paidos, Barcelona

Jordán, J A (1998) *Multiculturalisme i Educació*, Editions de la Universidad Oberta, Barcelona

Muñoz, J A (1997) *Educación Intercultural: Teoría y práctica*, Escuela Española, Madrid

Páez, Gonzalez y Aguilera (2000) *Identidad Cultural, Aculturación y Adaptación de los Inmigrantes Latinoamericanos en el País Vasco*, Centro cultural chileno Pablo Neruda, Universidad del País Vasco, País Vasco

13. Algeria: striking a balance between tradition and modernity

Sassia Ghedjghoudj

Introduction

This chapter will examine dilemmas and prospects for Algerian teacher education at present, and for the next decade or so. It will be argued that not only should policy for teacher education be directed towards developing future teachers who need to be conversant with new information technologies, but also that teachers should be trained to be better professionals with a wide set of knowledge and skills to support new ideas in teaching and learning. The chapter will first examine the socio-political and educational background to Algeria, and then discuss current issues and dilemmas in teacher education. The chapter will conclude with an examination of the prospects for the future training and education of teachers.

Background to the education system

Algeria, as a developing country, is facing the challenges of the new century with the ambitious aim of catching up with the rapid developments the world is undergoing. Education has constituted a source for the greatest hopes in the process of national construction. It has therefore constituted a central issue in national policies since the country's access to independence in 1962. Education continues to be seen today as the key factor in the acquisition of scientific and technological knowledge, and the major means to achieve social change and modernization. However, education in Algeria has been subjected to the control of a highly centralized political system and used as a means for ideological rather than practical considerations. The aims and content of education were not as much concerned with the development of the individual, as they were geared towards disseminating the ideology of the governing elite and their need for legitimacy (Haouam, 1990).

The educational system has remained an arena for intensive debate. Today it clearly reflects the contradictions and tensions of a society emerging from a long period of colonization and still in search of an authentic cultural identity.

A continuous confrontation has opposed traditionalists and modernists in terms of social and educational policies. This has greatly affected the content of education. Ambivalence between Western and Arab-Islamic values and norms has characterized education policies in this country. This has led to many of the problems and contradictions the educational system is facing presently. The most important contradiction has been the strong emphasis on modernization and development on the Western model, and the equally strong emphasis on the need to re-establish traditional cultural values. The nature of humanity and the nature of society remain problematic. Consequently, the nature of the knowledge that the educational system is to impart remains undefined. The most important issue, which has had tremendous impact on the development of the educational system, and mainly on teacher education and training, is the language question. The option for classical Arabic as the official national language has gradually replaced the use of French in education. But, the expansion of the Arabic language has been inefficient. Moreover, it has led to discrepancies, confusion and contradictions between the stated aims and reality.

The French language, deeply rooted in the society, continues to be largely used as the language of communication and work, and is the key to modern thought and practice. In addition to that, the important diglossia between the official Arabic and the colloquial Arabic has created an important gap between official and popular discourse. The Berber language (spoken by an important proportion of the population) adds to the complex linguistic situation of this country (Haouam, 1990; Grandguillaume, 1983). The problems and short-comings characterizing the Algerian educational system have hampered the achievement of the goals assigned to education in nation building. Three major aims were to be fulfilled by education (UNESCO, 1971):

- to re-establish national cultural identity;
- to change the structure, organization and curricula accordingly;
- to universalize education to all children of school age.

The achievement of these aims has led to increasing needs in terms of material and human resources. There has been, over the last four decades, a notable growth in educational provision, in quantitative terms. The number of primary and secondary schools has increased from around 3,000 to 20,000. The number of schoolchildren increased from around 800,000 to 7 million, and the number of teachers from 24,000 to 320,000 (MEN, 1997). In spite of this significant increase in terms of material and human resources, the demand for education has remained high mainly because of the pressure of numbers. The Algerian population has rapidly grown to more than 30 million during the last decades, with a birth rate of 3 per cent a year. More than 50 per cent of the population are under the age of 20 (ONS, 1998). The quality of education has been greatly affected by this increasing demand on the limited means of the country. Mass education has generated the recruitment of a high number of teachers with a low level of schooling and no professional qualifications. The majority of these teachers have not completed their secondary education; in-service training is provided for them by experienced teachers or inspectors. Moreover, teaching materials and pedagogical supports have been limited. They were produced in haste, and have consequently been of poor quality.

The Algerian educational system has not therefore achieved the objectives set for effective teacher performance. Repeat and drop-out rates are high among the school population. An official study undertaken during the school year 1988/89 by the Ministry of Education on a cohort of primary and middle school pupils showed that only 25 per cent had completed the compulsory period of nine years, 25 per cent had repeated at least one year, 18 per cent had repeated the same class twice and more than 32 per cent had dropped out before completing the cycle (MEN, 1997). The rate of wastage is even higher in secondary education, as less than 20 per cent succeed in the baccalaureate. This reflects just one aspect of the deficiency of the educational system. It is commonly admitted that the quality of education in Algeria is far below the standard required. Hence education is far from achieving the ultimate goals of individual and social development.

Reforms have been attempted to overcome the deficiencies of the educational system. These reforms were essentially concerned with changing the organization and/or the curriculum. The extension of compulsory education to the age of 16 and the introduction of new syllabuses (such as environmental and social studies, religious education and the use of Arabic in teaching) were among the major changes brought about by these reforms. Their major impact has been a burdening of the already encyclopaedic programme of teaching. The key problem underlying the failure of the Algerian educational system to meet desired standards has been, and remains, the low performance of teachers, which in turn is related to the poor quality of teacher education. Training and accreditation of teachers have been neglected. Relatively little attention has been given to the teacher as a central element in the educational process, which of course is the major determinant of the success of any educational system.

Issues and dilemmas of teacher education in Algeria

The educational policies, in terms of teacher education, are based on the old, but still persistent, view that the acquisition of a body of knowledge engenders the ability to transmit it. Hence the emphasis in teacher education has been on a disciplinary, or subject matter, basis rather than on professional training. Primary and middle school teachers are expected in their teaching to apply prescribed courses prepared for them in conventional teachers' guides. Secondary school teachers are generally recruited on the basis of a university degree in a given discipline with little or no professional training. Nevertheless, teacher education institutions have been established for the training of primary and middle school teachers. The number of these institutes, called *instituts technologiques de l'éducation* (ITE), has increased during the last four decades from 6 to 56 (MEN, 1997). Access to these institutions is dependent on success at the entry examination for candidates with a secondary level of education. The training these students receive lasts for a year, and consists essentially in strengthening the basic knowledge of the candidates in subjects such as language, mathematics and science. To prepare them for teaching, theoretical courses in child-centred psychology and teaching methods are provided.

However, the short length of training could not efficiently prepare teachers in academic as well as professional areas for their tasks. The institutes for primary and middle school teachers have produced more than 200,000 teachers, but this number remains below the number required. This has resulted in cramming the pupils into overcrowded classrooms of more than 40 per class, which adversely affects the quality of teaching and learning. Most secondary school teachers come from higher education institutions with little or no pedagogical training. Some are trained in high normal schools (*écoles normales supérieures*), of which there are only 12 for the whole country (MESRS, 1996). However, these normal schools provide the same academic education in different disciplines as in universities. Subject studies in psychology, pedagogy and didactics are taught but these are often too theoretical, and unrelated to practice. Thus, the academic as well as professional education provided in these schools remains unrelated to real teaching situations. Therefore, it does not constitute a real basis for teacher education and training.

The diversified profiles of teachers in the different stages of the educational system have led to fragmented and incoherent policies in teacher education and training. It is in the primary cycle that the low level of instruction and lack of pedagogical training of teachers are most acute. Pupils finish the cycle without fully acquiring the basic knowledge and skills required. The poor quality of education at this fundamental stage weakens subsequent phases of the educational system. This is reflected in the high rates of failure and dropout mentioned earlier. The professionalization of teachers is, therefore, still to be established through a unified initial training at university or in high schools (*écoles normales*). Decisions have to be made on who is to control this education and training. There are at present different centres for decision making between primary, middle, secondary and higher education institutions. The diversified centres of decision making have generated problems of coordination affecting their efficiency.

The role and status of the teaching profession have been declining in social and economic terms. The quality of teacher education and training and the role the teacher is expected to play in education, and in society, have largely contributed to an undervalued teacher role and status. Teacher education in this country is still perceived as essentially knowledge-based with the emphasis on academic knowledge only. The role of the teacher is therefore to provide learners with a given body of knowledge and little or no skills. The role of learners is passive; they are expected to memorize and reproduce faithfully the knowledge that is passed on to them. In this context, the teaching–learning process, in Algerian schools, remains rather archaic in its contents and methods.

The encyclopaedic curriculum, the poor quality of teacher education and training, and limited materials have constituted the major obstacles in the development of the individual and the society in accordance with desired goals. An emphasis on moral and religious education, throughout the whole educational system, reflects the traditional perception of the teacher as a model, spiritual guide and shaper of desired behaviour. The development of the personality of learners, though stated in official statements and curricula, is not provided for in the teaching process. The education and training of teachers is the core dilemma in the development of the Algerian educational system, and remains a prerequisite condition in any educational reform. A clearly defined strategy of teacher education is urgently needed to raise standards in the educational system and achieve the goals of individual and social progress.

The new political and economic options of the last decade have generated radical social changes. A political system based on a single party has evolved towards a plural political setting. In economic terms, there is a clear move from a centralized economy, grounded in Marxism, to a liberal and market-oriented economy. In social terms, a developed modern society is still the stated official aim. It is realized that modernization of society is a necessary condition of the country catching up with the developed economies of the world.

In educational terms, there is an explicit dissatisfaction with the educational system as a whole. Its shortcomings are officially stated in the national press and media. The National Commission for Educational Reform (CNRSE) was officially set up by the president in March 2000, and is composed of scholars and political, social and educational representatives. It is expected to analyse the deficiencies of the educational system and propose an overall reform with new requirements in terms of political, economic and social orientation. However, its preliminary report shows that its concern remains the structure and content of education. Teacher education and training are again relegated to low priority. In this reform, emphasis is put on the necessity of integrating new information communication technology in education. This would be attained by providing schools with computers and networks, and by introducing technological knowledge and skills in the curriculum (CNRSE, 2000).

However, while the integration of new technologies in education is a necessity, its realization remains uncertain. The limited resources of the country cannot cater for the provision of basic educational needs, such as sufficient school buildings, pedagogical materials and teachers. The acquisition of computers and related new technological devices will constitute a heavier burden for the country. But the major problem remains the provision of teachers with the necessary teaching qualifications: academic, pedagogical and didactic knowledge and skills.

The future prospects

The introduction of new information communication technologies implies new educational aims, new curricula and especially new teaching approaches for Algeria. It also implies reconsidering, readapting and developing the educational system in a global way. A clearly defined strategy for teacher education and training remains the essential condition for educational development. This strategy has to be based on the acquisition of adequate knowledge and skills, in line with new educational objectives.

The social and cultural problems the country has been facing since independence have to be rationally and definitely resolved. The language question, in particular, has adversely affected the quality of education in Algeria. Constantly used as a political issue, language has been a means for political legitimacy rather than educational efficiency. Even a little knowledge of the Arabic language has been considered a sufficient licence to teach, whereas qualified French-language teachers have often been excluded from the educational system or relegated into a secondary role because of their lack of mastery of the Arabic language. The use of the French language, as the first foreign language in the country, needs to be reinforced in the educational system. Its role will be to promote the acquisition of new information technologies and therefore access to the Western world. It is also necessary to develop the teaching of other foreign languages such as English, German and Spanish.

Educational issues in general and teacher education in particular need to be exempt from ideological considerations. The conflict between 'traditionalists' and 'modernists' in terms of culture, language and education constitutes an important obstacle to development and innovation. However, equilibrium can be achieved between valuable traditional values and modern thought and practice. The problem is that of pragmatic adaptation rather than blind adoption. The experience of Japan can be enlightening in this context. A symbiosis of specific cultural values and adapted Western knowledge and know-how can prove not only enriching but even more effective in social and cultural development.

A programme of teacher education should be based on two related and interdependent factors, namely 1) the acquisition of useful and practical knowledge and 2) the acquisition of professional skills. The most important aspect of teacher education is, in fact, a global approach within the educational process as a whole. To provide teachers with the knowledge and competencies required is necessary for their role as agents of social change. Higher education will have an increasing role in the initial training of teachers to provide them with the necessary academic knowledge for their teaching. Normal schools will be responsible for the professional training to qualify them for teaching. They will also have an important role in the in-service and continuous training of teachers to update and renew their knowledge and skills. The organization and control of teacher education is naturally managed by public institutions, but an independent commission could be involved, as is increasingly the case in countries such as the United States, France and Great Britain (Wise, 1990). Such a commission would also supervise and evaluate the progress of teacher education and ensure qualification standards.

The development of Algeria today depends on its capacity to integrate and absorb new technological developments. This implies changes in normative as well as in institutional terms, in the control of national policies to redefine the concept of the individual and society. The educational system has to keep pace with the changing and expanding demand for scientific and techno-logical progress. This will require a re-examination of the transmission of knowledge, skills and values. The problem will be to find a balance or a link between valued cultural traditions and desired modern developments.

Teacher education has to make provision for technological acquisition and the use of new communication and information technologies. These will enhance education and training. Simulation, role playing, microteaching and interaction analysis are among the simple means to help initial, in-service and continuous education. Distance learning techniques will play an important role in expanding teacher education nationwide by satellite instruction television (SIT). These programmes are already used in many developing countries. The increasing importance of new information communication technologies in the society, the introduction of multimedia in schools and the inclination of the young generation to use these technologies make it necessary for teachers to integrate technology-related knowledge and skills. New information technologies will constitute only one aspect of the education of teachers.

What is also needed today is a new paradigm for the future that includes theoretical as well as practical knowledge and skills. Teacher education needs to be conceived in the context of global, social, cultural, political, economic and educational desired changes. To educate teachers and prepare them for their multifaceted tasks is a long and continuous process, involving a clear option of investing in human resources rather than just in material resources. Teacher education should be the key in this development.

The scarcity of the country's resources, in human and financial terms, requires a more rational policy to achieve desired educational changes. An open policy towards accepting international and global contributions in the form of financial aid is also necessary. A call for foreign cooperation and investment will be needed to ensure an adequate teacher education for Algeria in the years ahead.

References

CNRSE (2000) *Rénovation du Système de Formation des Formateurs: Preliminary report*, Commission Nationale de la Réforme du Système Educatif, Algiers

Grandguillaume, J (1983) *Arabisation et Politique Linguistique au Maghreb*, Maisonneuve, Paris

Haouam, S (1990) Language, education, and modernisation in the Maghreb: a comparative study, Unpublished PhD thesis, University of London, Institute of Education, London

MEN (Ministère de l'Education National) (1997) *La Formation des Personnels de l'Education National: Bilan et perspectives*, ONPS, Algiers

MESRS (Ministère de l'Enseignement Supérieur et de la Recherche Scientifique) (1996) *Resean Universitaire et Points de Formation*, ONPS, Algiers

ONS (Office National des Statistiques) (1998) *Statistiques de la Population en Algérie*, ONPS, Algiers

UNESCO (1971) *World Survey of Education: Algeria*, UNESCO Publications, Paris

Wise, A E (1990) Policy for reforming teacher education, *Delta Kappa*, **72** (3), pp 2000–02, PIB

14. Cultural and linguistic minority language issues in Florida's public high schools: from cultural impact to inequality to enrichment

George L Iber, Norma Martin Goonen and Richard Moreno

Introduction

This chapter is about the cultural and linguistic minority language issues in Florida's public high schools, which are examined in the context of cultural impact, social and educational inequalities, and how enrichment may be attained through the prospects of improved teacher education. The chapter will first examine the historico-cultural background and its impact on education provision in what is a dynamic multicultural environment. This will be followed by an analysis of educational inequality based on quantitative and qualitative data collected by the authors that demonstrate the need to support Florida's limited English proficiency (LEP) population. The chapter will conclude by examining the notion of enrichment with reference to future prospects for teacher education

Cultural impact

The state of Florida is a rich example of cultural diversity and language amalgam, which has been the subject of numerous studies. Some of these studies focus on how the educational system has dealt and is dealing with a sudden and massive influx of immigrants, who bring with them the diversity that is reflected in its school systems. Some would think that the history of this cultural and language diversity dates to the 1960s with the influx of Cuban, Haitian and Central and South American immigrants. Indeed, those who would believe that the beginning of cultural and language exchanges in Florida began in the middle of the 20th century are not considering the long history of Florida as a culturally and linguistically diverse region. Historically, for example, the use of Spanish preceded the use of English in the peninsula eventually known as La Florida. Spain claimed the state as part of its empire in 1512. Florida's history and current status have always included a significant number of minority language groups. Historically, schooling was not always viewed as a prerequisite for participation into the mainstream political and economic institutions of the day. An LEP student was not always expected to complete secondary education. Unskilled working-class jobs were plentiful through the 1960s, and many drop-outs found employment. Beginning with the Civil Rights Act of 1964 and then building upon the Supreme Court decisions of *Serna* v *Portales* (1974), *Lau* v *Nichols* (1974) and *Plyer* v *Doe* (1982), Florida designed its Education Equity Act of 1984. The Act specified the broad framework for equal access to education within the state. At this point, individual schools and districts were left to resolve their perceived dilemmas regarding student difficulties.

In 1990, the League of United Latin American Citizens (LULAC) and others brought a court case against the Florida Board of Education, claiming that students whose first language was not English were not being provided with a fair and equal education. This was because English was the only mode of communication in most classes and that fact seriously jeopardized any chance for a non-English speaker to receive an education. Recognizing the strength of the case, Florida's State Board of Education sought a consent decree with the parties. The decree became the LULAC META Consent Decree and is now the current framework for compliance with state and federal education laws in Florida. While Florida instituted the LULAC META Consent Decree in 1990 to aid all non-English-speaking students in their transition to academic fluency and school success, it seems that it is far more successful for students who enter the system in the elementary grades.

However, the operationalization of the decree has been uneven in its benefits. Nevertheless, the decree's mandates coupled with the time provided to an entering elementary school student generally provide sufficient remediation and positive results. It falls short, however, when dealing with entering secondary students in programming, equal access to all programmes, personnel, monitoring and student outcomes.

An analysis of educational inequality

This second section presents quantitative and qualitative data that demonstrate the need for further support for Florida's LEP population. Let us examine the quantitative data first, followed by the qualitative case studies.

The quantitative data

Florida's student population is diverse. LEP students come from 252 countries and speak 202 languages within its schools. Table 14.1 shows the main countries of origin. LEP students are facing new challenges in terms of state examinations, public schools are being asked to be more accountable and universities are

Table 14.1   Countries of origin and percentage
of population of LEP students in Florida schools

Country of Origin 1998/99	Number	%
United States	124,264	52.41
Cuba	18,849	7.80
Haiti	14,975	6.32
Puerto Rico	13,255	5.59
Mexico	12,907	5.44
Colombia	7,242	3.05
Venezuela	4,971	2.10
Brazil	4,546	1.92
Dominican Republic	3,582	1.51
Nicaragua	2,923	1.23
Vietnam	2,857	1.20
Peru	2,761	1.16
Honduras	2,741	1.16

Source: Florida Department of Education (2000)

taking on more responsibility for training teachers. In addition, the schools have become more crowded, and student–teacher ratios are higher. There is some evidence that early entry into the school system with well-trained teachers of English for speakers of other languages (ESOL) is producing a group of successful bilingual students, while at the same time the problems of LEP students' late entry into the school system have not been adequately addressed.

Surprisingly, the largest group of LEP students in Florida, about half, is born in the United States; they are US citizens. The largest single minority language spoken is Spanish.

One alarming statistic concerns the number of drop-outs in the LEP populations (see Table 14.2). According to state record management, LEP populations who are enrolled in an LEP programme (LY) have almost twice the drop-out rate of an English speaker (ZZ). Usually drop-out occurs while the students

Table 14.2   Graduation and drop-out rates for 1998/99

LEP Status	Number of Graduates	Drop-out Rate
LY	2,077	8.4%
LF	1,288	6.9%
LZ	5,816	7.4%
ZZ (non-LEP)	86,789	4.4%

Source: Florida Department of Education (2000)
LY = LEP students currently enrolled in classes designed for LEP students
LF = Former LEP students who exited programme within the last two years
LZ = Former LEP students who exited programme for at least five years
ZZ = Non-LEP student

are in high school, after their 15th birthday. What this indicates is that an older student in high school who is involved with learning English, but has not yet attained the requisite fluency needed for academic success, is twice as likely to decide to leave school prior to graduation (see Table 14.3).

Again, the trends of success and failure emerge along ESOL entry and exit lines. LEP students who entered their ESOL programme as young students and have left the programme for at least five years are having results closest to the native English speakers. The other LEP categories lag way behind the ZZ and LZ norms. In part this should put to rest the myth that one can 'do maths' even if one doesn't know English. A review of the reading and maths problems on these tests reveals the need to make many fine discriminations between word meanings, a cognitive ability difficult to achieve in one's native language and much more difficult in a second language. When effecting a comparison, one sees again that average scores of LF students and LZ students are close to the ZZ average, but LY students have the most difficulty (see Table 14.4).

The implications of these figures for the recent immigrant high school student are not encouraging. In fact, these standardized tests may be viewed by some students as impossible hurdles. It then becomes only a matter of choice for these students to decide to drop out. If they sense that the system will not provide a means for them to be successful in school, it is logical for them to decide to begin a work career and pursue an alternative degree, such as a high school equivalency degree (GED). The realization

Table 14.3   10th grade Florida writing scores

LEP Status	% score < 3	Average score
LY < 2-year programme	67%	2.2
LY > 2-year programme	51%	2.6
LF	27%	3.1
LZ	11%	3.5
ZZ (non-LEP)	11%	3.6

Source: Florida Department of Education (2000)

Table 14.4   10th grade reading and maths standardized scores

LEP Status	Reading Average	% score < 3	Maths Average	% score < 3
LY < 2-year programme	247	96%	272	78%
LY > 2-year programme	250	99%	265	88%
LF	280	91%	293	77%
LZ	295	79%	300	65%
ZZ (non-LEP)	310	65%	315	56%

Source: Florida Department of Education (2000)

that success at school is limited may also serve to increase the sense of isolation or anomie.

The qualitative studies

The following qualitative case study subsection illustrates what high school teachers and students say about their daily struggles in teaching and learning. The first two studies look at the dilemmas from the teachers' perspectives; the third study involves three student cases.

Teacher case study 1: the need for personalized instruction

There is a need for personalized instruction... a supportive family / home environment that fosters a successful ESOL student. The state demands so much of them, such as the English curriculum and passing the FCAT to earn a standard diploma. These are overwhelming hurdles for them; let's stop being in denial about this.

At the high school level, I am teaching all levels of ESOL in one class, that is the class is broken down by class level, not by English proficiency level. My job is to teach 10th grade curriculum to an ESOL student who is in their second year of high school. It does not matter that they may have only been in this country for two years or less. But the reality is that most of these students are not ready for this curriculum, even with the appropriate adaptations.

Some of these students are illiterate in their home languages and some lack sufficient training in their home language for the transference of skills and knowledge of the second language, English. They are not ready for the high school language arts curriculum which I am to follow and then adapt with ESOL methodologies. There needs to be a way to meet their needs in learning the second language before we bombard them with the English curriculum and with preparing them for a standardized test like the FCAT.

Most of our LEP students did not have these types of standardized tests in their native countries, where so much of our teaching emphasis is placed. We should stop being in denial about what their true needs are. There needs to be a special programme where these children can build these basic English skills before being forced into the standard curriculum. This is not about equal access or the denial of equal access; it is about addressing some very basic student needs as it concerns their second language development.

My experience with children at the elementary school level is that they catch up on social language quickly and do not lag behind too much when acquiring academic language. They adapt faster to the school environment and they seem to bond to the teacher, especially if the teacher is from the same ethnic group as the student. At the elementary level you teach the student the whole day and all subject matters, so you can arrange the class according to their needs; you see the big picture. Co-teaching with other teachers can take place with much more ease than at the high school level. The mainstreaming of the elementary ESOL student is done in incremental stages. There is a much closer monitoring of the student's progress. The teacher at the elementary level is aware of the student's progress and the English proficiency level in all subject matters. In high school the situation is not the same, and at times it can be the opposite.

You, as the ESOL teacher, may understand the needs of these students [English proficiency needs], but the science teacher may ignore them or not recognize them as needs they need to address, or they may not be aware that the student is an ESOL student recently exited from the programme and still in need of guidance and monitoring.

Some students are more successful than others. This teacher believes it has a lot to do with the family support students receive, the environment they have at home, how well their parents are educated, and their particular academic preparation in their home language. All these components translate into how successful and motivated an ESOL student will be at the high school level.

Teacher case study 2: home language preparation
'The ones who are prepared in their home language will eventually make it. It is the ones who have no or very little preparation in their home language that I worry about.' The teacher interviewed is a full-time high school ESOL teacher. She often finds, when she is ready to exit a student from ESOL, that the mainstream teachers do not understand the differences between social and academic language. She thinks that many teachers believe that children should be exited from the programme once they have social language in place, or that they no longer need extra support and guidance once they have exited.

She thinks that this misconception exists because many staff members don't usually understand second language acquisition. They feel a newly exited ESOL student is just as ready as a monolingual English speaker and does not need further support concerning basic assignments and lessons. She goes on to say that some students see their own needs in a similar way, that is, that once social language is in place they no longer see themselves as in need of the ESOL programme to help them with their academic language development. She observes that many of these same students see a stigma with being an ESOL student and in ESOL classes and want out of the programme as soon as possible. So you have teachers, as well as students, rejecting ESOL principles and support once social language has been acquired, and rejecting the obvious need for academic language development, even when the reality hits that these students are not passing the courses into which they have been mainstreamed.

She too feels that the ones who are prepared in their home language will eventually be successful. It is the ones who have no or very little preparation in their home language that she worries about:

There are many children who come to my classroom who are illiterate or pre-literate, who have so much catching up to do. They try so hard but they are faced with an overwhelming task.

Along the way I was helping a child who is essentially just learning to read and write, and I worry – how will she pass the English portion of this test? But then on a day when I started to review math word problems, I realized that this child had never learned a number system nor did she know how to do basic math computations. So all along I thought, just teach her how to read and write. It just didn't hit me that if you had no previous schooling in your home language, not only can't you read and write but you don't know your numbers and that you also have been missing out on math preparation for all your life.

What we are doing for them does work. But we need to support that process a lot more, not criticize it, build on what works and revise what doesn't and revisit the tenets of bilingual education in general.

Just as the teachers express a sense of frustration, so do the students. They find it difficult to succeed with the combined agenda of academic and social adjustments.

Student case study 1: the sense of anomie
This student, a female, is 16 and has been in the United States for three years:

Originally I wanted to go back; I couldn't get used to it here. I only live with my mom and my stepfather. My sister and father are still in Cuba. I miss them very much. I am used to it a little. I would love to be able to go back to visit, but not to live.

The language here is hard to learn. The people are so different, I feel so strange as if I don't belong here. I miss my family; I want to return to visit. At first in school, it was strange. Sincerely I don't like school because of the language problem. I wasn't passing my classes. I like Spanish more. I feel embarrassed when I speak English. If someone knows Spanish, I go into Spanish. In English, I am embarrassed. I feel like if I make a mistake I'll be made fun of. But also I love my language and I love to speak it. As time went by I tried to speak more English and my English got better, and I was able to get better grades. I got used to the system. I have adapted. I am not saying I like it. You have to put yourself out there and push; if you don't, just forget it. I had no alternative, you become accustomed or you go crazy.

Student case study 2: home support
This student has been in the United States for three years. She is 16 years old:

In the beginning, I thought it was a big vacation, but after a while you realize it is something else. Then comes the depression; you miss your home, family and friends. And you realize that people and life have changed. Then you go to school. The first week of school I didn't know any English (I took English in Colombia, but it was only grammar), but when you're here you actually don't understand anything, even though I took English in my country. What really helped me is that my stepfather is American. He taught me English and helps me with my homework. If I had not had him it would have been hard because there was no other English speaker in my home, and when you come to school you hang out with Spanish-speaking friends.

Student case study 3: peer pressure
This student has been in the United States for two years. She is 16 years old and in 10th grade:

> When I originally arrived, my family that was already here helped me and new friends helped with English. The most important things that helped me were friends and some teachers. My Spanish teacher and ESOL teacher helped the most. They are both Hispanic and knew what was happening to me and could help me. Some of the hardest things were understanding the different accents in English and here the students are always trying to be so cool.
>
> Here students were different; they were trying to get out of work and really not being serious about school, like in Cuba. Peer pressure was hard. Other students know you don't speak English, so other students make you feel bad. They would belittle you even in the hallway going to class or the cafeteria. One time it was bad; I was walking down the hallway, going to the cafeteria and a bunch of girls started calling me 'stupid' and ugly things like 'bitch'. I just kept on walking. I didn't know why they were calling me names so aggressively and trying to trip me. I guess it was because I was different.
>
> I couldn't understand some of the teachers because of the language. The students would make me feel out of place and were mean to me. The classes were not challenging. In math I knew everything, so I wanted to go to sleep in that class, but in ESOL (English) I needed more time in it, to learn the English.
>
> What got me through all of this is that I got new friends, Hispanics who spoke English. They would talk to me and help me. I got an American boyfriend, so I had to speak English. I liked English. I also went to my Spanish teacher (Spanish for native speakers class) at lunchtime, and I would tell her everything that happened to me that day and she would listen and give me advice. Also, I told my mom. My mom and my uncle would help me. In my home my family would support me. Most importantly at school and during my first year at school I had a strong desire to learn English, so bad that I began to do better.
>
> You know, when I was in Cuba, I knew everything about Cuba; I had knowledge from Cuba and I was an advanced student. So here, I knew a lot of the material but I didn't know the language fluently and I still don't, so people sometimes think I am less intelligent than I really am.

Academic English demands not simply a basic communication but includes a sophisticated vocabulary, the ability to write in a formal manner, specific subject area knowledge, and content mastery oriented towards the US perspective. For most students, this is a daunting task. To make matters worse, there is a dearth of bilingual teachers and role models in secondary schools as compared to the elementary levels. It is not enough for teachers simply to know how to speak another language; they must also be biliterate in their specialized content area if they are really going to help the non-English-speaking student. Without teachers to turn to as resources, students become disenfranchised from the complete learning experience.

Enrichment: the prospects for teacher education

The lessons learnt have not come easily. Clearly addressing the needs of the non-English speaker is a 'work in progress'. While the META Consent Decree was a significant step in the legislative foundation supporting ESOL programmes, much work remains. Test scores reveal both success and concern. While younger students with more time in the school system are making appropriate advances, the student who enters the system at the high school level appears to need more support. As revealed in the case studies, the high school experience of large classes, academic discourse, intense peer pressure and a dearth of bilingual subject area teachers leave high school ESOL students in the position of relying on their own networks of friends and peers to help master English. Not all students even have the time to make the best use of a peer network, especially if the academic preparation in their home country was minimal.

While entering LEP high school students do receive special support, if they are identified as LEP, there is a distinct gap between the ESOL teachers' abilities and concerns, and those of the subject area teacher. A lack of ESOL training required by subject area teachers is evident by their minimal understanding of the language learning process. The incorrect perception that social language skills equate to academic language skills appears still to be the operational assumption used in many subject area classes. As stated by one of the teachers, 'We should stop being in denial about what their true needs are'. To remain in denial is to continue to deny a portion of the students' fundamental access to an equal education. What then might be done to improve the academic experience of LEP students?

As is currently being done in Florida, all teacher training institutions should require a series of courses designed to give new teachers the cultural awareness and methods training needed to work most effectively with non-English-speaking students. Focused sensitivity sessions that include ethnic and language diversity issues (eg language and cultural immersions) for two or more weeks as an in-service or as a summer programme could be developed. Improved access to ESOL courses through online Internet platforms may be a valuable methodology for teachers not able to attend a traditional class.

Requiring bilingual training that specifically includes several years of second language training in a targeted language would facilitate a tremendous awareness of the complexity of second language learning as well as the obvious links between the home language and English. In conjunction with the language training, special programmes could be designed for teachers to have a guided visit of the 'home country' of some of their students. Expanding on the visitation idea, formal year-long exchanges of teachers and university professors between countries might do more to facilitate cross-cultural understanding between cultures than any other measures.

Within the school facility itself many options also exist. In large secondary institutions the 'school within a school' concept might be considered. To help eliminate student anomie, 'houses' with greater student support could be structured to provide maximum student enrichment and academic success. Teachers on the secondary and elementary level should work as a team that would include an ESOL specialist. Competency-based assessment of high school graduation requirements in the major languages of LEP students might be considered in districts with large numbers of LEP students. Specialized or advanced coursework taught in other languages could be provided for all students. These advanced courses might be a part of an advanced international baccalaureate programme associated with a school in another country. Thus the 'disadvantage' of a non-English speaker becomes instead a valuable resource with the reward of a double graduation certificate.

Florida, from its earliest days, has been enriched by the constant tide of new immigrants. The unique cultural features of Florida would not exist without the dynamic exchange of abilities and ideas brought to the state from many peoples and lands. The efforts by the schools to ensure that all children and citizens receive a fair and enriching education will continue. One thing is certain; Florida will continue to have an increasing number of students whose first language is not English and the needs of this dynamic multicultural environment will continue to affect educational policy for the foreseeable future.

15. Cultural perspectives and teacher education: indigenous pedagogies in an African context

Ladislaus M Semali

Introduction

The notion of indigenous pedagogies captures the locality and diversity of current approaches to African teacher education – approaches that have been in theoretical, practical and political contest with one another. By indigenous pedagogies I refer to the ways of teaching that are enhanced by local knowledges and found among indigenous peoples. In the school context, for example, these non-Western education traditions and thought consist of a complex set of processes or abilities, ways of knowing and ways of being that students bring to the classrooms, abilities that span their lifetime – from employing their indigenous languages to relating their history.

The legitimization of indigenous ways of teaching and the education of teachers in this area are contested issues. Some scholars contend that the interference of one world-view over another in the learning of science concepts is perhaps similar to the interference of a first language in the learning of a second (Jegede, 1999). However, a research study to investigate such interference in the cultural learning environments of diverse populations including indigenous children has not been given much attention. Further, a project aspiring to integrate indigenous methods of teaching in the school curriculum is not popular among curriculum planners. Collectively, these perspectives present distinct, untested hypotheses of how teachers and teachers' colleges can meet students' needs in diverse cultural settings.

In an attempt to shed light on this much-neglected area, I present in this chapter my reflections on the possibilities and dilemmas teachers and teacher education programmes face in many African countries. My task here will be to provide a qualitative analysis based on veteran teachers' narratives about their teaching of indigenous children and how their current teaching practice is a mirror image of their own training. The narratives tell the stories of teachers who have been immersed in schools for five years or more. These schools are located in remote areas and in communities of ethnic groups that are native to the area but far away from the teacher's home. The reflections I present here, albeit a partial presentation, are results from these narratives, which were the outcome of interviews that I conducted between 1998 and 2000 in Southern African countries.

The principles guiding my reflection and thinking in this chapter derive from contemporary research on knowledge production, critical theory, post-colonial theories of subjugated knowledges, and radical curriculum theory. Through these principles, I envision that an indigenously informed educational context of students' lived experiences takes on more importance, as teachers connect them to the larger epistemological and cultural dynamics they are helping the students analyse. Radical curriculum theory opens the way to looking at the production of knowledge with new eyes. When curriculum, as a forum of knowledge production, is viewed in this new light, it moves beyond the traditional notions of curriculum as simply a course of study or a compilation of data to be learnt. As defined here, a curriculum immersed in indigenous pedagogies involves epistemological questions relating to both the production and consumption of knowledge, the relationship between culture and what is defined as successful learning, the contestation of all forms of knowledge production and the purposes of education itself. The curriculum development we propose in this vein aims to critique the process of the generation and validation of curricular content, and the ways that groups of people benefit from the 'certification' of some forms of knowledge while other groups do not.

Two knowledges collide: indigenous pedagogies and the school curriculum

The practice and teaching of indigenous pedagogies in the schools I visited in sub-Saharan Africa present a situation of two epistemologies at war, two knowledges on a collision course. Unfortunately, in this 'conflict' the casualties are the indigenous children. This phenomenon of two epistemologies or dual ways of knowing has been studied by social theorists and educators since the early 1900s. Overall in these studies, social theorists acknowledge the existence of a form of dual or separate socialization process involving indigenous or non-mainstream populations. They refer to a variety of constructs used in these studies to describe the personality development, identity or traits of non-white/non-European children. These constructs include concepts like: *double consciousness* (Du Bois, 1903), *double vision* (Wright, 1953), *bicultural* (Valentine, 1971; De Anda, 1984; Ramirez and Castaneda, 1974; Red Horse *et al*, 1981; Rashid, 1981), *diunital* (Dixon and Foster, 1971), *multidimensional* (Cross, 1978) and other references that closely resemble notions of *duality* and *twoness* (Memmi, 1965; Fanon, 1967; Kitano, 1969; Hsu, 1971; Sue and Sue, 1978). The question that needs to be asked today is: what can teachers and administrators do to eliminate further division, conflict and casualties in the schools of the 21st century? How could a teacher education programme help?

In my estimation, the epistemological war began some 500 years ago with the first encounter of Western and American Indian civilizations, and of Europeans with African cultures and with Asian communities. Western Europe imposed on indigenous cultures completely different world-views, definitions, norms and values, languages, and political, religious and academic ways of living in society. But, within indigenous peoples, a holistic world-view expressed through oral tradition, rites, and agrarian and health practices has endured locally. Whether in Tanzania, Botswana, Zimbabwe or South Africa, you are likely to find that the teaching of science, for example, has been defined in terms of Western traditions (AAAS, 1989, 1993). But because the Western world-view has dominated the teaching of maths and science for many years, it becomes extremely difficult to unravel cultural factors from the learning variables. Critics of Western education are quick to point out that the colonizing and civilizing view of Western science is basically responsible for the transfer of the curriculum reforms of the 1960s in maths and science to non-Western classrooms. Such transfer was characterized by little concern or disdainful disregard for indigenous cultures and the world-views that students brought from them to the study of Western science (Semali and Stambach, 1997).

Perhaps the blame need not be placed entirely on intruding foreign colonial powers. Rather, I would argue that one of the underlying difficulties with promoting indigenous pedagogies in schools (and instead preferring Western instructional approaches) is that teachers who have been educated in Western institutions or socialized with ideas such as 'West is best' are either unprepared, uncomfortable or simply prefer to hold tightly to their language and cultural biases. In addition, because science reflects the thinking of Western society, the norms and values of science are more familiar to students from the mainstream middle class than to students from indigenous communities or from diverse languages and cultures (Eisenhart, Finkel and Marion, 1996). Although these observations are more visible in science classrooms, they are not in any way limited to science teaching alone, but occur across all content areas.

Some of the teachers I met in schools, particularly in East Africa, explained to me that the Western systems of formalized school instruction take little account of local cultures. These teachers argued that many African governments tend to promote teaching methods in non-Western schools within a model of curriculum based on a nationalist view of history and a universal interpretation of the sciences and mathematics. Unfortunately, such a curriculum does not take account of local languages and teaches only the official or national language. Sometimes, such models of school curriculum deliberately dismiss or eradicate local culture, by excluding it completely from the classroom as if it were irrelevant to the concerns and lives of local populations. As cautioned by Shiva (1993), local knowledge of any kind is compelled to disappear when the dominant system negates its very existence or when such systems erase or destroy the reality that the local knowledge attempts to represent.

Destruction of indigenous epistemologies

When I talk about dilemmas and possibilities of indigenous pedagogies in an African context, I do not wish to imply that these examples are limited or are exclusive to the African continent. In fact they are not. In indigenous studies, such as the Native American academic programmes, emerging new political awareness has been expressed in terms of the existence of a global Fourth World indigeneity. Proponents of such a view claim that Fourth World peoples share the commonality of domination and are constituted by indigenous groups as diverse as the Indians of the Americas, the Inuits and Samis of the Arctic north, the Maori of New Zealand, the Koori of Australia, the Karins and Katchins of Burma, the Kurds of Persia, the Bedouins of the African/Middle Eastern desert, many African tribal communities, and even the Basques and Gaels of contemporary Europe. In this context it is important to avoid the essentialistic tendency to lump together all indigenous cultures as one, yet at the same time maintaining an understanding of the nearly worldwide oppression of indigenous peoples and the destruction of indigenous knowledges.

A few examples will illustrate what I mean by tension and dilemmas that exist between Western and indigenous epistemologies, and how students must cope with the two contexts. The first example refers to Tanzania. In the case of Tanzania, the tension rests between the relevance of the school curriculum and the life in the villages where students live. In this regard, I have documented elsewhere how Nyerere (1968) introduced education for self-reliance (ESR) in Tanzania. This initiative focused on the many aspects of local African education principles of familyhood, self-reliance, cooperation and collective work (Semali, 1999). However, this idea of aligning village life and education for self-reliance was met with resistance from both teachers and parents. Some policy makers as well as curriculum planners misunderstood this idea. The idea to prepare young people for the work they will be called upon to do in the society that exists in Tanzania was misunderstood to mean being withheld from rapid progress (Nyerere, 1968: 274). This reform idea was to develop the rural sector by, among other things, training primary and secondary school students in agriculture and other practical skills.

Unfortunately, right up to the present, students continue to be short-changed by a curriculum that teaches them skills and languages they cannot use, and uses classroom examples that are foreign and unrelated to the local situation (Semali, 1999). For example, the use of narration as a mode of teaching and learning is mightily ignored in the learning of maths and science. As a traditional teaching tool, narration is a broad term that includes myths, proverbs, legends and fictions to tell a story or teach a moral. According to Mosha, the main function of narration is to contribute in a very special way to the holistic formation process known as *ipvunda*. Narration has always been part and parcel of the African tradition and plays an indispensable role in indigenous education for life, as well as education for a living (Mosha, 2000).

The second example refers to the use of body language as a mode of learning. As explained by Da Silva (1999), educators do not value this indigenous method. She explains that the notion of corporality, which was used as a mode of learning in the Amazonian cultures of Brazil, is ignored in Western education. She argues that the human body, as the space and language of the social and symbolic structure, is described in the context of the Akwe culture. Movement, action, the senses, art and emotion are combined, she suggests, in techniques that are both educational and cognitive, and that take place both in everyday interaction and during the great ritual ceremonies. Less concerned with verbal language, these cultures construct and communicate knowledge through music, drama, gesture, aesthetics and body decoration.

The third example is from the Desana people of the Colombian rainforest. In this example, Classen (1999) shows that students in maths and science classrooms experience a conflict between so-called 'traditional' ways of education and Western ways of schooling. Classen argues that in Western culture the senses of sight and hearing have been stressed as ways to knowledge over and above the other senses. Our bodies provide us with many ways to learn about and interact with the world. Through the sense of smell, taste and touch, many non-Western cultures acquire and transmit knowledge.

Therefore, the conflict between traditional ways of narration, corporality and sensual learning, and Western ways of schooling illustrates in significant ways the war that goes on when children socialized within these indigenous contexts enter formal schools to learn science. The use of body decoration, beads, stories, proverbs, herbs and much more, prevalent among the Irawq and Maasai of Kenya and Tanzania, the Zulu of South Africa and other peoples of Africa, is systematically ignored in the school curriculum as a mode of learning and teaching of school subjects to this day. Further, as expected, these modes of learning are not valued in teacher education programmes. As explained by Nyerere, the students from indigenous communities 'get the worst of both systems' (Nyerere, 1968: 274).

Teaching and practice of indigenous pedagogies

Why focus on indigenous pedagogies? What philosophy should drive native education policy and practice? Why are indigenous pedagogies important to teachers and teacher education programmes? Arguments supporting the view to integrate indigenous pedagogies in schools and in teachers' colleges are based on the understanding that knowledge does not exist in objective, decontextualized forms, but is intimately linked to specific contexts, people and issues (Semali and Kincheloe, 1999). This understanding is particularly relevant in non-Western contexts in which you find indigenous people whose systems of knowledge have been subordinated by the forces of colonization that have consistently worked to subvert the indigenous world-view – the social, political, economic and cultural life.

Recent literature reveals a growing interest in understanding the educational needs of learners from other cultures and a growing awareness that methods to help learners from non-European cultures should be anchored to indigenous critical ethnographic research (Brokensha and Warren, 1980; Knuth, 1998). New publications show that teachers are reading about the progress being made in this area. For example, in 1999 the *International Review of Education* devoted an entire special issue on learning, knowledge and cultural text. In this issue, several case studies were presented from non-Western countries illustrating indigenous pedagogical models and their political contexts. Other works such as Brokensha and Warren (1980), Semali and Kincheloe (1999), Warren and Rajasekaran (1993) and Warren, Slikkerveer and Brokensha (1995) are rich with examples and definitions of indigenous knowledge from a wide range of geographical regions and topics. Central to these studies is a reversal of years of bias, a departure from the perception of millions of native people simply as irrational peasants in need of development and from the unquestioned importation of modern technologies into non-modern contexts. The main conclusions from these studies is that local people do know a great deal about their environment, in which they have lived for generations; and this knowledge must be taken into account in the teaching, planning and implementation of classroom practice as well as development of educational policies (Semali, 1999).

Having been born and raised on the slopes of the Kilimanjaro, where the Chagga people have lived for hundreds of years, I cannot resist reflecting on what the notion of 'going to the source' means for me or for the teachers I met over there. The Chagga refer to the concept of teaching as *ipvunda*. The wisdom contained in this concept is itself telling in terms of what it means to children and adolescents growing in this region, as a basis of their formation and increasingly for the mentoring of future teachers. According to Sambuli Mosha, the process of *ipvunda* illustrates the *heartbeat* of a healthy society and the interconnectedness between life in the community and the knowledge within and outside its borders. For Mosha, there are three educational tools in the *ipvunda* process: 1) linguistic tools – stories, riddles, song and dance; (2) spiritual inspiration of rituals – word and action; and (3) role-playing. These tools help to awaken in students and teachers their potential for hard work and hospitality, and then continue to nurture thsis human potential to 'do good', to become the best they can be.

What might these reflections mean to teachers of the 21st century? Perhaps, what the native educational leaders and Mosha are saying, as stated previously, is that teachers must take a hard look at their classroom practice. They must examine their relationship with indigenous children. They must look at their own education and how it matches what they practise in the classrooms with indigenous children. They must understand the complex relationship between the indigenous knowledge and insight they are passing along for students to grapple with, and the indigenous cosmology that grants contextual meaning to the concept. Therefore, it becomes necessary for the modern African school to encourage and allow parents, families and communities to participate more fully in education and to play an active role in the areas of values education, formation of curricula and hiring of administrators and teachers of virtue.

Also, African teachers need to know that Western science is an established field of study, with its own protocols for judging evidence and establishing truth. For non-Western students, with limited science experience, and unfamiliar with the Western protocols, engaging in inquiry may be challenging. A lack of adequate preparation to engage in inquiry, to interact and to communicate in the Western ways of judging evidence can become sources of frustration and failure. But in addition to an appreciation of students' cultures and languages, teachers also require knowledge of the nature of science as defined by Western tradition. Such knowledge may be incompatible with the cultural values and interaction styles of some teachers and students (Lee and Fradd, 1998). For example, the rules of science inquiry, including the use of empirical evidence, logical arguments, scepticism, questioning and criticism, may be incongruent (or in conflict) with the values and norms of cultures favouring social consensus, shared responsibility, emotional support and respect for authority. In contrast, teachers who are knowledgeable about science, but not about the cultures of their students, may emphasize inquiry without making science relevant to students. They must be able to help their students grasp the connections between the indigenous understandings and the students' lived experiences and school activities. Admittedly, such pedagogical abilities are intellectually demanding and will take much time and detailed study for everyone involved, including teachers' colleges.

Conclusion: prospects of indigenous teaching methods

I have outlined in this chapter the arguments in favour of indigenous pedagogies in African schools. As explained previously, to urge teachers to integrate indigenous pedagogies across the curriculum is tantamount to pushing them to rendezvous with a dangerous memory. In some of the Africanization literature that emerged in the early 1960s, indigenous or folk education was often confused with colonial ethnic education or native schools (Cross, 1985).

Because of such confusion in much of the literature, few debates have considered indigenous education outside the colonial context. In the native school system, a second-tier education was designed for 'natives' or the local people. The goals of such education in many countries of pre-independent Africa, for example, were to provide a curriculum that was to fit non-European populations. The main thrust of the curriculum aimed at producing graduates who would do manual labour and engage in subservient jobs. The assumption of such education was that even though both native schools and European formal schools had the same objective of training for employability, the outcomes were designed differently. The planners made sure that the 'natives' would not compete with their European counterparts for the job market within the country or abroad. Thus, native education was seen as a separate and inferior education.

My goal in this chapter is to confront these dangerous memories. I argue that students' and teachers' rendezvous with indigenous pedagogies in the curriculum can expand their perspective with a vantage point from which to view Eurocentric discourses, a starting point for a new understanding about the world and the human being's role in it. I believe that familiarity with indigenous knowledge will help both students and teachers see previously unseen problems and develop unique solutions to them. While deconstruction of these dangerous memories and self-reflection are important, the broader goal is to initiate a conversation that leads to a critique of Western science that results in a reconceptualization of the Western scientific project, around issues of multiple ways of seeing justice, power and community. For this reason, therefore, there is need to legitimate the ways of seeing that were forbidden in the curriculum, imported and fashioned after the outlook and model of Western educational systems. The quest of restoration of indigenous images and metaphors that were in the past suppressed in the curriculum finds new meaning in these arguments, which opens the way to look afresh at real curriculum reform.

In the present context of contemporary sub-Saharan Africa, language continues not only to provide a central identity variable but also to constitute a key means by which people can either gain access to power or, conversely, be excluded from the right to exercise control over their lives. This situation highlights the fact that local languages – such as Zulu, Setswana, Kiswahili, Khosa and so on – are constituted in multilevel power relations. Furthermore, contrary to the belief of some sceptics, students studying indigenous discourses of knowledge production would learn that the various categories of knowledge delineated by modernist science are not separated by indigenous ways of knowing. The two are perceived to be constantly informing and interacting with one another. By insisting that indigenous pedagogies become integrated in the school curriculum, for example, I envision a teacher education programme that advocates a new conversation between indigenous and Western peoples. Such a dialogue would serve numerous purposes, not the least of which would be to provide Westerners with a picture of how they appear to non-Westerners. The Western ignorance of indigenous knowledge holds profound consequences for everyone (Semali and Kincheloe, 1999). Therefore, it is only by integrating indigenous instructional methods in the social realism of learning that students can gain confidence to move from what they know to what they want to learn in maths and science. Students coming from indigenous communities and minority language backgrounds cannot achieve academically well in maths and science in mainstream schools unless schools stop ignoring the local reality of students and teachers.

As educators engage students in the historical development of ideas in any field of study, they can bring in indigenous perspectives to show students that ways of understanding particular phenomena can be different, that intellectual progress can take diverse directions and that different perspectives can create a critical consciousness that single perspectives cannot. Such a consciousness can change university, secondary and elementary curricula in unprecedented ways. Advocates of indigenous pedagogies contend that an indigenously informed curriculum not only can change education at the macro-level but holds profound implications at the micro-level as well. An awareness of these indigenous dynamics helps teachers adapt programmes to the special needs of local cultural settings or specific students. Teachers operating in this manner become far more aware of the relationship between the purposes of their curriculum and the interests, needs, problems and unique talents of their community. Such awareness allows for educational innovations unthought of by most schools and colleges.

References

American Association for the Advancement of Science (AAAS) (1989) *Science for all Americans*, Oxford University Press, New York

AAAS (1993) *Benchmarks for Science Literacy*, Oxford University Press, New York

Brokensha, D and Warren, O (eds) (1980) *Indigenous Knowledge Systems and Development*, University Press of America, Lanham, MD

Classen, C (1999) Other ways to wisdom: learning through the senses across cultures, *International Review of Education*, **45** (3/4), pp 269–80

Cross, M (1985) Open the parcels and check inside before you stick on the labels: a response to Penny Enslin, *Perspectives in Education*, **8** (3), pp 54–172

Cross, W E (1978) The Thomas and Cross models on psychological nigrescence: a literature review, *Journal of Black Psychology*, **4**, pp 13–31

Da Silva, A L (1999) Enfants autochtones et apprentissage: la corporalité comme langage en Amérique du Sud tropicale, *International Review of Education*, **45** (3/4), pp 251–68

De Anda, D (1984) Bicultural socialization: factors affecting minority experience, *Social Work*, **2**, pp 101–07

Dixon, V and Foster, B (1971) *Beyond Black or White*, Little Brown, Boston

Du Bois, W E B (1903) *Souls of Black Folk*, A C McClurg, Chicago

Eisenhart, M, Finkel, E and Marion, S F (1996) Creating the conditions for scientific literacy: a re-examination, *American Educational Research Journal*, **33**, pp 261–95

Fanon, F (1967) *Black Skins, White Masks*, Grove Press, New York

Hsu, F (1971) *The Challenge of the American Dream: The Chinese in the United States*, Wadsworth, Belmont, CA

Jegede, O (1999) Science education in non-Western cultures: towards a theory of collateral learning, in *What is Indigenous Knowledge? Voices from the academy*, ed L Semali and J Kincheloe, Garland, New York

Kitano, H (1969) *Japanese-Americans: The evolution of a subculture*, Prentice Hall, Englewood Cliffs, NJ

Knuth, R (1998) Building a literate environment: using oral-based reading materials to facilitate literacy, Paper presented at the 64th IFLA General Conference, 16–21 August

Lee, O and Fradd, S H (1998) Science for all, including students from non-English language backgrounds, *Educational Researcher*, **27** (4), pp 12–21

Memmi, A (1965) *The Colonizer and the Colonized*, Beacon Press, Boston

Mosha, R S (2000) *The Heartbeat of Indigenous Africa*, Falmer Press, New York

Nyerere, Julius (1968) Education for self-reliance, in *Freedom and Socialism/Uhuru na Ujamaa: Essays on socialism*, Oxford University Press, New York

Ramirez, M and Castaneda, A (1974) *Cultural Democracy: Bicognitive development and education*, Academic Press, New York

Rashid, H (1981) Early childhood education as a cultural transition for African-American children, *Educational Research Quarterly*, **6**, pp 55–63

Red Horse, J *et al* (1981) Family behavior of urban American Indians, in *Human Services for Cultural Minorities*, ed R Dana, University Park Press, New York, Baltimore

Semali, L (1999) Community as classroom: dilemmas of valuing African indigenous literacy in education, *International Review of Education*, **45** (3/4), pp 305–19

Semali, L and Kincheloe, J (1999) *What is Indigenous Knowledge? Voices from the academy*, Garland, New York

Semali, L and Stambach, A (1997) Cultural identity in an African context: indigenous education and curriculum in East Africa, *Folklore Forum*, **28** (1), pp 3–26

Shiva, V (1993) *Monocultures of the Mind: Perspectives in biodiversity and biotechnology*, Zed Books, London

Sue, S and Sue, D W (1978) Chinese-American personality and mental health, *Ameresia Journal*, pp 36–49

Valentine, C (1971) Deficit difference, and bicultural models of Afro-American behavior, *Harvard Educational Review*, **41**, pp 137–57

Warren, M and Rajasekaran, B (1993) Putting local knowledge to good use, *International Agricultural Development*, **13** (4), pp 8–10

Warren, M D, Slikkerveer, L and Brokensha, D (1995) *The Cultural Dimension of Development: Indigenous knowledge systems*, Intermediate Technology Publications, London

Wright, R N (1953) *The Outsider*, Harper & Row, New York

16. Toward a culture-sensitive teacher education: the role of pedagogical models

Elwyn Thomas

Introduction

The need to have an understanding of cultural contexts by teachers poses a key dilemma for their training and education, insomuch that their training should reflect sensitivities to cultural diversity in school and society, while also meeting challenging global changes that will affect future education practice. In this chapter we will examine three issues related to the prospects for a teacher education that attempts to resolve this dilemma. The first issue relates to the need to make educational provision flexible enough, to accommodate changes brought about by the cultural diversity within the school population. The second issue concerns the extent to which certain pedagogical models may enhance teacher education to be a more culture-sensitive process within culturally diverse systems, and the third issue deals with the prospects of using the pedagogical models in the furtherance of a culture-sensitive training and education for teachers.

The basic assumption that underlies this chapter is that culture is an ever-changing, reciprocal process involving transient and durable social encounters, which can be replicated, but which are also capable of being recreated, adopted and adapted in both time and space. In other words, culture is not a static, purist concept, but a dynamic one. The origins of this dynamism often come from sustained cultural contact between peoples of different ethnicity, religion, gender and traditions, and the day-to-day use of one or more languages within and across populations (Thomas, 2002).

The dilemma of cultural diversity and the diversification of education systems

Corson (1998) has argued that if differences that exist between a minority of educationally diverse students and the main body of students in a given population are educationally relevant, then some different type of educational provision is warranted. This line of argument is certainly becoming more common, when it comes to discussing the education and schooling of multi-ethnic populations and newly immigrant groups. Cultural diversity is no longer a marginal issue linked with a few immigrant groups and small numbers of ethnic minorities within a larger society. It has become an important issue in the provision of education, so much so that societies have had to face the fact that educational provision may itself have to be diversified, in order to meet the very real challenge of multicultural education that embodies much of cultural diversity. According to Corson (1998), post-modernity has two distinct but conflicting features, on the one hand a trend away from centralization, mass production and consumerism, which embrace national schools and state health services, and on the other hand a development of flexible technologies and an emphasis on accountability, diversity of educational provision and more school autonomy.

This means that, while cultural diversity has begun to be addressed as an issue in curriculum planning in several Western countries, the need to equip students to survive in the ever-competitive marketplace has understandably become the priority, and the special cultural needs of pupils are in danger of being ignored. Therefore, any society that recognizes the need to address the issue of cultural diversity as part of a policy of education for diversity must seek a consensus between the conflicting demands of postmodernism outlined above. Achieving this consensus means that education and schooling needs to be diversified, reflecting a cultural sensitivity for both teachers and learners, as well as preparing children for the 'Internet' world of the new millennium. A key determinant in attaining the success of any consensus depends on the way teachers will be trained and the extent to which teacher educators are sufficiently prepared for the task. This raises the need for a different form of teaching and teacher education reflecting cultural diversity and thence cultural sensitivity.

Teaching and teacher education as culture-sensitive processes

If teachers find difficulty in meeting the challenges of cultural diversity in school, this means that not only do these teachers need training, but the training should be part of a wider process of a more culture-sensitive education (CSE), in which stakeholders such as pupils, headteachers, teacher educators, parents and the community need to be involved. The underlying philosophy of such a culture-sensitive education needs to spell out at least three parameters before it can be viewed as a sound and effective component within formal schooling. The three parameters are:

- *Cultural inclusivity*. An educational process that purports to be sensitive to cultural influences raises the question, namely, should it include all cultural influences whether they be culture-specific or culturally universal? The answer probably would be both. For instance, it is clear that modern-day school curricula must take into consideration elements of the global culture as manifested in the instantaneous effects of the Internet and its impact on human information processing. In other words, schooling must be sensitive to the age of information technology (IT), and the new cultures that stem from it. These new cultures are not only enveloping industry and the world of commerce, but increasingly becoming part of schooling and home life as well. On the other hand, the new cultures should not be allowed to erode cultural traditions that provide security, continuity and richness to the life of a society (Thomas, 1994). This is particularly pertinent in an education system that aims to uphold cultural and moral values in a given society.

- *Cultural sensitivity*. Being sensitive to something means being aware of an object, or of someone's feelings, wishes and values. But sensitivity is more than this: it is also about actively engaging people and objects in the dynamics of education. Sensitivity also entails that cultural selectivity would be necessary, for it is not possible or even desirable to include all aspects of local culture in schooling.
- *The nature of the cultural dynamic*. The nature of cultural processes needs to be understood for any culture-sensitive process. It might be useful to think of culture as a set of encounters (Gearing, 1979; Thomas, 1992) that take place between people over time, some being short-lived (transient), others more enduring. Durable cultural encounters tend to be passed from generation to generation through modes of communication such as language, thinking, dance and drawing. These observations reinforce the view expressed at the beginning of this chapter that culture is certainly not a static concept but a dynamic process that results in a diverse mosaic of patterns and activities. The transnational nature of the school has meant that both schooling and the school are becoming increasingly universalistic in nature, reflecting similar outcomes throughout the world. Many of the cultural encounters that take place in school are formative and durable. The case, therefore, for a culture-sensitive education is a fairly strong one, especially if content and process are able to bridge the gaps between cultures new and old. The teacher's role would be pivotal here in cultural bridge building, and the place of pedagogy crucial.

The three parameters of a CSE in the context of teacher training

The three parameters discussed above are not only essential hallmarks of a culture-sensitive process of education, but they also relate closely to the development of a relevant culture-sensitive education and training for teachers (see Figure 16.1). The training curriculum will need to reflect quite closely the cultural inclusivity of the school curriculum. Not only will the teacher need to be trained as an effective agent in the art of cultural transmission, but he or she will also need to have an education and training in pertinent cultural knowledges and skills, which form a natural and necessary background to understanding the cultural diversity of the children who are being taught. The parameter of cultural sensitivity would occupy a salient place in the training of teachers, as it is part and parcel of the processes of teaching, learning and thinking that accompany the study of content and skills.

The highly socio-interactive nature of cultural sensitivity would also figure prominently during the practical training and in further practical training as part of in-service programmes. For this parameter to be successfully incorpo- rated into the development of a culture-sensitive teacher training, a knowledge about the values and beliefs of pupils, which are often intertwined within the cultural diversity of classrooms, would be desirable if not essential. A recog- nition of the third parameter, namely that of the cultural dynamic, which entails both transient and durable encounters, would assist teacher educators to make their training more pragmatic, meaningful, flexible and reflective, four features essential for an effective culture-sensitive training.

The role of pedagogy in establishing the presence of these three parameters in the educative process would clearly be very crucial. However, it needs to be emphasized that there is not just one pedagogical model that would realize this aim. The use of different pedagogies and their possible amalgamation would not only enrich the culture-sensitive nature of teacher training but also act as catalysts to initiate innovative teaching about cultural diversity, and stimulate interesting intercultural discourse during training as well as in classrooms. Therefore let us examine, in the next part of this chapter, some pedagogical models that could be used in a culture-sensitive training for teachers.

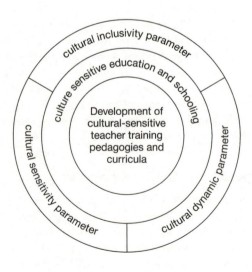

Figure 16.1 The relationship between culture parameters and a culture- sensitive education and training

Models of pedagogy as part of a culture-sensitive teacher education (CSTE)

The sheer complexity and cultural variety that we often find in multicultural classrooms provide a stiff challenge for any teacher. The multicultural classroom may consist of different ethnic groups, with their own languages, dialects, religious persuasions and cultural traditions. In order to help teachers meet this challenge, it may be necessary to identify models of pedagogy that are able, in the first place, to meet the basic requirements of formal education and, in the second place, to allow children the opportunities to maintain their socio-cultural identity, wherever and whenever possible, during their years of schooling. We will examine briefly five pedagogical models that would enhance the development of a culture-sensitive training for teachers.

Folk pedagogy model

The folk pedagogy model developed by Olson and Bruner (1996) puts the learner at the centre of teaching, following on from the child-centred approach in education pioneered over the years by Dewey, Piaget and the earlier work of Bruner in the 1960s. In collaboration with Olson, Bruner has more recently again provided educators with further challenges about making teaching and learning more relevant and effective, by exploring the relationship between children's minds and the instruction they receive from not only teachers but parents and significant others in the cultural world of the child. The kernel of Bruner and Olson's approach is based on shared experiences, beliefs, goals and intentions, which to these workers means that teaching and learning behaviour is a dynamic cultural process.

The first perspective emphasizes the way children may be perceived as doers, imitating the behaviour of adults and peers by being socialized into a cultural way of doing some activity. This imitation would include anything from learning how to utter sounds to speaking a language or performing a skill such as holding a pen or brush to paint with. It is a type of demonstrational apprenticeship that is common amongst young children before and after they enter school. The second perspective views the child as a knower, in which he or she acquires information either informally or formally (ie by being taught). The information is built up over time and acts as a basis from which new knowledge fits into the context of existing knowledge. A pedagogy that serves to recognize the fact that children know more than is credited to them is in contrast to the stance taken by most psychologists and many teachers, namely that the child's mind starts as a *tabula rasa*. In this perspective to pedagogy, the teacher not only recognizes how the child's knowledge capacity increases, but actively tries to match instruction to that capacity in order to enrich the child's cognition. A third perspective emphasizes children as thinkers, in which they not only develop theories about the world around them but have ideas about the mind and how it works. The pedagogy that accompanies this view would emphasize the importance of discussion, collaboration and argument between the teacher and the child, as well as amongst other children. A fourth perspective sees the child as an expert by virtue of the fact that he or she has acquired objective knowledge and expertise, and is able to contribute to the culture. The role of pedagogy in this situation is to act as a means of assisting the child to evaluate and construct his or her understanding of the world. This model of pedagogy is one that emphasizes facilitation and consultancy rather than didacticism.

Culture-sensitive pedagogy model

The culture-sensitive pedagogical model that the author has developed (Thomas, 1997, 2000) points to the fact that pedagogy can no longer be considered as just an instructional process, with broadly accepted methods of delivery and predictable learner–teacher interactions. Pedagogy is far more complex. This view of pedagogy identifies four main components, which interact with one another. The first component is the *epistemological* component and refers to the knowledge base that all teachers need; a second component is the *process* component, which includes activities such as planning, instruction, managing, evaluating and reflection. The third component is *contextual*, which includes language, religion and cultural traditions, while the fourth is a *personalistic* component and refers to the part played by a teacher's personal development. Six main factors may affect one or all of the four pedagogical components; these include political, economic, societal, research and innovation, teacher professionalism and, finally, cultural. Making teaching more sensitive to cultural contexts and the factors that determine these contexts is what the task of developing a culture-sensitive pedagogy is about. It must be emphasized, however, that a culture-sensitive pedagogy is one that should complement existing pedagogies. It is unlikely that it would replace other pedagogies. The essence of a culture-sensitive pedagogy would incorporate the best ideas and practices from all types of teaching, but at the same time it would ensure that the cultural context of teaching and learning would be pivotal.

A pedagogy that is culture-sensitive can be perceived as one in which the four pedagogical components discussed above are so integrated with one another that they actively reflect culture-specific knowledge, behaviours, attitudes and skills. These culture-specific attributes should complement the basic learning requirements common to all schooling. However, two prerequisites need to be considered before a culture-sensitive pedagogy can become a reality. The first prerequisite is an *analysis* of the cultural context of a particular situation, and involves the identification of needs and goals: this is termed *cultural analysis*. The second prerequisite involves the *selection* and processing of the information obtained from a cultural analysis, and is in reality a process of *cultural selectivity*.

A cultural analysis is an extensive examination of the cultural context of a community, small group or even an individual. A cultural analysis that involves schoolchildren would probe in depth what each pupil would bring in cultural terms to the classroom, eg language skills, type of dialect, making toys and other skills learnt at home. The outcome of a well-conducted cultural analysis should ultimately enrich curriculum planning, through the adoption and adaptation of ideas and practices specific to a particular cultural group. Cultural selectivity, the next stage after a cultural analysis has taken place, should provide appropriate knowledge and experience for making the pedagogical components, discussed above, more sensitive to the cultural needs of learners and teachers. For instance, let us examine the case for developing a school curriculum for the early primary school years. The rationale for including numeracy, literacy and writing is relatively easy to establish. However, the way children engage in different learning styles and strategies to achieve success in the 3Rs as their preferred culture-specific route to this achievement is more complex and time-consuming. The work of Carraher, Carraher and Schliemann (1987), and Nunes (1994) with Brazilian street children, concerning the learning of mathematical operations, gives testimony to the arduous task of combining careful analysis and selection from a particular cultural context.

Integrated pedagogy model

A third model, namely an integrated pedagogy, is strongly associated with bilingual teaching. However, teachers who practise an integrated pedagogy, especially in a multicultural society, are not only involved in teaching two languages but are actively engaging pupils and themselves in acquiring two cultures. Integrative pedagogy can also embrace different pedagogical traditions. For instance, the recent academic successes of secondary school pupils in Singapore, Taiwan and Japan reflected their top positions in the international league tables in subjects like mathematics and science. This prompted educationalists to examine the reasons for this success. Factors such as close interest and supervision by parents of their children's homework, and the fact that high school achievement is prized above all else may be responsible. Another observation has been the emphasis in the classrooms of these countries on full-frontal or whole-class teaching, featuring a strongly didactic pedagogical approach to classroom learning. These may also be reasons for this success story. This pattern of pedagogy is the result of a historical development that accompanied the growth of Western educational traditions, in which the didactic process was formalized, and instruction gradually became a large-group affair, with the attendant matching of instruction to the age of the learners. Features such as moral perfectibility, emulation (imitation of role models), diligence and effort typical of Confucianist cultures have been integrated into the former didactic European model of pedagogy, so giving the teacher more control over the learning process.

Intercultural pedagogy model

An intercultural pedagogy is the fourth model in our discussion about the role of different pedagogies in the development of a culture-sensitive teacher education. Few societies nowadays can be insulated from the influences of foreign cultures. Schoolchildren, especially in many developing countries, experience very marked cultural changes, even on a daily basis. For instance, a child leaves his or her 'home culture' at one part of the day and enters the very different culture of the school sometime later. The child is confronted with different value systems, organizational procedures and styles of learning, and is often taught in a different language.

An intercultural model of pedagogy aims to assist the teacher to understand the cross-cultural interface of how pupils experience the complex cultural dynamic of the school. Intercultural pedagogy, unlike the other models we have discussed, is mainly socio-cultural in nature. The model attempts to develop a better understanding amongst different cultural groups, hopefully engendering positive attitudes and resulting in a more effective and meaningful multicultural education. The teacher has a salient role in fostering cross-cultural interaction through the medium of an intercultural pedagogy in multicultural classrooms.

There are many forms of, and approaches to, multicultural education. Eldering and Rothenburg (1997) distinguish between four perspectives, disadvantage, enrichment, bicultural competence and collective equality groups. The disadvantage perspective has a built-in assumption that different cultural groups are in educational arrears, and there is a need for catching up with the dominant culture. Multicultural education for enrichment relates cultural diversity with enrichment, and so enrichment could be aimed at either a particular ethnic group or all the school population. Multicultural education that emphasizes bicultural competence refers to situations in which pupils coming from two different cultures have the strong likelihood of being doubly acculturated. Where multicultural education emphasizes the equality of groups, the aim is to develop a collective equality between cultures, ironing out the cultural gap between school and society. As an example, let us examine the use of an intercultural pedagogy in the case of biculturalism.

Teaching foreign languages is a common feature of most secondary school curricula and, in many countries, foreign languages are also taught at the primary school level. However, in countries like the United States and Britain, being bilingual or multilingual is often seen as overburdening the rest of the curriculum and unnecessary. However, in many countries children are often taught in a language that is culturally and linguistically different from the one they experience at home. This imposes many disadvantages on children, one of which would be that it is a barrier to better academic achievement. Another negative outcome would be that the indigenous language is perceived to be second-best, and would not figure very much in teaching. However, there is also growing evidence that being bilingual confers considerable advantages on pupils, not least providing a greater degree of authority and empowerment (Serpell and Hatano, 1997; Mohanty and Perregaux, 1997). Learning even one's own language is a significant cultural event for a child; learning two or more languages provides an even greater cultural enrichment, as well as a challenge for both learner and teacher. Bilingual teachers are able to act as a bridge between two cultural systems. The analogy of the bridge allows for an intercultural flow to take place between children who come from different cultural traditions, enabling them to experience both their own culture and that of others. This opportunity for bicultural exposure, through bilingualism, is a key element in an intercultural pedagogy, which could result in a well-balanced bicultural integration within the school.

The work of Gumperz (1982) has shown that language used by multilingual individuals in multilingual societies often results in different forms of psychological integration. Such integration entails different types of socio-linguistic interaction between persons coming from a different cultural background. These interactions often result in the adoption and adaptation of language use and cultural traditions across communities. Such studies and more of their kind will be able to promote the development of an effective intercultural pedagogy, and hopefully a better understanding amongst different cultural groups in the future. There is a discernible overlap between an intercultural pedagogy and that of the integrated model. However, a key difference lies in the fact that the former goes beyond the linguistic, emphasizing psycho-cultural as well as the socio-cultural dimensions to pupil learning, thinking and, of course, teaching as well.

Instructional objectives pedagogy model

An instructional objectives pedagogy is the fifth type of pedagogy in our discussion about the role of pedagogical models in developing a more culture-sensitive teacher education. Pupil learning is concerned with the mastery of concepts and principles that form the building blocks within each subject discipline. When Benjamin Bloom wrote his now famous *Taxonomy of Behavioural Objectives* in the mid-1950s, its impact on teaching and learning in the classrooms of the United States was immense. The effect was also felt in many countries throughout the world as a blueprint for curriculum design. Behavioural objectives were set out in pupil learning guides and became translated into instructional objectives, which appeared in teacher guides.

However, there are many instances where children from different cultures have been able to bypass the formal teaching of rules and principles of curriculum subjects altogether. This is because pupils did not attend school or had dropped out. The research of Nunes (1994) and Schliemann, Carraher and Ceci (1997) is well known in this area, where they studied child vendors making a living on the streets of Brazilian cities. The children used everyday mathematics to sell their wares. It seems from this research in Brazil and other countries that street children can perform quite complex calculations without having to be taught the appropriate mathematical rules. These observations are explained in terms of the importance of the 'immediacy' of situation in which these children operate. Some educators have advocated that classroom activities should be redefined and reflect what goes on 'out of school'.

Schliemann (1995) has warned, however, that mathematics (and other school subjects) should not be over-supplemented with imitations of 'out of school' situations, as they focus too narrowly on an immediate application to a particular problem. The challenge for teachers who may adopt this pedagogical model will involve making decisions about where and when children's everyday activities can be usefully included or omitted in the instructional process, so that they will enrich rather than hamper the learning and development of higher-order concepts and principles.

Model melding as part of a culture-sensitive teacher education

The five pedagogical models discussed in this chapter provide sufficient choice for teachers, whether they are teaching in a monocultural or multicultural classroom. There are cases where the application of one model may be sufficient to meet the needs of the school curriculum, eg the instructional objectives model. However, some of the other pedagogical models discussed earlier have become more high-profile in recent years, because schooling is increasingly seen as a social preparation for adulthood as well as a process of skill and knowledge acquisition for the workplace. The folk, culture-sensitive, intercultural and integrated models would provide teachers with the possibilities of developing teaching strategies that emphasize the socio-cultural development of pupils during their years of schooling.

It is unlikely in meeting the challenge of cultural diversity in schools that any one of the five models used alone would meet the demands of cultural diversity, so teachers will need to be able to make choices about which specific teaching model(s) might be melded, and under what circumstances. Figure 16.2 shows that culture-specific teaching strategies may be developed if such choices need to be made.

For instance, it might be necessary to harness parts of the epistemological or process components of a culture-sensitive pedagogy with the intercultural model, in order to realize intercultural enrichment with reference to visual learning cues or developing partnerships for class practical work. Melding is not an easy task as it requires considerable teacher knowledge, experience and

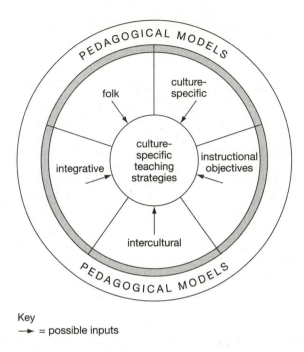

Figure 16.2 Pedagogical models and the development of culture-specific teaching strategies

sensitivity towards the cultural contexts in question. It also requires teachers to be good at selecting which pedagogical model would be the most appropriate to meld with another, and how that meld could be delivered in the classroom. This would indeed be a real challenge for a culture-sensitive teacher education curriculum.

The prospects for a successful melding of different pedagogies could be achieved by developing modular training strategies, which would include identifying and applying prognostic and diagnostic competencies, so that the teacher could find out as much as possible about the background of the cultural contexts that make up the pupil classroom profile. The use of self-assessment and case study critical incidence would also help in the training of prognostic and diagnostic skills (Brislin *et al*, 1986; Cushner, 1994). Having a component for field exercises would further develop observational diagnosis and the opportunities to apply culture-sensitive instruction, including the use of indigenous languages and the development of teaching materials that reflect traditional customs and traditions. These and other training strategies would strengthen the prospects for developing a relevant culture-sensitive curriculum, which would be a significant step on the road towards developing the notion of a culture-sensitive education and training for teachers.

References

Brislin, R W *et al* (eds) (1986) *Intercultural Interactions: A practical guide*, Sage, Newbury Park

Carraher, D W, Carraher, T N and Schliemann, A D (1987) Written and oral mathematics, *Journal for Research in Mathematics Education*, **18**, pp 83–97

Corson, D (1998) *Changing Education for Diversity*, Open University Press, Buckingham

Cushner, K (1994) Preparing teachers for an intercultural context, in *Improving Intercultural Interaction: Modules for cross cultural training programs*, ed R W Brislin and T Yoshida, pp 109–28, Sage, Thousand Oaks, CA

Eldering, L and Rothenburg J J (1997) Multicultural education: approaches and practice, in *Educational Dilemmas: Debate and diversity*, vol 1, *Teachers, Teacher Education and Training*, ed K Watson *et al*, pp 306–16, Cassell, London

Gearing, F (1979) A reference model for a cultural theory of education and schooling, in *Toward a Cultural Theory of Education and Schooling*, ed F Gearing and L Sangree, Mouton Press, The Hague

Gumperz, J J (1982) *Discourse Strategies*, Cambridge University Press, Cambridge

Mohanty, A K and Perregaux, C (1997) Language acquisition and bilingualism, in *Handbook of Cross Cultural Psychology*, vol 2, *Basic Processes and Human Development*, ed J W Berry *et al*, pp 217–54, Allyn & Bacon, Boston

Nunes, T (1994) Cultural diversity in learning mathematics: a perspective from Brazil, in *International Perspectives on Culture and Schooling: A symposium proceedings*, ed E Thomas, pp 357–70, University of London, Institute of Education, London

Olson, D R and Bruner, J S (1996) Folk psychology and folk pedagogy, in *Handbook of Education and Human Development: New models of learning, teaching and schooling*, ed D R Olson and N Torrance, pp 9–27, Blackwell, Oxford

Schliemann, A D (1995) Some concerns about bringing everyday mathematics to mathematics education, in *Proceedings of the XIX International Conference for Psychology of Mathematics Education*, ed L Meira and D Carraher, vol 1, pp 45–60, Recife, Brazil

Schliemann, A D, Carraher, D W and Ceci, S J (1997) Everyday cognition, in *Handbook of Cross Cultural Psychology*, vol 2, *Basic Processes and Human Development*, ed J W Berry *et al*, pp 177–216, Allyn & Bacon, Boston

Serpell, R and Hatano, G (1997) Education, schooling and literacy, in *Handbook of Cross Cultural Psychology*, vol 2, *Basic Processes and Human Development*, ed J W Berry *et al*, pp 340–76, Allyn & Bacon, Boston

Thomas, E (1992) Schooling and the school as a cross cultural context for study, in *Innovations in Cross Cultural Psychology*, ed S Iwawaki *et al*, pp 425–41, Swets & Zeitlinger, Amsterdam

Thomas, E (1994) Overview, in *International Perspectives on Schooling and Culture: A symposium proceedings*, ed E Thomas, pp 4–30, University of London, Institute of Education, London

Thomas, E (1997) Developing a culture sensitive pedagogy: tackling a problem of melding 'global culture' within existing cultural contexts, *International Journal of Educational Development*, **17**, pp 13–26

Thomas, E (2000) *Culture and Schooling: Building bridges between research, praxis and professionalism*, Wiley, Chichester

Thomas, E (2002) The case for a culture sensitive education: Building bridges between traditional and global perspectives, in *Asian Migrants and Education*, eds Michael C Charney *et al*, Kluwer Academic Publications, Dordrecht, the Netherlands (forthcoming)

Section IV
Training challenges for teachers and teacher educators: ongoing projects

17. Multigrade teaching: implications for the continuing professional development of teachers in the Caribbean

Chris Berry

Introduction

The aim of this chapter is to assess the extent to which multigrade teaching is supported in selected states of the Caribbean. The underlying thesis is that, in order to improve the quality of teaching and learning in primary schools, policy makers need to acknowledge the important place that multigrade teaching has in many Caribbean education systems. It is argued that this will assist not only teachers who are working in multigrade settings, but also those who deal with monograde classrooms consisting of students with diverse attainment. 'Multigrade' is defined as the situation where more than one grade level of pupils is of necessity placed in the same classroom with one teacher. This situation most frequently arises in small primary schools where there are fewer teachers than grade levels. In such schools, a single teacher may have to deal with three or more grade levels at the same time.

In line with Thomas (1996: 15), teacher education will be defined as 'a process of life-long training and personal development, during which teachers and teacher educators are exposed to new ideas and practices with the ultimate aim of improving their self-esteem and professionalism'.

The emphasis in this chapter is therefore on the continuing professional development of teachers. This chapter includes reference to the following Caribbean states: the Turks and Caicos Islands, Belize, Dominica, Guyana, Trinidad and Tobago, and Jamaica, mainly drawing on the author's own experiences of working in these countries. The chapter will address three questions:

- Why should multigrade teaching be an important issue for teacher educators in the Caribbean?
- What are some of the dilemmas in, and prospects for, the provision of multigrade teacher education in the region?
- What conclusions can be drawn for the continuing professional development of multigrade teachers?

One reason why multigrade teaching is an important issue is its extent. Figures quoted by the Commonwealth Secretariat (1997) indicate that in several Caribbean states multigrade schooling is almost as common as monograde schooling. A second reason why multigrade organized classes are important is because of what they might be able to tell us about how to manage and teach monograde classes. Teaching in monograde classes in the Caribbean generally appears to be characterized by didactic and teacher-directed approaches (CARICOM, 1993). Recent research conducted in the Caribbean by Kutnick, Jules and Layne (1997) and Berry (2001) tends to support this view.

Dilemmas in the training and ongoing support of multigrade teachers

Caribbean teacher educators who wish to support multigrade teachers face two major dilemmas, namely 1) availability of training materials and expertise and 2) the primary school curriculum does not support multigrade teaching. Let us first examine the former dilemma.

The first dilemma is that multigrade teaching is usually peripheral to the education process. It is mostly carried out in small isolated schools, and policy makers may view it as an anomaly within a predominantly graded education structure. This leads to its marginalization in education systems, and may make it difficult to design and implement teacher education programmes that are more sensitive to multigrade settings. In relation to the design of courses, educators in the Caribbean generally know little about how multigrade teachers manage their classes, and even less about how they could be better supported to do this. Although this situation is slowly beginning to change, it remains an obstacle to the development of initiatives in this area. In the absence of a knowledge base with which to work, it is difficult to see how appropriate and high-quality training materials can be produced to support multigrade teaching. Educators need both to look at international research and to develop their own research agendas in this regard. Studies by Nielsen, Gillett and Thompson (1993) in Belize, and Berry (2001) in the Turks and Caicos Islands give some possible future directions.

Where appropriate training materials can be developed, their implementation may be affected by the physical location of multigrade teachers. As already mentioned, they are frequently working in the most isolated and remote areas of the country. It may, therefore, be difficult to reach them with traditional modes of training. Innovative strategies may need to be developed that involve taking the training to teachers and making it as relevant as possible to their setting.

The low status afforded to multigrade teachers indicates that attention should be paid to promoting more positive attitudes. One way to do this is by improving the general policy environment for multigrade teachers and ensuring that teachers are supported in their efforts to differentiate instruction. In many Caribbean states this will require a shift in thinking as regards the structure and content of the primary school curriculum. This brings us to the second dilemma, namely that the curriculum used in many Caribbean states is graded and does not lend itself to the introduction of multigrade teaching techniques.

Such graded curricula tend to assume that pupils of any particular grade level will be at a similar level of attainment at any one time. They therefore contain material considered appropriate to that level. The structure of the primary school curriculum has three potentially negative consequences for the multigrade teacher.

Firstly, graded curricula are likely to be assessed in a summative way. At the end of the term or year, students are given an examination on curriculum content on the basis of which the teacher makes a judgement of whether the pupil has achieved the curriculum objectives and covered the curriculum content. Pupils will probably be given a percentage mark that allows their progress to be compared with that of their peers. Tests focusing on grade level coverage are problematic for the multigrade teacher because they mean that he or she has to set multiple tests for each grade level in the class, regardless of whether the test is pitched at the attainment level of the pupils. They give the teacher little information on individual children's learning needs. More useful are formative approaches to assessment that are tied to the pupils' current level of attainment and can be used to give feedback to guide future learning. Unfortunately, there is not a strong tradition in formative assessment in the Caribbean. This is partly because the focus on the common entrance examination (CEE) as the means of selecting pupils for secondary school entrance has caused the system to lose sight of other forms of assessment used for determining levels of achievement appropriate for different grade levels (CARICOM, 1993).

Secondly, graded curricula are often 'content heavy', as they include a body of skills and knowledge that is considered appropriate for delivery at any one grade level. The most efficient way to deliver such content is through a didactic approach. As previously mentioned, one consequence of this is that much of teaching and learning in Caribbean monograde primary classrooms is teacher-directed (CARICOM, 1993; Kutnick, Jules and Layne, 1997; Berry, 2001). It is difficult for multigrade teachers to be effective if they attempt to use didactic teaching methods. With two or more grades in the class, direct instruction aimed at one grade level means that the other grade levels are not receiving instruction at all. More appropriate teaching methods for multigrade teachers include cooperative group work, peer tutoring and self-directed learning (Collingwood, 1991; Miller, 1991; Rowley and Nielsen, 1997).

Thirdly, the main teaching tool tends to be the textbook. These are usually produced for a graded school environment and are designed for delivery and explanation by the teacher. Activities in the textbooks are rarely self-correcting, nor are they suitable for self-study. They are also not written at an appropriate level of difficulty for the range of attainment in any one grade level group. The reliance on graded textbooks as an instructional tool is problematic for the multigrade teacher, who needs additional resources that pupils can use independently.

Prospects for resolving these dilemmas

The dilemmas outlined in the previous section indicate a range of obstacles to promoting conditions that are more conducive to multigrade teaching and learning in Caribbean primary schools. However, there are examples of initiatives from the region that may help to resolve, or at least reduce, the effect of these dilemmas. The dilemmas can be grouped broadly into four areas, namely 1) development of teacher training materials, 2) curriculum reform, 3) innovations in national assessment and 4) teaching materials development. Each of these is now considered in turn.

Development of teacher training materials

One response to the needs of multigrade teachers comes in the form of training materials that have been produced under the aegis of the Commonwealth Secretariat (1997). These materials were developed collaboratively by teacher educators from Trinidad, Guyana, Belize, Dominica, Barbados, and the Turks and Caicos Islands. They indicate four areas in which multigrade teachers may need support: planning from the curriculum, approaches to instruction, assessing students and managing resources.

The materials have been produced in a modular format, and this enables them to be delivered through a distance education mode. Consequently, they are potentially a very useful resource for multigrade teachers who are posted in difficult-to-reach areas. A teacher educator from Belize gave her country's experience in implementing these modules during a recent conference (Wright, 2000). She described how the teacher training college incorporated the modules into the classroom organization and management course. Only modules focusing on timetabling and scheduling, managing resources, and teaching strategies were used. The modules were found to be useful because they expose teachers to factors that must be considered in both multigrade and monograde teaching. Wright stressed the importance of introducing in-service training to support teachers operating in multigrade contexts, and to engage in further research to find out the kinds of teaching strategies that are actually used in multigrade classrooms. Beyond the Belize experience, the Commonwealth Secretariat materials do not appear to have been extensively trialled.

Curriculum reform

As we have seen, reform of the national curriculum is a priority area for Caribbean states wishing to support multigrade teaching. More appropriate curriculum designs for multigrade classrooms should have the following two key characteristics: flexibility and integration (Birch and Lally, 1995). Flexibility means that the curriculum gives teachers more scope for developing content and materials that are relevant to their particular school and classroom. Integration means that the relationship between different subjects and grade levels is more clearly articulated than it is in many curriculum documents currently in use. Two examples of curriculum reform efforts that fulfil these criteria are outlined below. One comes from Jamaica and the other from Belize. Neither was developed with the needs of multigrade teachers specifically in mind, but both show how curricula might help to support teaching and learning in multigrade classrooms.

The Jamaican experience is described by Bailey and Brown (1997). This curriculum reform was a response to a perception that there was a need for a more 'integrated' approach to curriculum design and delivery in Jamaica. A sample of themes and sub-themes from the new curriculum for grades 1 to 3 shows how it might be more sensitive to the needs of multigrade teachers. The same theme is spiralled across three grade levels, and there are clear linkages between the sub-themes for the different grades. This would make it much easier to plan from the curriculum for a multigrade class. One difficulty might arise if the multigrade class was split across grades 3 and 4, but this is an organizational issue that can be avoided unless the school is extremely small.

The Belize curriculum reform was a response to a mid-project review, which indicated that the previous primary curriculum documents were fragmented and lacked integration (DFID and World Bank, 1995). Using as a curriculum platform UNESCO's four pillars of education (learning to be, learning to do, learning to know and learning to live together), educational goals were developed for the whole of primary education. These were then further broken down into a set of 'specifications' for primary education. On the basis of these, learning outcomes were specified for three levels of primary education. A sample of outcomes taken from the revised mathematics curriculum is shown in Table 17.1 (derived from Berry, 1998).

The Belize curriculum is helpful to multigrade teachers in at least three ways. First, the outcomes for each level span more than one grade level of schooling. Second, the outcomes for each of the levels are related to one another. Third, the curriculum framework is flexible enough to generate different schemes of work depending on the school context.

Innovations in national assessment

As mentioned previously, the approach to the assessment of pupils is another key area in which primary school teachers need support. The priority given to

Table 17.1   Sample of Belize curriculum document

| Specification: Know the number system | | |
Lower (end of grade 1)	Middle (end of grade 3)	Upper (end of grade 6)
Understand place value in one-, two- and three-digit numbers.	Understand place value in numbers up to five digits.	Understand place value in numbers up to ten digits.
Understand the consecutive sequence and position of numbers 1–999.	Understand the consecutive sequence and position of numbers 1–99,999.	Understand the consecutive sequence and position of numbers 1–999,999,999.

summative forms of assessment in Caribbean education systems leads to a situation in which students are viewed as being in competition with one another rather than as having individual learning needs. This is especially problematic for low attainers because they will frequently be confronted by tests that are too difficult for them and then be given no information on how they might go about improving their performance in future. As a result, they can become demotivated and lose their capacity to learn.

This situation is exacerbated by the emphasis traditionally placed on the common entrance examination (CEE) as a means of selecting primary school students for entry to secondary school. There are encouraging signs from a number of Caribbean states that the CEE is gradually being replaced by some kind of test of primary school achievement. This means that national assessment can potentially focus on measuring what has actually been learnt rather than on what should have been learnt. This is a key feature of formative assessment approaches that encompass 'all those activities undertaken by teachers, and/or their students, which provide information to be used as feedback to modify teaching and learning activities in which they are engaged' (Black and Wiliam, 1998: 6).

Teaching materials development

In the majority of Caribbean states, the main teaching aid is the textbook. However, because this is designed for use in a graded classroom, it tends to be inappropriate for use by the multigrade classroom teacher. In addition, it encourages the monograde teacher to deliver the same instruction to the whole class. Regionally produced books also tend to be written with the needs of teachers who work on the larger islands, and are usually more suitable for use with students living in urban areas. Two examples of efforts to widen the resource base for primary school teachers may give an idea of what is possible in other Caribbean states.

The first example comes from the Turks and Caicos Islands. It shows how self-instructional materials can be cheaply produced for use in classrooms.

The Peripatetic In-service Teacher Education Project (PINSTEP) included a focus on developing additional self-study materials for use by students. The materials were produced so that they were tied more closely to the local context (Berry, 1997). They consisted of workbooks to support the graded reader, giving additional comprehension exercises at a range of different levels. They were produced at very low cost using desktop publishing facilities in the Department of Education. It was possible to distribute these workbooks free of charge to all students.

The second example relates to the development of classroom libraries. These are a crucial resource in the multigrade classroom (Thomas and Shaw, 1992), and also in the monograde classroom where classroom libraries have been linked to higher reading achievement amongst students (Elley, 1994; READ, 1999). They can be used to support individualized or group reading programmes and to provide additional learning opportunities for advanced or motivated students. Developing classroom libraries is, however, expensive since books usually have to be imported.

These examples of materials development share three important characteristics. They involve teachers in the development process, thereby increasing the chances that the materials meet the needs of students in the classroom. They focus on being relevant to the locality. They try to ensure that the process is sustainable so more materials can be produced in the future.

Conclusions

What conclusions, if any, can be drawn from the foregoing discussion regarding the continuing professional education needs of multigrade teachers in the Caribbean? Examples have been included from only a limited number of Caribbean states, so the extent to which these experiences can be applied more generally is open to question. However, the author believes that there are enough points of commonality to make generalizations worth while. These are outlined below.

Firstly, the reform of graded curricula has been presented as a key area in which Caribbean states can assist their multigrade teachers, and examples of curriculum renewal have been provided from Jamaica and Belize. Curriculum reform efforts have several implications for the continuing professional development of the teaching force. Teachers need to be exposed to a variety of different possible curriculum structures in order for them to input into the curriculum development process. In this respect, a modular curriculum would be worth considering. Teachers also need help in planning from whatever type of curriculum structure is adopted. Finally, if curriculum designs are more integrated, then multigrade teachers need to be trained to plan lessons that are relevant to several grade level groups simultaneously.

Secondly, in order to support student learning, the purpose of school-based assessment has to change so that the summative function becomes less important and the formative function more so. To achieve this, teachers will need extensive training in the use of formative assessment strategies, as they have generally had little exposure to them. Miller (1989) suggests developing checklists and self-assessment strategies for students, using peer assessment, observation and anecdotal notes. These ideas need to be treated cautiously as they may be time-consuming and difficult to implement across several different grade or achievement levels. Decisions on appropriate assessment strategies would need to be made in conjunction with any curriculum reform and in collaboration with practising teachers.

Thirdly, if the teacher is effectively to instruct more than one grade level group at the same time, then he or she needs training to help to reduce the amount of 'dead time' in the classroom. This is time when one or more grade level groups are not engaged in doing any work. Given that one of the 'prospects' for the support of multigrade teachers is low-cost materials development, it is necessary to consider how these resources can be managed in the classroom. One way to manage the multigrade classroom is to develop learning areas that the students have independent access to. Teachers should be aware that students need to be taught to use the materials independently, and that some record should be kept of the work that they do.

Finally, more effective multigrade instruction rests crucially on the teacher being able to reduce the amount of time that he or she engages in directly instructing students. This is because it is difficult for direct instruction to reach the range of grade levels in the class. Two strategies that are frequently promoted for use in the multigrade classroom are cooperative group work (Cohen, 1994) and peer teaching (Topping, 1988, 1998; Nielsen, Gillett and Thompson, 1993). The promotion of either of these would require some commitment to the in-service training and development of teachers. These teaching strategies are equally relevant to both the multigrade and the mono-grade teacher. If teachers can begin to move away from teacher-directed strategies, then this will help to promote the academic and social progress of all students. A three-pronged approach, involving curriculum reform, materials development and targeted in-service teacher training may be the most effective way to achieve this.

References

Bailey, B and Brown, M (1997) Reengineering the primary curriculum: improving effectiveness, *Caribbean Journal of Education*, **19** (2), pp 147–61

Berry, C (1997) Improving reading attainment in a small island state, *Reading*, **31**, pp 25–28

Berry, C (1998) *Report on the Curriculum Development Process*, Government of Belize/Department for International Development, Belize

Berry, C (2001) Achievement effects of multigrade and monograde schools in the Turks and Caicos Islands, Unpublished PhD thesis, University of London, Institute of Education, London

Birch, I and Lally, M (1995) *Multigrade Teaching in Primary Schools*, Asia Pacific Centre of Educational Innovation for Development, Bangkok

Black, P and Wiliam, D (1998) Assessment and classroom learning, *Assessment in Education*, 5 (1), pp 7–71

CARICOM Advisory Task Force (1993) *The Future of Education in the Caribbean*, Caribbean Community Secretariat, Trinidad

Cohen, E G (1994) Restructuring the classroom: conditions for productive small groups, *Review of Educational Research*, 64, pp 209–13

Collingwood, I (1991) *Multiclass Teaching in Primary Schools: A handbook for Vanuatu*, UNESCO Publication, Apia, Western Samoa

Commonwealth Secretariat (1997) *Teacher Education Modules for Multi-grade Teaching*, Commonwealth Secretariat, London

Department for International Development (DFID) and World Bank (1995) *Belize Primary Education Development Project Mid-Term Review*, Department for International Development, London

Elley, W B (ed) (1994) *The IEA Study of Reading Literacy: Achievement and instruction in thirty-two school systems*, vol 11, Pergamon, London

Kutnick, P, Jules, V and Layne, A (1997) *Gender and School Achievement in the Caribbean*, Serial No. 21, Department for International Development, London

Miller, B A (1989) *The Multi-grade Classroom: A handbook for small rural schools*, North West Regional Educational Laboratory, Oregon

Miller, B A (1991) A review of the qualitative research on multi-grade instruction, *Journal of Education in Rural Education*, 7, pp 3–12

Nielsen, D H, Gillett, E and Thompson, E (1993) *Multigrade Teaching in Belize: Current practice and its relation to student achievement*, Ministry of Education, Belize

READ (1999) *Annual Report 1999*, Read Educational Trust, Braamfontein, South Africa

Rowley, S D and Nielsen, H D (1997) School and classroom organisation in the periphery: the assets of multigrade teaching, in *Quality Education for All: Community based approaches*, ed D H Nielsen and W K Cummings, Garland Publishing Inc, New York

Thomas, C and Shaw, C (1992) *Issues in the Development of Multigrade Schools*, World Bank, Washington, DC

Thomas, E (1996) Issues and developments in teacher education in Commonwealth and other countries, in *Caribbean Issues and Developments*, eds L Steward and E Thomas, p 7, Commonwealth Secretariat, London

Topping, K (1988) *The Peer Tutoring Handbook*, Croom Helm, Beckenham, Kent

Topping, K (1998) *Paired Reading, Spelling and Writing: The handbook for teachers and parents*, Cassell, London

Wright, W (2000) The Belize experience with multigrade teaching, Paper presented at the Commonwealth Secretariat regional workshop on multi-grade teaching, 17–21 July, Gaborone, Botswana

18. Practical and theoretical problems in training teachers to confront HIV/AIDS

Roy Carr-Hill

Introduction

The HIV/AIDS pandemic continues to ravage sub-Saharan Africa (SSA): at least 40 million people are infected. Children will be the most affected as a result of HIV/AIDS as they live with sick relatives in households stressed by the drain on their resources. They will be left emotionally and physically vulnerable by the illness or death of one or both parents. Children, and especially girls, who have lost one or both parents are more likely to be removed from school, to stay home to care for the sick and to be pulled into the informal economy to supplement lost income.

In the first part of this chapter we show how the AIDS epidemic is likely to have a serious impact on the demand for, the supply of, and the management and quality of education provided at all levels. The pandemic impacts not only on the numbers and availability of teachers, and thence on the quantitative need for teacher training but also on the quality of education that teachers can provide in the schools. The second part of the chapter first describes the optimistic approach that involves using teachers to inform and counsel pupils and students using participatory methods about HIV/AIDS. We argue that there are several practical and theoretical problems with this view, and suggest a more realistic approach. Finally, we discuss what would be involved in institutionalizing a response to HIV/AIDS and how to implement such a programme.

The impact of HIV/AIDS on education systems

The HIV/AIDS epidemic has a multiple impact on education and not only on national and regional or local levels – but also down to each single family and child (see Figure 18.1). On the demand side, decreased fertility (estimated at around 30 per cent of HIV-infected women) and increased infant and child mortality through vertical transmission of the virus mean that projected numbers of children fall.

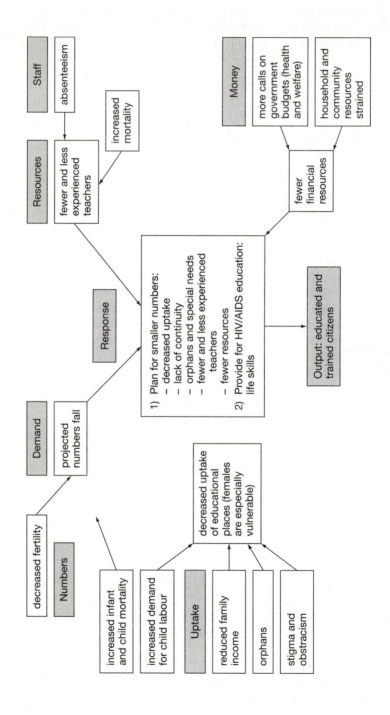

Figure 18.1 The impact of HIV / AIDS on education

At the same time, orphans and those from families where one of the parents is suffering from AIDS are less likely to go to school because of both stigmatization and the increased demand for child labour as a result of reduced family incomes. On the supply side, there will be increased mortality among teachers, and absences due to illness; and because there are more calls on government budgets (for health and welfare provision), and household and community resources are strained because of medical expenses, there are fewer financial resources for education. In the remainder of this section, we examine the impact on teachers and on the quality of education that they can deliver, in more detail.

Obviously, the most important impact is illness and then death. There have been suggestions that, whilst teachers are more highly educated and therefore more aware of the risks of unprotected sex, they may, at the same time, be at higher risk from HIV than other groups. This is both because they are often posted away from their own families and also because they have higher incomes than other people in rural areas and therefore have greater possibilities of visiting urban centres, which is a known HIV risk factor. Sichone and Haworth (1996) report that in Zambia HIV infection levels in those who have received higher education are in the region of 40 per cent or more (as compared with general population levels of 25 per cent for urban dwellers and 13 per cent for rural dwellers).

Indeed, the number of teachers dying from AIDS is greater than the output from all teacher training colleges (Kelly, 2000). In Namibia, the incidence of HIV infection among teachers is assumed to be well above that for the population as a whole, which is currently between 20 and 25 per cent. By 2010, therefore, at least 3,500 serving teachers may have died in Namibia, but the figure could be as high as 6,500 (Coombe, 2000). In Tanzania, it is estimated that 27,000 teachers will have died from AIDS by 2020. Data from Mozambique show a very rapid acceleration in deaths amongst working teachers.

Even where teachers are healthy and fully functioning, their performance may also be affected in communities where an extended family system is still practised, because of their commitment to the extended family members. Teachers are faced with a dilemma: do the job for which they are paid or fulfil their family responsibilities. For example, attending relatives in a critical condition will take away time from school activities. Inevitably, the school curriculum suffers.

Clearly, whether or not teachers have higher rates of infection, these perceptions are important issues for those educating teachers, and important workplace rights issues for their employers – in developing countries, usually the Ministry of Education. But there are several other knock-on effects, such as:

- Teacher posting becomes increasingly difficult (Kelly, 2000).
- The loss of trained and experienced teachers and interruption of teaching programmes due to illness will reduce the quality of education (Sifuna, 1996).

- There is a change in the content and role of education. Curricula must be changed to meet the pupils' needs, and must focus more on life skills such as decision making and interpreting social settings.
- The role of the teacher also changes. HIV/AIDS necessitates psychological support for the children from affected families, and teachers find that they are increasingly being used as counsellors for pupils. In Zambia, programmes in counselling are being established at the tertiary level in order to prepare the teachers for this role (Kelly, 1999).
- There is teacher absenteeism. Sometimes the sick leaves are so frequent that the education office wants to give the teacher notice in order to employ a permanent replacement who can provide secure, stable schooling for the children (Odiwuor, 1999).
- There are changes in parental motivation for schooling. The lack of a teacher will diminish the pupils' returns from schooling, and reduce the quality of education as such. This reduction of quality will, in a longer-term perspective, reduce parents' willingness to enrol their children. Why use time and money on low-quality schooling, instead of keeping the children at home, where they can work and even add to the family income rather than school being a drain on household resources. Moreover, children from AIDS-affected families are under emotional strain; and if they have AIDS they are often kept home from school due to illness, or are taken out of school.

There are increasing problems of teacher absenteeism, and loss of inspectors as well as teachers, education officers, and planning and management personnel. As AIDS continues to take its toll, there will be schools with no headteachers and no inspectors of schools. The education system will not be able to plan, manage and implement policies and programmes. The school itself may also be affected by the psychological effects of having infection, illness and death in its midst. There is likely to be discrimination, ostracism and isolation in the classroom and school.

Teachers may face the suspension of social and health benefits and/or dismissal from the system. Pupils may face formal suspension by the system or be pressured to leave school if they have not already been pushed out or dropped out. In quantitative terms, with high death rates of teachers, there will be a less-qualified teaching force, as trained and experienced teachers are replaced with younger and less-well-trained teachers, which compromises quality. This may lead to poor school attendance for both teachers and pupils, with severe implications for the completion of the curricula: the quantity of education offered could be limited. The qualitative effects on teachers are clear. Mukuka and Kalikti (1995) write that AIDS cases and deaths among teachers have had various perceived negative impacts:

- Teachers become over-concerned about their health and therefore become nervous and depressed.

- Teachers are frequently absent.
- Teachers' attitudes to work deteriorate.
- Teachers become unable to perform well.
- There is a negative psychological impact on children.
- An average of four teacher-hours were lost per week per school in 1995 in urban areas.
- Combined morbidity and mortality rates represent a 25 per cent increase in public expenditure to maintain recruitment and staffing at current levels.

Teachers in these countries already experience a lot of stress and the same kinds of outcomes as a result of other factors (notably the absence of pay), and so the existence of AIDS will inevitably lead to greater stress. Thus, not only is HIV / AIDS likely to remove more teachers from education, but it also affects the atmosphere and mood of the classroom. Teachers who are sero-positive, not surprisingly, tend to become unconfident and unmotivated. There is also discrimination against teachers and pupils who are known to be infected. This in turn prevents disclosure, and is psychologically and medically problematic. It also has obvious cost implications.

Teachers and other educational personnel who eventually die of AIDS have to be replaced. Other costs relate to medical charges and benefits to the families of those who die. Two other issues that need to be considered are: 1) the potential relevance of multigrade teaching in order to keep open schools that are accessible to children as enrolments fall; 2) the potential importance of non-formal alternatives to schooling.

Multigrade teaching, whilst it might optimize resource use in terms of the number of teachers available at any one time, will require teachers trained in that approach to pedagogy, implying additional costs. There have of course been several successful experiments with multigrade teaching (before the term was invented) from the original village schools in most of Europe during the 19th century and missionary schools in many other countries. But organized attempts to introduce multigrade teaching into an existing one-grade-per-teacher system have not always been successful; and clearly, the presence of HIV / AIDS only adds to the complexity.

Non-formal alternatives to schooling are, in principle, more flexible, but have also had a chequered history over the last 30 years. The problem is that the carers may see this as a substitute, lower-quality form of education, and this may only add to the discrimination suffered by children who are already psychologically deprived.

This rapid review of the impact of HIV / AIDS shows how the problems of managing and organizing the teaching force are exacerbated and highlighted by the epidemic. In particular, those organizing teacher training programmes have to take into account the quantitative impacts of death and illness and, when planning the intake and output of their colleges, the curriculum and the impact on the quality of the learning experience that teachers can realistically deliver in the schools. It is imperative for planning purposes that we have accurate information on the impact of the pandemic on the teaching force. Estimates should be augmented with data collected specifically on deaths of teachers based on local registers.

The role of the education sector in preventing the spread of HIV/AIDS

It is often advocated by those debating and writing in the area that the educational systems could and should do more to help prevent the spread of the pandemic among the 'generation of hope' (those who are not yet sexually active). The dilemma is that, in many countries, repetition rates are high, so that this would mean introducing discussion of HIV/AIDS into the primary school, and this is likely to encounter strong resistance from some communities. In this part of the chapter, we will first consider the official optimistic view, then the practical and theoretical constraints on this approach and finally the implications for a programme.

The education sector is, by its nature, a unique tool for disseminating information and awareness about HIV/AIDS. It often receives the lion's share of public revenues and is usually the major employer of public staff in a country. The main advantage of using the education sector as the vehicle is that it already has an existing – even if degraded – infrastructure, so that using it as a channel for education about HIV/AIDS would be cost-effective compared to other proposed vehicles. One would reach a very large audience: not only teachers and administrative staff could be reached, but also pupils at all levels and, eventually, their parents and extended families. UNAIDS therefore argues that the education system can be used as a tool for information, awareness campaigns, etc, reaching out to each village. This involves:

- rapid development of HIV/AIDS teaching and learning materials for integration into the curriculum at all levels, including teacher training;
- training peer educators;
- getting pupils involved through participatory teaching methods;
- training teachers to use new materials, handle new curricula and use participatory techniques, perhaps through training them as peer educators and getting them to practise participatory methods;
- awareness campaigns to reach parents and the local community;
- including the topic in headteacher training and in-service training of teachers;
- commitment throughout the system and of course extensive collaboration between the ministries of education and health (although often unspoken).

There are several examples of attempts and innovations in each of these areas in the literature, although rather fewer evaluations of their effectiveness (see below). There is now a new initiative, Focusing Resources on Effective School Health (FRESH), backed by both UNICEF and WHO, to introduce life skills education into all schools. At the same time, they recognize that strategies must be developed to secure effectiveness and quality of the services in spite of illness and absenteeism, including strategies to promote more effective schooling in general (counselling, introducing more creative learning opportunities, flexibility, smaller classes, better community liaison, etc). There are also strategies for the replacement of staff at all levels, strategies for the development of multi-skilled teachers and strategies for the management of staff in order to make staff more interchangeable. It is recognized that capacity among school teachers, educational administrators, religious leaders and the community at large has to be built to cope with the pandemic. Training involves encouraging a positive approach to living with AIDS, support to those affected and how to deliver AIDS prevention education.

If schools are to become an open channel for information, teachers are the keys to success. But, the issue of HIV / AIDS requires a different methodology from the usual curriculum. Most teachers therefore need to be (re)trained to use new material, to handle new curricula and, not least, how to communicate with children and adolescents on these topics. HIV / AIDS touches upon very sensitive issues and taboos like sexuality, power relations and gender equity. Participatory learning and teaching techniques using discussion, communication and action are needed. UNAIDS suggests that one way of preparing teachers for this new methodology is to train them as peer educators, practising participatory methods to train the pupils as peer counsellors, and that music and drama teachers are crucial in this respect.

For some commentators, the HIV / AIDS epidemic has accelerated the need for curricula reform with an emphasis on life skills to encourage behaviour changes. But, in many countries, the curriculum is already overcrowded and often outdated, so comprehensive alterations are required. Moreover, writing appropriate materials for a new subject is time-consuming; writing a cross-cutting curriculum is likely to be even more difficult (see below). Then, in order for the new content to be effectively delivered, textbooks or other materials have to be produced and distributed, and teachers have to be trained to use the new materials in an interactive way with their pupils.

For those acquainted with the reality of teaching in the vast majority of primary schools in the most affected countries, this will all seem rather fanciful. There are rarely sufficient textbooks for pupils to have even shared access – many teachers rely on copying out materials from their copy on to the blackboard, and sometimes their own notes from their own schooldays – and 'interaction in the classroom' is usually restricted to chanting responses to a teacher's questions. The idea that new materials could be produced and distributed, and that teachers can be trained appropriately – all rapidly – again seems a little unrealistic.

Equally, there has been a long history of peer counselling, an obvious example being the Child-to-Child project. Many of these initiatives appear to work but they rely on the enthusiasm of a key person or persons in the community and/or school for the process to take off and be sustainable. It is, in any case, very difficult to programme for such charisma, enthusiasm or interest; and it will be especially difficult in the atmosphere of suspicion and distrust that is often generated by the HIV/AIDS epidemic. With multi-age grades (Carr-Hill, 2001), sadly, the prospects of successful peer counselling are further diminished, because the class peer-group is more likely to become a vehicle for spreading HIV rather than education about how to prevent it; and this is especially true in boarding institutions (Coombe, 1999).

Similarly, there have been hundreds of attempts and innovations involving pupils through participatory methods, often on quite a large scale. Whilst the innovatory schemes themselves rarely fail, they usually peter out, again because of a lack of sustained commitment and a lack of a realistic appreciation of the difficulties facing a teacher in ordinary times, let alone the 'extraordinary' situation of an HIV/AIDS epidemic (IIEP, 2000).

The point is that if the teaching profession has not, as a matter of course, involved students in teaching the 'core' subjects, it is very unlikely that they will be able to do so with such a delicate subject matter. Indeed, participatory approaches involving pupils and adults may, in some cases, be seen as culturally inappropriate for a teacher. Indeed, in many countries where the impact of the epidemic is largest, the bulk of teachers are not adequately trained for the existing curriculum (and often have not received any pre-service training at all), let alone being capable of delivering the complex package being promoted by UNAIDS/UNICEF etc. Moreover, teachers themselves are sometimes perceived by the community (although often wrongly) as guilty of introducing the epidemic into the schools, and therefore the most inappropriate adults in the community to explain and teach about prevention.

Even assuming that training can be provided to all teachers in the system – which is itself a tall order – the teachers will have to be trained in pedagogical approaches that will be very different from those that they themselves experienced when at school. It is simply not realistic. Donor agencies say that there has to be commitment at all levels of the system. It sounds fine and there has been plenty of rhetoric to support it. But, given the present levels of financing, there is a reality for government recovering (hopefully) from the rigours of structural adjustment that means that worrying about HIV/AIDS tends to be sidelined. Moreover, the presumption that there can be easy communication between the ministries of education and of health ignores the history of interdepartmental suspicion that many of these countries have inherited from colonial times.

Theoretical problems

These approaches have ignored some fundamental conceptual problems such as the different epistemologies of health and education, the conflicts over how to design a curriculum and the limiting role of education in changing behaviour, all discussed in the following paragraphs.

One set of epistemologies comes from theoreticians (academics) and senior policy makers over the concept of health (whether it is basically collective or individual; how to influence behaviour, etc). Another set of epistemologies comes from health workers and educationalists in which health education has to be treated as something like a subject. 'Health education' has to be more closely integrated into the fabric of the school with a wider concept of behavioural objectives. These contrasts are compounded by the frequent lack of any serious health institution's involvement when the education sector discusses the issue.

Curriculum planners argue over the width of the concept, scientific nature of curriculum planning and control of the school curriculum. Four strands have been emphasized at different times by different schools, namely health as hygiene knowledge, the inculcation of hygiene habits, scientific curriculum development and the primary school curriculum as preparation for further studies.

The resolution of these depends on society's conception of the role of the school: they cannot be treated as a simple technical issue. There have been many attempts to introduce health education into the school curricula. These vary according to the type of content and mode of delivery but, sadly, one constant is the relative lack of success. It is well recognized in the public health literature that, whilst health services can provide repair and comfort, they can only have a limited impact on the population's health (because they can only cure a minority of those who are chronically ill). This relative modesty (relative because it is not shared by the peddlers of hi-tech medicine) contrasts with the view of some in the education sector who appear to believe that what is taught in school is taken as gospel by the pupils. In fact, of course, there are many other influences on the child apart from both the school and the parents. The relative success in stemming the spread of HIV / AIDS in Uganda is, at least in part, ascribed to the mobilization of youth out of school.

None of this pessimism should be taken as an excuse for not trying. It is just a warning that preventing the spread of HIV / AIDS, whether directly through school systems or out of school, is difficult. An evaluation of UNICEF programmes such as those comprising action for youth in and out of school, and community-based orphan care reported serious shortcomings in their strategy and implementation, and lack of collaboration with other sectors. It is not a problem that can be solved or even tackled with top-down rhetoric; and the contribution of other sectors cannot be ignored. Whilst the situation is urgent, we must be realistic about what can be achieved.

Prevention of HIV / AIDS needs a lot less rhetoric and a lot more under-standing and confidence building with communities drawing on the few resources that do exist. This implies that any programme has to be based on existing activities and stakeholder interests in the communities. For example, if there already is an adult literacy class, it would be silly to reinvent such a class in order to discuss the problem of HIV / AIDS; similarly, if there already is a functioning community-based organization then, although it may not appear to be the most appropriate vehicle for prevention activities, it certainly cannot be bypassed.

All this, in turn, implies that, firstly, in any community activities there should be an inventory of existing resources including the local school resources. It is an essential prerequisite and, if organized locally, it does not take that much effort or time. Moreover, if HIV / AIDS prevention activities cannot be organized locally, then it is unlikely that they will be sufficiently accepted locally for them to work. Secondly, schools need the support of other actors to integrate health education into the school curricula. For example, community health workers are often ignored in much of the discussion, as is the positive role of the churches. It is only after this local institutional 'mapping' of the potential role of other sectors and, in particular, of the health sector and of religious organizations that a realistic programme, based on a careful analysis of the existing situation, can be devised.

All the implications in terms of the organization and pedagogical style of teaching are simply an exemplification of good practice when teaching. The HIV / AIDS epidemic has served to highlight the reality of the teaching–learning experience in schools, and the long route march towards good teaching practice that is needed.

Prospects towards a more realistic approach

HIV / AIDS preventive education programmes frequently have a wide range of targets. These programmes often involve new curricula, but the balance of experience is that inexperienced teachers communicating with pupils can be counter-productive, both because of misinformation and because their parents might react negatively. Furthermore, a thorough peer education of teachers is crucial for any programme to extend prevention activities to the students themselves, and this is rarely available.

At the same time, the ministry of education is responsible as the employer of a large workforce with their own rights; and, in the context of a severe teacher shortage, teachers have to be the priority as the main investment of the sector. On this basis, the first priority should be to reach the teachers. This does not mean that pupils should be ignored; on the contrary, informed teachers make for a safer school. Moreover, this approach ensures that, in addition to any other agencies' activities that should, of course, be encouraged, any eventual teacher input to HIV/AIDS prevention activities is of high quality and therefore sustainable.

Note that thoroughly educating teachers about HIV/AIDS and training them to deliver corresponding material in the classrooms are different exercises. The teacher has first to integrate appropriate attitudes and behaviour through basic understanding of HIV/AIDS, before learning how to communicate, in collaboration with others, these difficult issues to adolescents; and the capacity to counsel adults and students individually is a further (third) step again.

There also has to be careful attention to the scope and sequence of topics. For example, materials can be rather light on other sexually transmitted diseases (STDs) and, by describing characteristics of 'sufferers', can easily promote discrimination against those with HIV/AIDS. Materials should be reviewed both by local educators who are experienced in this area and by representatives of civil society in order to ensure their acceptability. Materials must be presented, at least initially, face to face rather than at a distance. Equally, it is not appropriate to use traditional cascade methods here: only those who are thoroughly conversant with the subject matter and completely comfortable themselves should present to students. Educators experienced in this area should be recruited to carry through this programme; any 'training of trainers' should include inspection and supervision as an integral part of the programme.

There are narrow economic arguments for focusing on secondary school teachers (because there has been more investment in them) and broader economic arguments for focusing on primary school teachers (because the long-term implications for society are greater). The eventual target group is, of course, the 'generation of hope', arbitrarily defined here as 12- to 15-year-olds. In general, we would recommend that primary school teachers should be taken as the first priority but this is a relatively finely balanced judgement.

References

Carr-Hill, R (2001) Multi-age grades and risk in schools, *Mimeo*, Education and International Development, University of London, Institute of Education, London

Coombe, C (1999) *Education Sector: Niassa Province 2000–2003*, November, Lichinga, Niassa Province

Coombe, C (2000) Managing the impact of HIV/AIDS on the education sector, Briefing paper prepared for African Development Forum, UNECA, University of Pretoria, South Africa

International Institute of Educational Planning (IIEP) (2000) *HIV/AIDS and Education: A workshop report*, 25–27 September, IIEP, Paris

Kelly, M J (1999) *The Impact of HIV/AIDS on Schooling in Zambia*, p 2, Ministry of Education, Lusaka

Kelly, M J (2000) Planning for education in the context of HIV/AIDS, *IIEP Fundamentals of Educational Planning*, No. 66, UNESCO, Paris

Mukuka, L and Kalikti, J (1995) *The Impact of HIV/AIDS on Education in Zambia*, Ministry of Health, Lusaka

Odiwuor (1999) *AIDS Scourge: Which way forward for Africa?*, *Studies in Comparative and International Education*, No. 51, IIE, Stockholm

Sichone, M and Haworth, A (1996) *The Impact of HIV/AIDS in the Education Sector*, National AIDS, STB, TB, Leprosy Programme, Ministry of Health, Lusaka

Sifuna, D (1996) *Academic Achievement as a Predictor for Teaching Effectiveness among Primary School Teachers in Kenya*, Kenyatta University, Bureau of Educational Research, Nairobi

19. The democratization of teacher education

Lynn Davies

Introduction

Within a context of worldwide moves towards democratization of political systems would go a parallel concern about democracy in education. Political and economic democracy are seen as central to development or transformation (Leftwich, 1996; Mehbrahtu, Crossley and Johnson, 2000), even if there is contestation between or within countries about definitions of democracy and about the types of participation, representation, decentralization or equity seen as viable (Davies, 1999). This chapter examines firstly the extent of democracy in teacher education in a range of countries, and secondly the possible dimensions of a democratic teacher education institution and system. It moves on to consider the processes through which teacher education institutions can democratize; this highlights some contradictions in control and implementation, and uses experience in the Gambia as an example.

The extent of democracy in teacher education

Teacher education institutions (whether in developed or developing countries) have often been characterized as authoritarian establishments. Teaching can be by mass lecture and passive learning; there may be minimum school experience; or assessment is done through matching against predetermined lists of 'competences'. The ideal of the autonomous learner who creates his or her own learning paths and engages in critical inquiry is far from the reality of much traditional teacher training (Harber, 1997; Davies and Iqbal, 1997). In some countries, this relates to the positioning of teacher training as simply an extension of secondary schooling, with similar 'discipline' for trainees and similar methods of control. Alternatively, it may relate to the contradictory function of schooling and its teachers both to preserve existing culture and to act as agents of change or modernization. In the end, the conservative and reproductive role of schooling is easier to manage and prepare for than one genuinely adaptive to unknown future economic, social and political shifts.

Teachers may in fact find themselves lagging behind radical educational movements. This has become apparent in England, with the advent of the new citizenship curriculum to be implemented in 2002. Although supposed to be a whole school development for all age ranges, teachers will vary enormously in their adaptation to this, according to their curriculum expertise and their own teacher training. They are also receiving mixed messages from government agencies. On the one hand they hear that there is nothing really new in citizenship that they do not do already (in history, geography and religious education, for example, or in personal and social education). On the other hand, there is a glut of citizenship conferences and workshops for teachers, accompanied by new manuals, schemes of work and guidelines. Clearly, there is more to preparing children to be democratic citizens than an amalgam of previous good practice, and teachers are becoming aware of the implications.

Studies of teacher training in different countries reveal that political socialization is deep but hidden and conservative. In Germany, for example, Raghu (1995) commented in her study of Catholic teacher training institutions that there was little attention in the official curriculum to the role of teachers as political actors; rather the programme emphasized professional and technical activities such as teaching methods, use of teaching aids, use of psychology with children and classroom management. The hidden curriculum transmitted similarly depoliticized messages. The students stated that they had been influenced by their professors as models to remain silent on controversial issues (such as gender relations).

An account of Sri Lankan teacher education also points up gender issues, in terms of the proletarianization of teaching and the preponderance of females in primary education. The claim is that females are less likely to challenge the status quo; certainly the fact that female teachers tend to stay at the primary level may fulfil the accumulation aims of the state of more work for less pay (Tatto and Dharmadasa, 1995). Such accumulation aims are also noticeable in education policy in Palestine, where there are proposals to encourage more women teachers into the primary sector (where their status and pay are lower) (Davies, 2000).

Teacher education ideology and practice therefore will be caught between three contradictory imperatives: preservation of customs and cultures, the need for modernization and the need for economic stringency. States may simultaneously centralize and decentralize, authoritarianize and democratize, for example insisting on national curricula and 'standards' for schools and teacher education while giving more autonomy to principals to manage their institutions and take responsibility for economic costs (as in South Africa, Sri Lanka and the UK). There would be spaces for staff and students to engage in critical democratic pedagogy within such contradictions, but this is not always easy or sustainable. It would therefore be unfair to blame teacher educators solely for social reproduction: they themselves are caught up in state regulation and control.

Dimensions of the democratic teacher education institution

If we were to move from this somewhat negative picture of teacher education to the portrayal of an emerging democratic institution, the dimensions could be put under three headings: *learning about democracy, learning democratically* and *organizing democratically*. My definition of a democratic teacher education would be one that is based on giving teachers experience of choice, decision making, participation and informed debate together with the acquisition of knowledge of political processes and rights.

Learning about democracy refers to the knowledge base for teachers, and their preparedness to engage for themselves as professionals and workers in the democratic state as well as 'transmit' knowledge to pupils. Such capacity requires at the very least a working knowledge of the political system of the country, and some notion of global citizenship. However, on initial teacher training courses, citizenship may remain an 'option' rather than a compulsory core of knowledge for all teachers. At the very least, all trainees should be aware of the many different ways of 'doing democracy' in the classroom and school, and of when a democratic or indeed an authoritarian response is more appropriate.

There are certain key elements in learning democratically. These are reflection, participation and contestation. Steiner (1996) has argued convincingly about the role of reflection during teacher training, which is echoed in research on women teacher educators' experiences of gender politics embracing exclusion or marginalization (Dillabough, 2000). For Steiner, learning for democracy and global citizenship is not solely about a course in civics, development education or critical pedagogies but is about unlearning the patterns of subordination and dominance that we bring from childhood. Few of us have experienced any real equality with others on a regular basis in our lives. 'Reflective practitioners' are therefore those who not only think about their daily practice, but also reflect on their own and others' biographies and how these shape their perceptions and behaviours within a political system.

Reflection of course is not enough: it must lead to informed action. This means taking responsibility for one's own – and others' – learning. Dove (1986) argued that teachers need to be stimulated through participatory forms of in-service training. One of the major skills to be developed within teacher education for democracy is that of contestation, or the disposition to challenge. Carr and Hartnett (1996) argue eloquently that a distinctive feature of a democratic society is that it accepts that no single image of the good society can be theoretically justified to an extent that would allow it to be put beyond rational dispute, and that such disputes as arise should not be concealed or repressed. Such skills, together with how to stimulate pupils' challenges, are arguably at the heart of a critical teacher education.

Democratic curriculum and pedagogy are more honestly and easily practised within a framework of democratic management of a college. The features that would allow students and staff to experience democratic politics would include the presence of student councils, representation on governing bodies of a college, participation in the appointment and retention of staff and emphasis on learning to work with parents and community. Paradoxically, such features are more often to be found in schools, with increasing good examples throughout the world (Davies and Kirkpatrick, 2000). In teacher education, they can be found in countries where the link between democratic school reform and teacher education reform is officially recognized, such as is the case in Colombia (Harber and Davies, 1997) and Mexico (Tatto, 1997).

One key principle is that of subsidiarity, that decisions should be taken at the lowest possible effective level, as near to the point of action as possible. It also means that decisions become more client-orientated in responding to regional professional needs and not just to central government requirements, as Sayer (1995) points out in relation to the Czech Republic.

Subsidiarity in fact would happen at a number of levels: relative independence or decentralization of teacher education from central ministry control; and devolved internal governance of a college to create structures of decision making that avoid hierarchy and bureaucracy and allow swift decisions to be made by those nearest to their impact.

A difficulty in subsidiarity is the control of teaching practice and of its perceived function. As Carr and Hartnett (1996) argue, the schism between 'educational studies' and 'teaching practice' has frustrated genuine curriculum change and undermined the development of democratic educational reform. The best and most democratic 'partnerships' between college and school would be those where both tutors and school-based mentors or training supervisors do theory and practice, on both sites, and neither is afraid to question state or institutional policy. As well as partnerships with schools, there are partnerships with other agencies such as supervisory bodies. One challenge is to resist the contemporary obsession with predetermined and homogenized 'learning outcomes' for each lecture, module and programme, as that destroys the possibility of learning going in different directions according to students' (varying) needs.

Processes of democratization

It is one thing to have a vision of what a democratic teacher education institution looks like and another to engage in bringing this about. This section examines the *process* by which democratization might occur, and some of the dilemmas and challenges involved.

The first dilemma is the question of *who initiates democratization*. If this is 'imposed' by a ministry or outside aid agency, then there is the issue of both imperialism and the possible lack of ownership from within that would ensure successful implementation. Democracy, like any other ideology, can be subverted or ritualized very easily, if the commitment or understanding is not there, as Banya (1995) describes in Sierra Leone. While democracy is a highly rational process to the converted, it may be far less so to those whose vested interests or power may appear threatened. It would appear supremely unde-mocratic to force a democratic process on an unwilling institution. Yet, as European legislation has demonstrated, requiring schools to have pupil repre-sentation on councils, school committees and governing boards has provided for a pupil voice and the rights of children 'to participate in decisions that affect them' (Article 12 of the United Nations Convention on the Rights of the Child), in ways that may not have happened if left for schools to decide (Davies and Kirkpatrick, 2000). Firm legislation can be one way to begin the process of power sharing.

A second dilemma concerns the *increasing use of distance education courses* for teacher preparation, which may not be that helpful in the processes of democ-ratization. The individualism, the isolation and lack of linkage to partnership and social movements would not give much support to the collaborative efforts and joint action needed to push forward real reform of a school, college or system. Distance education programmes have democratic elements, in the sense that they are broadening out access and knowledge and help equity, but there is little evidence that they act as a political catalyst. Tatto and Dharmadasa (1995) describe the 'carefully designed, self-instructional mate-rials' used by the in-service teachers in Sri Lanka, which contrasted well with the traditional teacher-centred, lecture format found in the colleges, but commented on the 'dual status' and lesser prestige attached to distance creden-tials and diplomas from teacher colleges (as opposed to colleges of education), and the teacher discontent and lack of unity that this is likely to aggravate.

A third dilemma concerns *action research as a better tool in democratization* in the way it stimulates reflection and collaboration. Dyer *et al* (2001), for example, give a fascinating account of their project with Indian teachers, outlining the processes of facilitation they engaged in, while not denying the political and cultural barriers involved. Yet Gore and Zeichner raise grave doubts about action research, emphasizing that 'there is nothing inherent to action research that makes it emancipatory' (1995: 206). Using Foucault's analysis of power–knowledge relations, where power passes through multiple points and turns on multiple axes, they show how the production of knowledge through action research has no necessary impact on social condi-tions or practices. Reports are not widely circulated in teacher education programmes, and students' knowledge production is not used in any systematic way. Gore and Zeichner therefore argue that, for action research to be more reflexive than it is in pre-service and in-service teacher education, it must be embedded in a programme context that itself has emancipatory goals towards social justice and where both colleges and schools are collaborative research communities reflecting on the purposes of education in a democratic society. Similarly, Sultana (1995) has cast severe doubts on some of the 'consciousness-raising' under the name of 'action research'. He argues that the exclusive focus on the local, and the fragmentary approach that does its best to utilize 'spaces' created by the predominant political forces of the time have grave political and strategic implications.

A fourth dilemma concerns the issue of *'working from within'*, which can often mean individualized responses, the very ideology that socialist educators should be challenging. 'Gone, in the teacher development discourse, are the political strategies on the Gramscian scale' (Sultana, 1995). This has certainly been borne out in contemporary England and Wales, where teacher educators appear to have been powerless to resist the ludicrous policing of their work by both OFSTED (Office of Standards in Education) and the QAA (Qualifications and Assessment Authority), let alone the insult of the imposition of numeracy and ICT tests on initial trainees. Individual critiques by academics have not led to social movements, the forging of alliances with other parts of higher education and with parents, teachers and students, which would enable concerted resistance.

In Malta, in contrast, Sultana (1995) described coalitions of students, teachers, heads and parents, who are developing radical ways to break down authoritarian school management, develop vocational schooling, draw up charters of student rights and develop their own skills in media and communication to promote the cause. Osler and Starkey (1996) suggest a different way into democratization through the introduction of human rights that are embedded in opportunities for a broad experience (which was one objective of ERASMUS programmes). Studying abroad gives student teachers better preparation for their future role as teachers, 'having had the opportunity to reconsider their own identities as a consequence'. Similarly, case studies of black teachers demonstrate that they are likely to have a good understanding of human rights issues and identities through their own lived experience.

Democratization of the Gambia College: a case study

To explore these different ways into the change process and exemplify some of the discussion in this paper, I now describe an interventionist research project being conducted in the Gambia by a team from the Centre for International Education and Research at Birmingham University, UK. The Gambia is committed to democracy as a political system and supports the value of democracy in education. As in many other countries, schools vary in the degree that they have taken on board the principles of democratic learning and management, and there is recognition of the need for teachers themselves to experience a democratic teacher education. We are working with the Gambia College at Brikama, the sole teacher training establishment, to assist in the processes of democratization there and to research the impact of the intervention on the college itself and on its trainees when they enter schools.

The college has many democratic features, such as an active student union, but equally has many traditional features of a testing regime and lack of student control over curriculum. It also lacks any resources on education and democracy, and hence would have difficulty in introducing democracy or citizenship as formal components of the curriculum for teachers. The 15-month project consists of workshops for staff and students, observation in college and local schools, interviews with staff, students and teachers by ourselves and college researchers, the provision of materials for the library and the trialling of a manual on 'Improving teacher education through democracy' for use in teacher education colleges and university faculties more widely.

We were very concerned, firstly, about whether this whole project was an imposition by a group of Western people, fervently committed to democracy and wanting to spread the word. The process of the project is gradually to hand over some control of workshops and research to the college, but certainly the initial planning and drawing up of the research and development design was almost entirely ours. Would participants object to the usual experts jetting in and telling them things they already knew? Gratifyingly, we have got no sense of this at all. Participants uniformly found the workshops valuable and even 'exciting', and have asked for more.

Secondly, we were concerned whether there would be any impact. A workshop can be enjoyable and stimulating, but participants may go away unchanged or even with their previous ideas and behaviours reinforced. Here, while participants were in the end very able to identify what democratic people, schools, teachers and teacher educators would look like in an ideal world, this is no guarantee that theory will be translated into practice. We therefore asked them to complete a personal action plan that stated what they would personally now do as a result of their experiences. The results were very instructive, including statements such as:

- 'I will serve as a role model for my students, eg practise what I teach.'
- 'Not allow male students to intimidate female students.'
- 'Delegate responsibility to students.'
- 'I will try to be less autocratic in my behaviour towards my students, especially in areas covering assessment and evaluation of the work already covered.'
- 'I will ensure that, at all times and situations, I make myself a guide, learner and a facilitator rather than a Mr Know-All.'
- 'Endeavour to consult more with colleagues with a view to allowing for more participation... as Head of School endeavour to network with other partners and stakeholders.'
- 'I have realized how autocratic our school atmosphere is in Africa... I have decided to try to help bring change.'

One interesting action point at the top of one participant's list was 'Be very democratic in running my family', which was significant in that we had not mentioned families at all. This participant had obviously translated the principles to other contexts. We noted, nevertheless, that he was still 'running' his family. Of course, it is one thing to make pledges in the heat of the moment and the immediate post-euphoria of workshops, and another to enact them in the cold light of day. Only one participant admitted a possible difficulty in making his teaching methods more participatory.

It will be very interesting to follow up the participants to see whether they were indeed able to effect any change in their own behaviour or style, or whether constraints of expectations (by students as well as college), organizational culture, time, additional efforts needed and the formal curriculum plus its assessment preclude any real inroads into the tried and tested.

Adaptation is a key issue, and there was a constant reminder by participants about needing to work within Gambian culture, which is a predominantly Islamic culture, with all that that means for issues such as modes of child rearing or gender roles. There is a massive innovation literature that points up the failures of good intentions and the inertia resulting from structural and psychological normalities. While pleased at the apparent success of the 'training' so far, we – and they – are not going to be over-optimistic about instant radical reform.

There is none the less a thirst for more exposure to controversial issues and the opportunity to air them in a safe environment. The next workshop will therefore tackle the concerns identified by participants themselves as future steps: how to develop a module on democracy for the professional studies unit; practical teaching and discipline in a democratic class; school governance; assessment; rural areas; multigrade systems; and contradictions in democracy.

At the moment then it would appear that workshops by outside facilitators do help in stimulating or even kick-starting processes of democratization, if such issues have never really been discussed in a collective way before. It will be important, however, that staff and students themselves take ownership of the process as soon as possible, deciding content of workshops and training modules, researching impact and barriers and convening groups that collectively can do more than individuals trying to fulfil personal action goals.

The prospects

Democratization of teacher education is yet another example of how it is possible to learn from international experience. England, for example, possibly fast becoming the least democratic teacher education system in the world, with its emphasis on 'low trust' and 'commercialised professionalism' (Furlong et al, 2000), can learn from the slightly more extended notions of professionality in Australia or the United States (Smyth, 2000), as well as from the collaborative and adaptive cultures of countries such as the Gambia. Work by Schweisfurth (2000) and Chisholm (1999) shows varied responses by teachers to the processes of democratization in South Africa and Russia, with resistances and shifting definitions and meanings. The role of teacher education in countries undergoing transitions to democracy still needs much research, to parallel such investigations of teachers in schools. This chapter has tried to identify some of the possibilities in the democratization of teacher education as well as some of the inevitable tensions and contradictions. What are the prospects for the future?

There appear to be five interlocking imperatives that will push teacher education into a more democratic operation. Firstly is the growing international concern and legislation about human rights, whereby teachers will have to have concrete knowledge for curriculum purposes, as well as understand the implications for both 'discipline' of pupils and for school organization in terms of structures such as learning contracts, charters and grievance procedures.

Secondly is increasing pluralism where teachers now work with multicultural, multi-ethnic and shifting populations, including migrant workers, refugees and nomads. This entails moving on from vague notions of 'tolerance' to specific skills and understandings of inclusion or inequality and of the positioning of 'self' and 'other' in terms of citizenship.

Thirdly, linked to the above, is the need for serious development of education in conflict and post-conflict societies. We have examples of this with teachers' groups in contexts such as Bosnia, Kosovo and Palestine, working on curriculum harmonization, or human rights or gender issues, as well as thinking about the contribution of the school to the perpetuation or reduction of violence.

Fourthly comes the impact of new technologies. Teachers are no longer sole experts in their field but facilitators of learning through different media, or even co-learners with the pupils. This is already demonstrating very different – and more democratic – relationships with pupils and between teachers, and is being foreshadowed in teacher education courses.

Fifthly is the spectre of globalization. Exposure to a range of cultures and media, together with international networking of pupils and teachers, can mean young people not only being exposed to global issues of peace and environment, but challenging traditional authority and gender roles. The impetus towards education for democracy may come at least in part from the young people themselves.

In spite of the dilemmas related to implementation, the author of this chapter would not back down from the position that some form of the principles of democracy is the only way to begin to resolve global tensions and global inequities. Teacher education is a conservative force, which has often acted to hinder such resolutions, but it will be forced to change – and there are many committed and radical teacher educators as well as young people who will be spearheading the transformations.

References

Banya, K (1995) The dynamics of extending an integrated rural teacher education project in Sierra Leone, in *The Political Dimension in Teacher Education: Comparative perspectives on policy formation, socialisation and society*, ed M Ginsburg and B Lindsay, Falmer Press, London

Carr, W and Hartnett, A (1996) *Education and the Struggle for Democracy*, Open University Press, Milton Keynes

Chisholm, L (1999) The democratisation of schools and the politics of teachers' work in South Africa, *Compare*, **29** (2), pp 111–26

Davies, L (1999) Comparing definitions of democracy in education, *Compare*, **29** (2), pp 127–40

Davies, L (2000) *Integration of Gender in Policy and Decision-making in the Ministry of Education, East Jerusalem (West Bank and Gaza)*, Report, British Council, London

Davies, L and Iqbal, Z (1997) Tensions in teacher training for school effectiveness in Pakistan, *School Effectiveness and School Improvement*, **8** (2), pp 254–66

Davies, L and Kirkpatrick, G (2000) *A Review of Pupil Democracy in Europe*, Children's Rights Alliance, London

Dillabough, J (2000) Women in teacher education: their struggles for inclusion as 'citizen workers' in late modernity, in *Challenging Democracy: International perspectives on gender, education and citizenship*, ed M Arnot and J Dillabough, Routledge, London

Dove, L (1986) *Teachers and Teacher Education in Developing Countries*, Croom Helm, London

Dyer, C *et al* (2001) Research and the participatory development of primary teacher educators in India, in *Learning Democracy and Citizenship: International experiences*, ed M Schweisfurth, C Harber and L Davies, Symposium, Oxford (forthcoming)

Furlong, J *et al* (2000) *Teacher Education in Transition: Reforming professionalism*, Open University Press, Buckingham

Gore, J and Zeichner, K (1995) Connecting action research to genuine teacher development, in *Critical Discourses on Teacher Development*, ed J Smyth, Cassell, London

Harber, C (1997) *Education, Democracy and Political Development in Africa*, Academic Press, Brighton

Harber, C and Davies, L (1997) *School Management and Effectiveness in Developing Countries*, Cassell, London

Leftwich, A (1996) (ed) *Democracy and Development*, Polity Press, Cambridge

Mehrbrahtu, T, Crossley, M and Johnson, D (eds) (2000) *Globalisation, Educational Transformation and Societies in Transition*, Symposium, Oxford

Osler, A and Starkey, H (1996) *Teacher Education and Human Rights*, David Fulton, London

Raghu, R (1995) Preparing teachers for gender politics in Germany: the state, the church, and political socialization, in *The Political Dimension in Teacher Education: Comparative perspectives on policy formation, socialisation and society*, ed M Ginsburg and B Lindsay, Falmer Press, London

Sayer, J (1995) The continuing professional development of teachers and the role of the university, in *Developing Schools for Democracy in Europe*, ed J Sayer, pp 97–102, *Oxford Studies in Comparative Education*, **5** (1), Triangle, Oxford

Schweisfurth, M (2000) Teachers and democratic change in Russia and South Africa, *Education in Russia, the Independent States and Eastern Europe*, **18** (1)

Smyth, J (2000) Review symposium, *British Journal of Sociology of Education*, **21** (4), pp 643–47

Steiner, M (ed) (1996) *Developing the Global Teacher: Theory and practice in initial teacher education*, Trentham Books, Stoke-on-Trent

Sultana, R (1995) From critical education to a critical practice of teaching, in *Critical Discourses on Teacher Development*, ed J Smyth, Cassell, London

Tatto, M (1997) Teacher education for disadvantaged communities, *International Journal of Educational Development*, **17** (4), pp 405–15

Tatto, M and Dharmadasa, K (1995) Social and political contexts of policy formation in teacher education in Sri Lanka, in *The Political Dimension in Teacher Education: Comparative perspectives on policy formation, socialisation and society*, ed M Ginsburg and B Lindsay, Falmer Press, London

20. A comprehensive prototype for urban teacher education in the United States

Ken Howey and Linda Post

Introduction

Four key areas of teacher education are identified in this chapter within the context of present dilemmas and future prospects in teacher education. The four areas include:

- theories and ideologies of teacher education;
- the control of teacher education by the state, with reference to the role of schools and higher education;
- cultural perspectives and the education of teachers;
- the notion of teacher education as an ongoing process.

These four areas are not mutually exclusive and can intersect in various ways. In this chapter they are addressed in the context of efforts to improve the recruitment, preparation and retention of teachers for urban schools and school communities in the United States. The particular focus is schools where, by economic standards in the United States, there are large numbers of students living in or on the margins of poverty. In some instances there is considerable pluralism in culture and language; in others there are very high percentages of youth from particular historically under-represented populations, primarily African-American and Hispanic-American ethnic groups.

Some might be ignorant of the scope of youngsters in need in the United States. Rentel and Dittmer (1999: 8) portrayed this condition with dry but nonetheless compelling statistics:

> More than 300,000 school-age children are homeless at any given time in the United States... Roughly four million children have been exposed to dangerous levels of lead, and health statistics indicate that some 300,000 newborns have been exposed prenatally to drugs including dangerous levels of alcohol... Many if not most of these children have joined a growing underclass of poor, often homeless, and increasingly rootless adults. As juveniles, evidence suggests that many of them will be noncompliant, aggressive, anti-social, and unable to communicate or to understand effectively. Contrary to media stereotypes, they are distributed throughout the population, not just concentrated in minority communities, although they are disproportionately represented among the *poor* [emphasis added].

The federal Department of Education projects that over 1.25 million new teachers will be needed over the next five years. The growing demand for teachers generally greatly exacerbates the problem of placing competent and caring teachers in urban 'high-need' schools and communities. This is a challenge of major proportions. Consider some of the following statistics. The American Association of Colleges for Teacher Education (AACTE) research about teacher education (RATE) studies in 1999 revealed over several years that only one in eight teachers had as their first preference teaching in a highly diverse, urban setting. The federal Department of Education school and staffing survey (National Center for Educational Studies, 1994) further revealed that the number of teachers who are teaching out of their field is considerably exacerbated in high-poverty schools, that is schools where more than 40 per cent of the students are eligible for free or reduced-price lunch. For example, almost one in five high-poverty schools have teachers of English who are not qualified to teach this subject. This is the situation with one in four teachers in the area of mathematics, an even higher percentage in biology and an incredible 71 per cent in physics.

This is to say nothing of the considerable shortages of teachers in the areas of bilingual education, special education and English as a second language (ESL). Beyond this, there is the unfortunate, stark contrast in demography between teachers and students in urban contexts. Zimpher (1989), a member of the RATE research team, portrayed prospective teachers in the United States generally as female, of Anglo descent, speaking only English and travelling less than 100 miles to attend college. The typical prospective teacher is raised in a small-town, surburban or rural setting, and wants to teach in a similar location. In fact this 'typical' teacher does not wish to teach students in a pluralistic setting or in a school that is organized in other than a traditional manner.

Ken Howey, one of the authors of this chapter, has for the last decade directed a network of partnership in over 30 urban settings across the United States dedicated to improving the recruitment, preparation and retention of teachers for these school communities. This confederation is known as the Urban Network to Improve Teacher Education (UNITE). Linda Post, the co-author, has now assumed co-directorship of this urban network. The hub of the network is the Milwaukee partnership where both authors are on the teaching staff of the School of Education at the University of Wisconsin–Milwaukee (UWM). Drawing on the best of practices and policies across UNITE, they are developing a prototype for urban teacher preparation in Milwaukee.

Guiding theory of teacher education

Two salient propositions guide the theory or ideology of teacher development, the notion of teacher education as an ongoing process and aspects of teacher preparation, which the authors were asked to address. The first proposition is that pre-service preparation has an overarching twofold mission: 1) to socialize novice teachers in collaborative structures so that their teaching is public (open to examination by others), and they are generally disposed to learn with and from their colleagues; and 2) to provide them with core strategies for learning to teach over time, on the job and with others. The second proposition is that effective teaching is best understood as a highly intellectual, problem-oriented and largely clinical endeavour – that is, if conducted properly. Teachers who can justify their teaching decisions with principled arguments and data, especially data derived from analyses of their effects on learners, are superior to other teachers. Howey (1997) reminded his readers that repeated studies have demonstrated glaring shortcomings when pre-service preparation does not fully take these propositions into account.

Limited and often misguided professional socialization in the abbreviated structure of pre-service preparation has led to countless examples of beginning teachers who are disposed to teach and plan alone. Negative enculturation in their early years of teaching reinforces this. The initial technical skills acquired by beginners commonly find no sustaining fit with the complexities of full-time teaching. Because novices have few abiding strategies for robust learning on the job and, most fundamentally, do not engage in professional discourse around teaching and learning, they are severely stunted as professionals. In order to redress these common short-comings in the United States, the urban prototype has put in place both distinctive inter-institutional collaboration and new infrastructures within the university designed to accomplish the following six interrelated goals:

1. enabling a new and more powerful P–16 (pre-school to grade 16) urban partnership governance arrangement;
2. implementing strategies to recruit both a more competent and a more diverse teaching force;
3. strengthening urban teacher education as an all-university endeavour;
4. achieving fundamental improvements in an array of professional programmes targeted for teachers in urban schools;
5. extending urban teacher preparation in a seamless manner into the first year(s) of teaching;
6. addressing both ends of the teacher education continuum simultaneously.

Teacher preparation too often is ineffective because of its abbreviated nature and its disconnection from the best of pre-school to grade 12 (hereafter P–12) practice. Simultaneous and aligned reform in the preparation of teachers should begin in general studies, proceed through professional programmes and continue programmatically into the first years of teaching.

The control of teacher education: stronger shared governance and mutual responsibility

A priority of the first order was to have the leaders of all of the organizations in the urban community with a vested interest in teacher quality meet on a regular basis. Their overarching mission is to address long-standing, pervasive problems afflicting teacher quality. Typical partnership arrangements in the United States are at the individual school level in the form of partner or professional development schools. Many schools or colleges of education also have advisory boards. In this instance a non-profit entity, the Milwaukee Academy, was created with the following membership: the president of the university, the superintendent of schools, the executive director of the teachers union, the president of the school board, the president of the local community college, the executive director of the metropolitan Chamber of Commerce, the director of the Private Industry Council, other key officials in the school district and the deans of the schools of education and arts and sciences.

How a prevalent problem in urban schools has been addressed by this expanded governance structure should illustrate why it is necessary for the leaders of the above organizations to meet on a regular basis. As indicated at the outset, recruiting and preparing caring and competent teachers for urban contexts is a very formidable challenge. In addition, needed diversity is lacking in the teaching force. The situation in Milwaukee is not unlike that in many major US cities.

Almost 85 per cent of the youngsters in this urban setting are from historically under-represented populations but only about 15 per cent of the teachers are, and most of them do not live in the immediate neighbourhood community surrounding the school in which they teach. This flies in the face of what empirical research suggests about two critical aspects of good instruction. First, institutional plans should be guided by an understanding of the lives of youngsters outside of school. Second, these plans and the teaching that derives from them often have the power and transportability to engage learners outside the classroom in authentic applications in the home, community and workplace. The UNITE network abides by the adage that you cannot truly understand youngsters outside of the context of their families and you cannot understand families outside the context of their neighbourhoods, in this instance distinctive urban neighbourhoods. Thus, providing career paths for 'paraprofessionals' becomes a moral imperative, which should reflect a local contextual understanding of culture, community and youth that is essential to good teaching.

In order to develop a career path for many of the over 2,000 teaching aides and paraprofessionals who work in the Milwaukee schools, a collaborative strategy calling for action by all parties in the Milwaukee Academy was initiated. Many of the individuals in these support positions are women who have limited economic income and who are members of ethnic groups that have endured prejudice both historically and even today. They live in urban neighbourhoods and their children attend the city schools. In order for many of these individuals to become licensed teachers and eventually employed by the school district, all of the organizations and agencies represented have to assume coordinated, complementary responsibilities. For example, considerable scholarship money is needed, and business and industry represented by the Chamber of Commerce and the Private Industry Council have major responsibilities in terms of fund-raising and financial support.

The post-secondary institutions have multiple but different responsibilities. For example, changes have to be made to accommodate non-traditional students in terms of when courses can be offered, so that these individuals can continue to work as aides and also have adequate childcare. There are curriculum articulation agreements and shared advising arrangements, which need to be negotiated between the community college and the university. Both the teachers union and the school board have to come to an agreement on differential job descriptions, roles and responsibilities for aides at various stages of their preparation, with concomitant increases in salary. A strengthened entry year or support system for these individuals when they take on full-time responsibility as novice teachers needs to be put in place as well.

It is one thing to talk about pipeline strategies and going to scale in the face of massive shortages; it is quite another to put in place inter-organizational structures guided by a mutual vision, collective will and, yes, adequate resources to make this pipeline a reality over time. Enacting teacher education as a major partnership endeavour extending far beyond the reaches of a school of education is the cornerstone of the prototype. This brings us to a second building block, that of making teacher preparation truly an all-university responsibility.

Strengthening teacher education as an all-university endeavour

There are four major ways in which teacher preparation can be enriched and expanded as an all-university endeavour. The four ways include 1) content preparation, 2) emphasis on school in the urban community, 3) cross-college leadership and 4) cultural perspectives. In this section we will consider the first three, and the fourth will be examined in the next section.

There is a considerable need to expand the content preparation of prospective teachers, and especially elementary teachers. This is widely advocated among 'reformists' in the United States (National Commission on Teaching and America's Future, 1996). Actually a more potent strategy would be to reconceptualize the elementary teachers' role so that no teacher taught more than two subjects. Dual majors could accommodate this alternative strategy very well. There are, for example, expanding and compelling data that youngsters in the formative, first years of schooling learn best when they remain with a team of teachers who complement one another through a thoughtful division of labour around different school subjects or disciplines. The youngsters remain with these teachers over multiple years, engaged with fewer concepts and ideas but studied in greater depth and with multiple opportunities for application both in and out of school. Teachers are not prepared in this manner because most schools are not organized in this way, or is it the other way around? The lack of aligned renewal between the P–12 sector and higher education in terms of school culture and organization as well as curriculum standards and testing is ample evidence of the lack of genuine partnerships across the country.

The second way is an emphasis on school in the urban community in which teacher preparation is an all-university endeavour. Many urban US schools have inter-agency linkages. These typically are not what they could or should be; none the less, good models can be found. Urban schools structurally interacting with these various community agencies are commonly referred to as comprehensive or wraparound schools. They coordinate and sometimes house a range of health, social, family and legal services. Better inter-professional preparation, however, is the key to enhanced inter-organizational cooperation. Inter-professional preparation is an all-university responsibility in close coordination with other agencies such as those represented in the Milwaukee Academy.

A third way in which teacher education is an all-university endeavour is cross-college and departmental cooperation on leadership training for urban districts. A particular problem in urban schools is stable leadership. Again there is mounting evidence that leadership teams, founded on the notion of shared leadership and with a reasonable division of labour, contribute immeasurably to school-wide success (Sergiovanni, 1994). These leadership teams vary in responsiveness to local urban school communities. Typically they include the principal, teacher leaders, community / parent liaisons and media technologists. Teacher leaders are central to this concept as they have primary responsibility for instructional leadership. Again multiple academic units across the campus can cooperate with urban districts and the private sector to move to a bolder and more potent form of leadership preparation than typically is provided, and which can address the challenges and complexities of urban schools and their communities.

The fourth way, on cultural perspectives for teacher preparation as an all-university endeavour, is discussed in the next section.

Cultural perspectives

Cultural perspectives are also important for teacher preparation as an all-university endeavour, from a cultural perspective in which liberal studies can be used as a foundation for understanding the multiple cultures and communities that define large urban settings. This is especially important for those Caucasian, middle-class prospective teachers who invariably have grown up in contexts other than urban settings. In the teacher education prototype at UWM, we have proposed a core series of courses referred to as 'Cultures and communities'. This core is designed to ensure that students enrolled in these courses are positively socialized in a planned manner through interaction with a sustained cohort or persistent learning group, which is purposefully structured to reflect differences in race, culture, gender, age and background experience. The courses are being designed so that students will gain an understanding and appreciation of both local and global diversity through scholarly study and first-hand experience. These cohorts will also serve as a source of support as well as a collaborative study group on occasion.

This series of courses will examine community contexts and cultural diversity through such lenses as those provided by the historian, the sociologist, the cultural anthropologist, the political scientist and the urban geographer. Literature, the fine arts, architecture, business, engineering, religion and education pertain as well to acquiring multiple interpretations and understandings of urban community. In addition to the wealth of resources across the campus who will contribute in manifold ways to this series of courses, there is a great range of talented and dedicated individuals who will be incorporated into these courses from the community, ranging from chief education officers to community activists. It will be essential in order to maintain a dynamic interplay with the community to have widespread and continuing involvement with these individuals from the community in the planning and delivery of these courses. Often student learning experiences will extend out into the community and be responsive to community interests and needs. Thus, there will be a degree of reciprocity as well as interaction between the campus and the urban community. Ideally many in the community will contribute immeasurably to the curriculum and instruction, and students in turn will contribute through some of the learning experiences back to the community.

Addressing fundamental improvements in professional programmes

The authors will not dwell at length here on the major reforms undertaken in the professional programmes adapted specifically to preparing teachers for urban contexts. Lessons learnt in the UNITE network are summarized elsewhere (Howey, 1997). The following are just some of the common features of programmes designed specifically to prepare teachers for urban contexts:

- Involving prospective teachers in a range of collaborative problem-solving activities in the community and stressing the relationships between youngsters' activities in the community and those in school.
- Developing guiding programme frameworks that explicitly address a conception of teaching and learning to teach in urban city contexts. For example, powerful out-of-school peer socialization needs to be considered in the development of learning communities inside urban classrooms and

schools. Diversity is a value-added aspect of constructivist approaches to teaching, especially those incorporating dialectic forums.

- Identifying a reasonable number of key understandings and abilities relative to the urban community addressed in a thematic approach over time. A common theme, for example, is that urban teachers should continually examine relationships between language, learning and culture in and out of school and in a continuing manner.
- Developing core learning to teach strategies focused on common urban school communities. Examples are conducting case studies of urban youth and mapping the many assets of urban communities. The latter is especially critical, given the negative stereotyping of many urban neighbourhoods.
- Employing exemplary, veteran urban teachers not just to 'supervise' student teachers but also to design, develop and teach in coherent preservice programmes that ensure good articulation between campus and urban school and community.
- Integrating authentic assessments throughout, tied directly to novice teachers' developing beliefs about and abilities to work with diverse learners and with youngsters who don't reflect middle-class norms.

Urban teacher education as an ongoing process

Extending teacher preparation programmatically into the first years of teaching is the final leg in the three-legged stool representing a more robust and protracted form of teacher preparation. This entry-year programming is also tied directly to the sixth and final goal mentioned earlier, as it is addressing both ends of the teacher education continuum simultaneously. Earlier the major collaborative strategy of recruiting and preparing aides and paraprofessionals for teaching was addressed. A key to that plan is recruiting and preparing outstanding veteran teachers who will work with these paraprofessionals throughout their preparation and then mentor them in the first year(s) of their teaching assignment.

Thus, the Milwaukee prototype extends from recruitment to induction and includes leadership preparation for outstanding veteran teachers. Thus, it also addresses a career lattice incorporating aides, pre-service teachers, novice teachers, veteran teachers and lead teachers. This major reform presently engages 19 teachers in residence working in every aspect of the developing prototype. That is to say, they are involved in the revision of course content and the preparation for the core cultures and communities courses in the arts and sciences. They are instrumental in the reconceptualization of the array of urban professional preparation programmes and they are key to rethinking the induction year and mentor preparation.

In order to assume these multiple responsibilities, they have been seconded for a two-year period to the UWM campus. During this time they are also engaged in the co-construction of a teacher leadership preparation programme. This is a coherent series of graduate, credit-bearing courses designed to prepare them to assume a leadership role at the all-school level when they return to their urban school district. Eventually they will teach part time while assuming a variety of other leadership functions. They will have primary responsibility for all-school renewal.

There is a variety of approaches to mentoring and mentor preparation documented in the literature (Fideler and Haselkorn, 2000). In the Milwaukee prototype, mentors will serve in a linking or brokering role for the novice teachers. This linking function is an integrative change strategy, for while mentors or, better, lead teachers engage novices with a range of teachers and other staff in the school, they are at one and the same time developing a collaborative school culture, hence the integration. In such a school culture and organization, teaching is more public and open to investigation and scrutiny than it typically is, and there is a collective approach to addressing problems common to urban schools. As lead teachers, they will, for example, engage one colleague to help the novice or novices with understanding the local curriculum guides, another colleague to help with technology, a third to help with orientation and understanding of the local community and a fourth to assist with making sure the beginner understands the local norms and customs of the school, such as how to dress, when to leave, where to park and so forth.

In order to take on these new and expanded responsibilities, these teachers in residence regularly engage in leadership preparation designed to increase their effectiveness in 1) providing leadership in school renewal, 2) modelling powerful teaching and finding time for teachers to work together, 3) assisting with job-embedded professional development, and 4) engaging school with the urban community.

Conclusion

In summary, there has been ample documentation of the problems associated with recruiting, preparing and retaining competent teachers for urban schools. This prototype is grounded in a vision of preparing teachers to be disposed and having specific strategies to learn on the job over time. Lead teachers will help organize schools so that they enable teacher learning on the job, as well as pupil learning. The prototype is supported by an inter-organizational partnership with leaders of all vested parties meeting on a regular basis and committed to mutual reform. It incorporates, in multiple ways, resources across the entire university and the urban district. Finally, it addresses all phases of the teacher education continuum from recruitment of new teachers to specific preparation for outstanding veteran teachers. It focuses on developing a career lattice consistent with a dynamic and fluid school organization and culture, which research supports as enhancing student learning.

References

Fideler, E F and Haselkorn, D (2000) *Learning the Ropes: Urban teacher induction programs and practices in the United States*, Recruiting New Teachers, Boston, MA

Howey, K R (1997) School-focused teacher education: issues to address, *Association of Teacher Educators Newsletter*, **4**, November–December, Reston, VA

National Center for Educational Studies (1994) *Schools and Staffing in the United States: A statistical profile*, US Department of Education, Washington, DC

National Commission on Teaching and America's Future (1996) *What Matters Most: Teaching for America's future*, US Department of Education, New York

Rentel, V M and Dittmer, A (1999) *Themes and Issues in Faculty Development: Case studies of innovative practice in teacher education*, University Press of America, New York

Sergiovanni, T (1994) *Building Community in Schools*, California UP, San Francisco

Zimpher, N L (1989) The RATE project: a profile of teacher education students, *Journal of Teacher Education*, **40** (6), pp 27–30

21. Borderless education: a new teaching model for United Kingdom higher education

Anita Pincas

Introduction

The task of the UK university teacher greatly increased in range and complexity over the last decade. Not only were additional administrative duties required, but new information, communication and technology (ICT) skills had to be learnt very quickly. Since higher education can no longer be seen as a sequestered academe, universities cannot remain isolated from social change, secure behind a brick cloister protecting intellectual exclusivity. Their physical and abstract walls have been breached, so that it is now impossible to draw the old borderlines between universities and other providers of learning. These changes are caused by social-economic shifts and by the new digital technologies, which have also opened many gateways. Higher education (HE) has become borderless in several ways:

- Universities' formerly special knowledge is now provided by others.
- Their activities are being made ever more transparent and accountable.
- Students and teachers have access to one another without constraints of space or time.

Academic teachers have no choice but to adjust to these enormous changes, particularly to the new structures of management they entail. In the United Kingdom there have been many initiatives designed to retrain university staff, but the process is proving to be time-consuming, protracted and painful. The next decade will see many different efforts to provide effective teaching with the help of ICT. More and more universities will strive to sell Internet courses globally, and maintain a distinction of quality between themselves and corporates. Worldwide virtual teaching is already accepted. Pedagogic alternatives in this borderless environment will present a rich source of ongoing debates for many years to come.

In this chapter a brief background to recent qualitative changes in UK higher education will be presented, followed by an overview of the socio-cultural changes in education. An examination will then be made of the areas of ICT and pedagogy, which are identified as the key dilemmas for teachers in British higher education. The chapter will conclude with a discussion of future prospects, and a model that can assist pedagogy using ICT.

The background

In the United Kingdom, all academics are expected to publish research papers to support their university's rating in the government's regular Research Assessment Exercises (RAE). At the same time, they collaborate both internally and externally in the drive to innovate attractive course offerings for home and overseas 'markets', and participate in focus and foresight groups, course team meetings and special seminars. They are asked to provide increasingly substantial formative as well as summative feedback to their students, with whom they must improve their relationships generally, but always being careful to keep detailed records of encounters. It is understood that they will manage their budgets, where possible including consultancy and research projects, and provide a large range of management information. It goes without saying that they will keep abreast of progress in their subject, and will strive to improve their own pedagogy while participating in regular peer reviews and self-assessment exercises.

At the same time, they are inspected by the Higher Education Funding Council's Quality Assurance Agency (QAA), which makes their institution's score public. The QAA:

> provides an integrated quality assurance service for higher education institutions in the UK using an assessment method [combining] self-assessment by the institution with visits by trained external assessors, inspecting six aspects of the learning experience and its outcomes: curriculum design and organization, teaching, learning and assessment, student progression and achievement, student support and guidance, learning resources, and quality management and enhancement. (QAA, 2001)

Many believe that the establishment of the government-sponsored Institute for Learning and Teaching in Higher Education (ILT), a professional body for people who teach, support learning and contribute significantly to the development and maintenance of learning environments, will help to rationalize the role and status of university teachers. It encourages membership, based on passing an accredited course (there are now over 80 available across the UK university sector) or showing evidence of experience and good practice. All new staff will be expected to undertake training. Thus for the first time, academics are in a similar position to school teachers.

The ILT reference to 'learning environments' presupposes the borderlessness of universities. There are many off-campus environments in which university learning can take place: the workplace, allied institutions of many kinds, the home and, of course, the virtual environment. In fact ICT has so greatly facilitated the expansion of educational opportunity that the UK government recently published a document called *The Business of Borderless Education* (CVCP, 2000), followed by a consultation document on information, communications and media (Hemmings, 2000). They are linked to the proposal for a business model for the e-university prepared by a multinational accountancy and management consultancy firm, PricewaterhouseCoopers (2000). At the same time, the last years of the 20th century saw many millions of pounds being spent on numerous central and local government initiatives, designed to develop education skills in ICT at all levels and sectors, as well as in the population at large.

Many governments across the world are likewise pouring resources into this area, and what we see in the UK is replicated elsewhere: the large-scale interpenetration of business and education where corporations, especially those dependent on increased use of digital technologies, are seeking to be involved in teaching well beyond their traditional concerns. Education is therefore increasingly dependent on ICT and open to corporate oversight and initiatives. Some corporations will take a much more pragmatic approach than schools or universities normally do. They are greatly concerned with keeping pace with the growth of relevant knowledge. At university level, they are likely to limit research contracts to areas they have a market for and where findings can be patented.

All these developments, however, need to be viewed in the light of the socio-cultural changes that have occurred within education. Let us briefly survey some of these changes before discussing the dilemmas that may be associated with them.

Socio-cultural changes in education

Probably the most significant social changes are the increasingly multicultural nature of societies across the world, economic globalization and the intensification of the new electronic information and communication technologies. All the above interact with one another in the context of education. Multiculturalism undermines older views of educational systems as transmission agents for the nation-state, and requires that courses are relevant to a range of contexts rather than being discussions of theoretical principles. Economic changes mean that borders between disciplines and professional knowledge are shifting as professional experience takes a central role. Employers are now influencing the curriculum, knowledge being seen as relevant for work rather than as a valued intellectual goal. Moreover, ICT is enabling people to turn more easily to public information as their source of just-in-time learning. As a direct consequence, knowledge has to a large extent also been dissociated from teachers or accepted scholarly texts.

Thus we see a change in the kinds of expertise that university teachers and their trainers must demonstrate if they are to maintain demand for their courses. The state needs to produce workers who can act independently of locality, often with globally defined work practices from other cultures, and this includes academics among them. Learners have come to be seen as knowledge seekers rather than students being taught by traditional methods. In this sense, they have now become more significant in the educational process than the teacher. The term 'education' is being replaced by 'learning', and 'teacher' by 'facilitator' or 'mentor'. Lecturers are now said not so much to teach but to 'support' learners, thus presupposing that students become independent and preferably autonomous. This is of course a logical consequence of the acceptance of group learning, peer collaboration and constructivist learning theories. It provides a theoretical justification for placing the burden of learning on students rather than on the teacher. It almost seems as if universities can only survive in the new conditions if students teach themselves.

We are seeing the growth of new cultures of learning and new communities of practice as individuals and communities are digitally networked in a globalized education 'market'. Universities are trying to reach this market, at least partly as e-universities, either alone or in consortia. Academics – experienced and new – now have to come to grips with different kinds of learning, both in their own methods and in the way they are preparing their students for diverse learning. In other words, they have to see beyond the borders of their universities to the workplace and to everyday life.

The key dilemmas

Educators thus face the dilemmas of wishing to maintain their traditional values, while under pressure to keep pace with the times and to adapt their pedagogy to change and innovation. To what extent can they allow business interests to override their academic concerns? To what extent are they in a position to reject the financial help that business offers? Most crucially, to what extent is it correct to assume that business involvement will have a negative effect on educational standards? Behind the dilemma is the ever-present importance of ICT and the role of pedagogy in this new environment. This section deals first with the dilemma surrounding ICT and the problems of pedagogy.

The gradual penetration of ICT into the UK education system has proceeded along different paths at the different levels. For primary schools, ICT started by enlivening the learning process with multimedia but is now accepted as contributing to artistic, literacy and learning skills, especially when used in group work. At upper levels, the emphasis shifts towards the information resources available on the WWW for subject learning and project work. There is widespread use of e-mail for links between individuals and schools. In higher education ICT has had a predominantly information focus, to help supplement library resources. At the same time, there has been a small but now rapidly growing trend to foster collaborative learning by Internet both in distance education and on campus. Since the late 1980s, asynchronous online discussions as part of course design have been gaining attention, aided by the ever-increasing software solutions for teaching on the WWW.

Innovations of the 1990s have resulted in an explosion of new learning initiatives such as the Teaching and Learning Technology Programme (TLTP, 1996) and the Computers in Teaching Initiative (CTI). Today, many universities as well as commercial enterprises are offering at least some fully Web-based courses, as well as mixed-media courses (both distance and on-campus), including CDs, video cassettes, print materials, face-to-face meetings, e-mail and videoconferencing. As would be expected, there has been a growing literature in the field of online learning, starting with Hiltz and Turoff's (1993) ground-breaking *The Network Nation*, originally published in 1978. Academics who previously took the traditional modes of instruction for granted (albeit not without dissatisfaction) are now debating different learning models in ways that were formerly the province of education faculties. Nevertheless, only insignificant attention is as yet given to the use of computers in classrooms, and a call for ICT in the lecture or seminar as opposed to the laboratory (Saunders, 2000) has to be seen as highly innovative, even revolutionary.

ICT is also having a small but growing effect on assessment procedures, since automated feedback and marking are now possible, both in computer laboratories and on the WWW (TRIADS, 2001). For distance education, they are seen by many as an alternative provision of formative feedback, thus holding down staff support requirements. For on-campus work they are often seen as a device to assist tutorial input by lecturers (Gannon, 2001). However, besides the need to reskill teachers in HE, the problems posed by ICT are fundamentally pedagogic, and as such have to take account of the wider context of social and economic change that is loosely pulled together under the term 'globalization'. This has contributed to fundamental socio-cultural shifts, and the perception of education as 'borderless' in geographical, epistemological and methodological senses.

There is at present a real danger that the new paradigm of the autonomous learner will be widely accepted for HE. This would constitute a radical break from traditional and well-understood concretely situated teaching modes. It would be a negation of the long history of education that all cultures have experienced. But the blueprint for the UK government-funded e-university is almost exclusively concerned with the quality of the resources and materials – mostly text – provided on the WWW (PricewaterhouseCoopers, 2000). This paradigm sees the demise of the teacher except as facilitator, and also the demise of the classroom. Learners, it is claimed, will have the benefits of independence, being left free to work in their own style at their own pace whenever and wherever is convenient for them.

A further 'edutopian' consequence may even transform the teacher into an automaton. Instead of human teachers, 'intelligent' software is being conceived to support educational dialogue. Such software will respond to and converse with learners, building up a profile of an individual's learning needs, perhaps sending new information to the learner's desktop every time he or she logs on to the Internet. It will present information according to the learner's own requests, provide practice material as and when required, correct the learner's mistakes, propose further avenues of learning and so forth. Thus, learners will be unconstrained by a pre-imposed syllabus, receiving automated formative feedback, and will exit with a qualification automatically titled to suit the topic. Serious research is under way to produce the underlying 'knowledge management' systems that will be required, that is, to identify and classify knowledge so that parcels of digital learning can be automatically realigned to suit individual learner needs.

At present, commercial interests are leading the way with short, sharp learning experiences in anything from business skills to more homely subjects like how to iron a shirt or lose weight. The courses are written to be easily followed by independent students for whom the help is often no more than a list of frequently asked questions (FAQ). An accessible example is BBC Online, which is in close collaboration with the UK Open University (OU) for joint development of Web-based learning opportunities for the general public, such as the recently launched first aid course developed jointly with a well-respected ambulance service. Recognizing that people need help in developing ICT and independent learning skills, specially equipped drop-in centres are being established where some tutorial assistance will be available.

Longer university courses on the WWW have thus far also consisted mainly of 'text online' (called 'lectures' by many institutions). These are traditional distance materials placed on the WWW with audio or graphic enhancements where appropriate. Discussion opportunities are normally offered but not usually made essential. It is assumed that students will be able to address questions to a tutor, who is not necessarily the specialist who wrote the materials.

It therefore appears as if borderless education of this kind can be cheaply delivered. Overheads are reduced by the lesser need for classrooms and other facilities, libraries are digitized to save physical space, and students become autonomous learners both on and off campus. Where course materials already exist, they are placed on Web pages for learners to retrieve, thus reducing the need for books or journals. In these ways, institutions can certainly provide 'university education' at dramatically lower cost than by traditional teaching methods. But it is far from self-evident that such courses are of equal value to traditional ones. It was clear from older distance education, with its low completion rates, that too many learners are not prepared to sustain autonomous learning over longer periods.

The dilemma for academics is whether to accept that WWW education should be based on a distance education model. There, an isolated learner worked through texts, receiving individual formative guidance from a remote tutor. Now, the model is enhanced by rapid student–tutor e-mail communication, by automated feedback and by the opportunity to share some aspects of the learning with fellow students if the course is in lock-step mode. But it is still the same model; there is no teaching in it. Fears have been expressed that academics will become materials writers, and that their work will be used by universities as saleable property over which they will ultimately lose control. To keep costs down, senior subject experts will not be used as tutors; these will be recent graduates.

The reaction has been either to try to resist the digitization of education or to improve the quality of the materials by adding, for instance, filmed lectures by well-known specialists. Videoconferencing is slowly becoming more common as a forum for students and tutors, but has the disadvantage of being time-bound. Some, like the UK Open University, have added a limited amount of face-to-face teaching, but this is clearly impractical for widespread global education. Others are therefore attempting to write special Web-oriented content and instructional material in a multimedia format that genuinely takes advantage of computing power. This is a lengthy, specialized, not-yet-well-understood and therefore much more expensive undertaking. It can only succeed with competent management of team effort among subject specialists, technical staff and academics experienced in online teaching. The numerous projects funded under the UK government's TLTP initiative during the 1990s have given considerable impetus to this movement.

But much remains to be understood, notably how teaching can be integral to, or integrated with, these materials. However lively and attractive they may be, however skilfully they may create the impression of a teacher addressing a student, materials as such are not courses. Whether the independent learning approach will succeed is an empirical question. Theoretically, because it does not take account of what is obvious about learning, one could expect it to survive for short 'just-in-time' learning, but to fail for the kind of sustained, academic or vocational learning that higher education offers. The next section bases a sketch of some realistic solutions to these dilemmas on an understanding of human learning processes in the changing context of what the technology of the future can provide.

Prospects and solutions

First, the distinction should be made between three major learning styles. The most systematic is the teacher–classroom–pupil style. It occurs in some form in most cultures, though the processes inside the classrooms may differ widely. Somewhat less systematic is apprenticeship, where a learner works closely with a skilled person, receiving informal instruction as required. Finally, there is the informal learning of everyday life, of which most people are perhaps not fully aware. This daily learning often depends on reading instructions or simply 'working things out'.

The last method is the 'just-in-time' kind in which people are accustomed to act independently and which is being very effectively assisted by information and short courses on the WWW. However, for more sustained learning needs, the role of other people has always been an essential part of common experience. This kind of learning is a deeply social process, involving models, mentors, teachers and other learners. All investigations of the learning process point to the important role of teachers and of social, cooperative or collaborative learning (Askew and Carnell, 1998). All societies have long and successful histories of oral explanation, of 'educational dialogue' of various kinds (Laurillard, 1993). Even the lecture has its place as an often very efficient method of explication of subject matter. The teacher's oral explanatory discourse shapes the learning experience.

It would seem fatuous to discard the pedagogic traditions and insights that most societies have developed during centuries of experimentation and for higher education to ignore the evidence and instead try to restructure student learning habits. We are likely to be more successful if we use technology to replicate what people already can do, and to enable them to use the skills they already have. This is as true for academic teachers as for their students. The technological method that allows them to build on familiar, tested modes of teaching and learning is likely to engage them more easily and more successfully.

The solution to the university dilemma is therefore most likely to be found in a replication of existing procedures. And this is now possible with the benefits of the Internet. We can combine its communication facilities with its information resources to create a virtual copy of our familiar contexts of learning. We can bring people together synchronously or asynchronously, visually, aurally and through text, without restriction of place or time. Thus, we can at last develop truly virtual learning environments (VLEs), which will probably be similar in many ways to those in computer games.

The author has already used a 'replication model' of virtual learning with simple technologies for an international Master's programme at the University of London, Institute of Education since 1994 (Pincas, 2001). It has shown an average of 90 per cent completion rates. Its strength is that it enables learners to feel as if they are in a classroom with other people, even when they are elsewhere with only a computer. Future technology will make it even more truly virtual. The replication model contains the accepted and acceptable teaching and learning practices familiar in universities across the world. It uses a lock-step syllabus and timetable in order to develop the virtual learning community. Lectures are provided as filmed classroom events provided on the WWW, CDs or cassettes, though occasionally as synchronous videoconferences where convenient. In either case, they are supported by very structured workshop or seminar discussions using asynchronous e-mail or computer conferencing software. Tutorial support, for individuals and groups, again using asynchronous e-mail or computer conferencing, is integral to the design. Since it incorporates teaching in the films, such a course does not require contrived instructional Web materials, but uses already existing written texts. This VLE creates a feeling of presence in a university learning space mediated by a combination of films and personal contacts that give an illusion of 'being there together'.

The attested value of the replication model is just that it brings otherwise isolated individuals into a learning community. It uses well-tried structures that are designed to assist and encourage learners to share their experiences and support one another in maintaining commitment to the pace of an ongoing course. The key to its success is the effective scaffolding of collaborative learning events and, especially, of the student–student–tutor discussions. Properly implemented, the model pushes communication towards a new form of discourse in the computer environment. The future will add many further dimensions, for instance the use of films available on demand, which can be stopped, started and replayed, as well as enhanced by interactivity and links to other resources. Delivery will be enriched by advances in knowledge management but will not be either transmissive or based on autonomous learning. The model fosters discussion and therefore also a spirit of inquiry and critical thinking.

It has in fact been shown that it is possible to create a satisfactory VLE through dialogue alone, as long as there is an abstract framework for a virtual community of learners and teachers. The present author's Certificate in Online Education and Training (Pincas, 2001) and the computer-supported cooperative learning model initiated at the University of Lancaster (McConnell, 2000) are two examples. Both use asynchronous, but well-structured, written communication without the benefit of filmed inputs. In both cases, participants value the virtual learning community that is created. The training that UK academics would require for the replication model is far simpler than any attempt to implement an ingenious new paradigm of teaching and learning. It can shift known practice smoothly into a new environment.

Let us now return to the three aspects of borderless education that were presented at the start of this chapter, namely 1) new provision of knowledge, 2) transparency and accountability and 3) access learning without constraints of space or time.

Lecturers will need to familiarize themselves with the knowledge available on the WWW and with various search engines to find it. They will have to evaluate for themselves whether existing resources can be incorporated into their own courses, or whether, if not, they wish to retain the use of textbooks and other materials rather than preparing new Web resources themselves. If they pursue work-based learning, they will need to develop new expertise themselves or learn to collaborate with workplace mentors.

Digitization of text and video has both the advantage and disadvantage of leaving a permanent record. Academic teachers may have to accustom themselves to highly visible 'performance', rather than the evanescence of the spoken word. Already, Web materials are subject to organized institutional editing or other scrutiny in a way that oral teaching never was. But since self-assessment, peer review and team teaching are now common, lecturers will need to learn to present themselves in improved ways, and the new transparency may bring many benefits. However, the eccentric scholar in tattered clothes and open sandals may be left in peace with traditional, on-campus students.

Academics will need to develop course designs that hold their workloads at acceptable limits. If student collaboration is combined with pre-filmed lectures, as in the replication model already described, they need not fear a constant deluge of e-mail messages. In fact in that model, the academic's task is somewhat lighter than in traditional teaching. Creating new systems to deal with routine tasks will further improve the situation.

Global communication will demand understanding of diverse cultural and linguistic backgrounds. UK universities have developed considerable sensitivity to the needs of overseas students, supported by the United Kingdom Council for Overseas Student Affairs (UKCOSA). But the new educational colonization will require courses to be as culture- and value-free as possible. Universities will also need to accept that, while English is the dominant international language, many do not find 'standard English' useful or even valuable.

The HE training being developed under the ILT umbrella will in time develop in range and depth to encompass e-learning as well as traditional teaching. Research into methods of teaching at this level have lagged behind other educational research, but are given a new impetus in the present climate of innovation. HE, like virtual teaching, is in a state of flux and transition. But the future holds promise that the university academic's task will become a renewed pleasure.

References

Askew, S and Carnell, E (1998) *Transforming Learning: Individual and global change*, University of London, Institute of Education/Cassell, London

Committee of Vice-Chancellors and Principals of the Universities of the UK (CVCP) and Higher Education Funding Council for England (2000) *The Business of Borderless Education: UK perspectives*, Summary report, Higher Education Funding Council for England (HEFCE), http//www.cvcp.ac.uk

Gannon, M (2001) Advanced composition with computers, A course offered by the University of South Dakota, USA, http//www.usd.edu/engl/gannon_ac.html

Hemmings, P (ed) (2000) *Foresight: Making the future work for you*, Information, Communications and Media (ICM) Panel, The Learning Process in 2020 Task Force, Department of Trade and Industry, UK, http://www.foresight.gov.uk

Hiltz, S R and Turoff, M (1993) *The Network Nation: Human communication via computer reading*, MIT Press, Cambridge, MA

Laurillard, D (1993) *Rethinking University Teaching*, Routledge, London

McConnell, D (2000) *Implementing Computer Supported Cooperative Learning*, 2nd edn, Kogan Page, London

Pincas, A (2001) http://www.ioe.ac.uk/english/Apincas.htm

PricewaterhouseCoopers (2000) *Business Model for the E-university*, Higher Education Funding Council for England, Bristol, http://www.hefce.ac.uk

QAA (2001) Extract, http://www.hefce.ac.uk/learning/quality/quality.htm

Saunders, G (2000) *Getting Started with On-line Learning*, Learning Partners, UK

TLTP (1996) The impact of TLTP, *Active Learning*, **4**, pp 3–5

Tripartite Interactive Assessment Delivery System (TRIADS) (2001) http://www.derby.ac.uk/ciad/lough99pr.html

22. Teacher education in India: status, problems and prospects

V K Raina

Introduction

In this chapter we will examine a number of key areas related to the status, problems and prospects of teacher education in India. The first part of the chapter will examine the context to current issues underlying Indian teacher education, and this will be followed by a more detailed discussion of the structure and processes that affect the training and status of teachers. The author will further examine the relevance of programmes and the role of teachers in urban and rural areas. The final part of the chapter will identify the future prospects for teacher education with reference to the creation of new institutions for improving the quality of teaching in the country.

The context

India is a land of paradoxes. While on the one hand it can claim a high level of industrial and technological progress, on the other hand a good number of its people – roughly 30 per cent – still live below the poverty line (CSO, 1995) and roughly 48 per cent of its population is illiterate (Premi, 1991). Similarly, there are some cities like Bangalore and Hyderabad, which are internationally known for the production of computer software, often hailed as being the 'silicon valley' of India, yet there are places like Kalhandi and Sabarkantha where people do not get two square meals a day. While India can be proud of its good number of institutions of higher learning, such as the Indian institutes of technology, at the same time a vast number of its primary schools are still ill equipped and impoverished. Even though the country and its constitution are strongly committed to promoting social and economic justice, the fact remains that we are not as yet fully free from caste and gender disparities.

Although a major achievement of our education system since independence is its incredible expansion (Adiseshiah, 1986), the country so far has not been able to fulfil its constitutional commitment to provide free and compulsory elementary education to all the children in the age group 6 to 14 years.

Historically also, it has been observed that the singular characteristic of Indian tradition, as Verma (1997) points out, is that the past and the present are not divided in historical fragments but are integral and intimate parts of the same flow. Culturally, tradition in India is not seen merely as memory of time past, which is kept safely in a museum and got rid off. On the contrary, tradition actively and creatively intervenes in all its contemporary conflicts and concerns. Thus, the Indian nation during the post-independence years has made rapid advances in various fields, including school and teacher education. However, as with the national scene, the field of school and teacher education also reflects similar kinds of paradoxes and dilemmas, and yet looks forward to vibrant changes and progress.

After the defence services, teachers in India constitute the largest workforce. The number of teachers and all those involved in the teacher education system of India may be one of the largest in the world, having more than 4.5 million teachers in over 0.6 million primary schools and 0.17 million secondary schools (Walia and Rajput, 2000). Table 22.1 shows the number of male and female teachers, and the percentage of trained teachers, working at the primary, middle, secondary and higher secondary level.

There is a large network of institutions, both pre-service and in-service, responsible for the preparation of teachers. Such institutions function nationally, regionally and at state and district levels. Let us examine each: first pre-service preparation and then in-service training.

Every year more than 2,000 (1,200 primary and approximately 800 secondary) teacher training institutions prepare 200,000 trained teachers through pre-service teacher education programmes. Nearly 90 per cent of teachers in schools possess a training qualification acquired either before joining the system or during their in-service period. The spread of trained teachers and training institutions in the country is not uniform. Several states, particularly in the north-eastern region, have a paucity of trained teachers, while in certain other states the percentage of trained teachers is around 97 to 98 per cent. While there is a surplus of trained teachers in certain regions, others are struggling to prepare more trained teachers using various alternative strategies. Added to this, the regional diversities, cultural pluralities and geographical variations confront

Table 22.1 Number of school teachers in India (in millions)

Stage	Male	Female	Total	Percentage of Trained Teachers
Primary	1.20	0.59	1.79	88
Middle	0.77	0.43	1.20	88
Secondary	0.60	0.33	0.93	89
Higher Secondary	0.41	0.21	0.62	89
Total	2.98	1.56	4.54	88

Source: Selected Educational Statistics 1996–97, Ministry of Human Resource Development, Government of India, New Dehli

the system with unique problems. Pre-service teacher training is provided through the university departments of education, colleges of education affiliated to the universities, and primary teacher training institutions managed and recognized by the state governments. All training qualifications are either approved by the universities or by the state level agencies.

The government of India continues to be a major player in the field of education by providing large-scale funds and policy directions. Teacher training institutions are at present either assisted by the state governments and universities or are dependent solely on the fees levied on the trainees. The number of self-financed institutions has grown and this trend is likely to continue in the future. The government of India has also assisted the state governments by providing resources for staff, equipment and other support under the centrally sponsored scheme for restructuring and strengthening teacher education.

The existing programmes of elementary teacher preparation are recognized and approved by the state governments or state-identified agencies. The secondary stage programmes are given recognition and approval by the various universities. At the pre-school stage, the situation regarding the recognition of institutions is different. There are a large number of private institutions providing training for nursery and pre-school stages with no mechanism to approve and recognize their qualifications. A major factor responsible for this situation is the lack of state-sponsored learning centres for the pre-school stage.

The admissions to the teacher training institutions are usually made on the basis of marks obtained in the qualifying examination at the school or university. In some institutions, admissions are made on the basis of specifically designed entrance tests. It has been found that not all of those who seek admission to pre-service teacher preparation programmes are necessarily interested in teaching. It has been realized that the pre-service teacher preparation is not an end in itself, and does not provide an all-time expertise to the teachers. The National Policy on Education (MHRD, 1986a) and various commissions have very strongly supported an ongoing in-service teacher education programme updating the professional competence of teachers.

The pre-service education programmes for teachers face some interesting paradoxes. These programmes have been primarily designed as induction programmes for fresh graduates. A large number of Indian states, as Parhar and Mukhopadhyay (1999) point out, offer the same induction programme to both fresh candidates and working teachers. In other words, the same inputs are offered at pre-service and in-service levels, despite leading to different qualification and certification. By default, it fails to derive the strength from the experience of the teachers that in-service education can.

Another important paradox is the variation in emphasis. The maximum emphasis is on pre-service education for teachers for the primary and secondary level. This is evident from the well-laid-out institutional network, clearer policies about duration, curriculum structure and compulsion on pre-service education as a required qualification for teaching. Becoming a teacher at the elementary and senior secondary levels is covered by the same degree (the BEd) more by default than by design. In most of the states, pre-service teacher training is not a required qualification for teaching at the senior secondary grades. One of the possible reasons for this could be that the senior secondary classes are also held in the degree-awarding colleges and in some states, like Haryana, Uttar Pradesh and West Bengal, teacher training is not a prerequisite for college teachers. The status of the in-service education of pre-primary teachers and that of higher professional teachers is quite different. For pre-primary teachers, the desirability of pre-service education has been well acknowledged, though this is not compulsory for primary education. The debate on the desirability and relevance of pre-service education at the higher and professional level continues.

Teachers in India are hired for teaching at various school stages like primary (including upper primary), secondary and senior secondary. The primary and upper primary stage are referred to as the elementary stage, which consists of eight years of schooling. This is followed by two years each of the secondary and senior secondary stages. Those appointed to teach at the elementary stage are required to have 12 years of schooling, followed by two years of pre-service training in a teacher training institution. The teachers of the secondary stage are required to be graduates, having had 12 years of schooling and three years in college or university followed by one year of teacher training. Those teaching at the senior secondary stage are supposed to possess a two-year postgraduate qualification in their respective disciplines. The nature of the one-year teacher training programme largely remains the same for both the secondary and senior secondary stage.

At the primary stage, while a large number of teachers are qualified and trained, the number of those who are under-trained, under-qualified or ill trained is also considerable. Teacher effectiveness at the primary stage suffers considerably because of certain practical factors like the inevitability of multi-grade teaching. There are nearly 130,000 primary schools that were once single-teacher schools but have now become two-teacher schools. The two-teacher schools look after all the instructional needs and requirements of children of the first five grades. This improvement has been possible because of a massive scheme launched by the central government, to support more than 0.5 million primary schools in terms of staff, equipment and other infra-structural support. This scheme, which provided the single-teacher schools with an additional teacher, is popularly known as 'Operation Blackboard'. Attempts are also being made, through use of alternative and innovative in-service programmes, to upgrade the qualification and competence of teachers to make use of new teaching strategies.

The teachers in India, besides classroom teaching, also have to undertake several other responsibilities like participating in literacy drives, family-planning programmes and census activity. The secondary teachers may also have to teach subject areas other than the ones in which they are professionally competent. This is usually because of the non-availability of adequately qualified teachers. Conditions such as these often exercise a demotivating influence on teachers, and reduce their effectiveness and sometimes even interest.

Teachers also often work under compelling circumstances and with serious handicaps. It would be easy to find primary teachers who may not have seen the prescribed curriculum and the syllabus before they start teaching. Moreover, there are several distinctions between the working conditions of primary and secondary teachers. In comparison with primary school teachers, secondary school teachers are somewhat better placed in their access to reading materials and libraries. Secondary schools, often being located in urban areas and small towns, provide better opportunities for teachers to interact, get information and enhance their awareness as compared to the primary teachers. The existing situation at the primary stage warrants greater attention and inputs. However, it is somewhat encouraging to note that the focus of educational planners has shifted to the primary stage in view of the national resolve to achieve universalization of elementary education and also to ensure acceptable levels of quality at this level. During the past few years, under the 'Operation Blackboard' scheme, every primary school has been provided with some reading material for the children.

The quality of teacher education often heavily depends on both the physical and financial resources and on the professional and academic capabilities available in teacher training institutions. Gunnar Myrdal (1971), in his famous book *Asian Dilemma*, identified these institutions as 'power plants' for generating labour. However, the reality remains that teacher education has not assumed the requisite status as a profession like engineering, medicine, law or business management. The community and parents also do not attach as much importance to the teachers as they ought to do. Even within the larger field of school and teacher education, it is the schools and their problems that get greater recognition and importance than the teacher preparation institutions. One may explain this phenomenon in India and other developing countries as a part of sociopolitical neglect. While school and teachers in these countries have greater political visibility, teacher training institutions and teacher educators do not enjoy such status. Analysing teachers and teacher educators in developing countries, Dove (1986) observed that building schools is often a highly popular measure. There is usually a blaze of publicity when a new school is built. In contrast, the training of teachers is a behind-the-scenes process, without much scope for dramatic popular gestures. Apart from the general apathy towards the teacher preparation institutions, there are some endemic and deeper problems that the teachers and teacher education system in India suffer from. These problems are not in any case new but they continue to plague the system.

It is indeed paradoxical that while several ancient texts and folk stories speak volumes about the high status teachers enjoyed in India in the past, the status of teachers at present is rather low. Status is very much linked to salaries but is not exclusively influenced by them. To some extent the low status of teachers in India is a result of lower entry requirements, shorter training periods and considerably lower salaries than those for professionals with comparable training and experience. Low salaries and few opportunities, as Lockheed and Verspoor (1990) observe, affect both teacher morale and their status amongst other professionals, as well as their teaching performance. This contributes to the relatively high annual rate of teacher attrition, which in some states reaches 9 or 10 per cent. Part of the reason for the low status of teachers, as Kumar (1991) has pointed out, is that the academic challenge involved in teaching children has not been well recognized. While teaching at the college level was perceived as an intellectual job, teaching in schools was treated as on a par with low-ranking office jobs. Secondary teaching was somewhat less spoilt by this association because it was closer to college-level education. The association was thus at its strongest at the primary level and, since teachers in this category were far greater in number than those working at secondary and college levels, it was they who shaped the popular view of teaching as a low-status profession. As teaching is a low-status job, it is also the case that those who get into the profession are often not able to get a better job. In order to attract people with better credentials, it is absolutely essential that the salaries and working conditions are improved substantially.

Lack of relevance of programmes

An important reason why people in general perceive the teacher preparation programmes to be weak is because of their lack of relevance for the actual classroom. Teacher preparation programmes in India by and large, even after more than five decades, continue unchanged. Batra (1995), making a critical analysis of teacher training programmes in the country, agrees that we are currently training teachers based on a model that has changed little since the 1950s. The present teacher training patterns in India are based on the system of training introduced by the British missionaries in the late 19th century. The two general features of the colonial legacy that continue to persist even now are: 1) the isolation of teacher training from academic and professional institutions and 2) teacher training being considered inferior to professional institutions such as schools of law, medicine and business administration. In addition, teacher training still tends to be conducted in specialist institutions where intending teachers have few opportunities to gain wider experience and to break the school–college–school circuit (Dove, 1986).

Even though with the passage of time teacher training programmes have undergone some cosmetic changes, the colonial influences have persisted.

Although a lot of the material imported from metropolitan countries has been purged, much still remains unquestioned. For instance, outdated psychological theories based on research from foreign cultures continue to be an integral part of our teacher training curricula. Teacher training programmes, as Raina (1999) points out, have not been in tune with the real needs of classroom teachers and have not contributed to their professionalism. It is a sad fact that, at the moment, much training is a ritual necessary for obtaining the teaching certificate and worth very little else. Whilst it may satisfy political and professional sensibilities to claim that a high proportion of the teaching force is certified, in the long run this is an expensive effort unless real gain in teacher effectiveness is achieved (Dove, 1986). Partly the situation can be greatly improved by having an indigenous model of teacher education (Raina, 1999). Indigenization of teacher education envisages a paradigmatic shift, taking an inner view of the situation, giving importance to socio-cultural realities and making use of culture-sensitive pedagogies. It discourages modelling programmes and research on 'borrowed consciousness' rather than rooting them in the local context.

Teachers for rural and urban areas

Teacher training programmes in India have largely remained uniform, not paying any special attention to the needs of teachers who have to work in settings that are other than urban. Teachers, both for rural and urban areas, are generally prepared in urban situations and surroundings in training institutions mostly located in towns and cities. Even their practice teaching and internship in teaching take place mostly in urban schools, which are comparatively better equipped and better staffed. There is hardly any provision for providing initial practical training in single-teacher schools and multigrade teaching situations for teacher trainees.

Understanding of the basic differences in rural and urban societies is rarely highlighted in teacher training institutions in theory or in practice. It has been observed that, even when sincere attempts are made to give adequate focus to work experience and working with the community, certain significant factors often get ignored. It would be rare to find teacher training institutions that lay emphasis on agriculture and related areas in work education programmes. Making an observation about the out-of-tune Primary Teacher Certificate (PTC) courses being offered in the Gujarat state, Dyer (1996) reported that most teachers she had interviewed felt that the training was not suitable for the situations in which they worked, since training colleges have a strong urban bias, despite the fact that five-sixths of teaching posts were in rural areas. Reportedly, trainees were not in touch with the realities of small schools with a single room and no facilities. It is ironic indeed that we learn from the World Bank report (1997) that in India teachers need – but do not receive – preparation for teaching in the situation that two-thirds of them have to face: multi-age, multilingual, multigrade classrooms, with many first-generation learners.

In fact it would appear then, as Avalos (1991: 16) points out:

> that in defining the focus of teacher training, there is a need to keep in mind the broad requirements of the educational system as well as those specific to rural and urban contexts. What is indeed needed is not two types of teachers, but opportunities in training institutions for trainers to focus closely on the sorts of knowledge and skills that can help them work with either rural or urban communities, depending on their own interest and past experience.

Despite so many problems and challenges, the teacher education scene in India is poised for a bright future. Concerted attempts are now being made to improve the situation by large-scale funding of programmes in the field of teacher education.

Future prospects

The past decade has witnessed some major developments taking place in the Indian teacher education system. It was the National Policy on Education (MHRD, 1986a) and its associated Program of Action (MHRD, 1986b, 1992) that suggested a total restructuring of teacher education in the country. Most importantly, it was perhaps the first time that a policy statement of this kind was followed by some concrete programme of action to improve the status of teacher education in the country. As a consequence of this, the government of India initiated a centrally sponsored scheme of teacher education that aimed at providing mass orientation to school teachers to sensitize them to this major national policy and the improvement of the content and process of school education. It also suggested the establishment of an innovative institution called a District Institute of Education and Training (DIET) at the elementary level. The whole idea of establishing this institution is to improve the state of elementary teacher education in the country, and contribute towards achieving universalization of elementary education.

The other components of this centrally sponsored scheme were to upgrade some secondary teachers training institutions into comprehensive Colleges of Teacher Education (CTEs) and Institutions of Advanced Studies of Education (IASEs) to carry out multiple functions such as pre-service and in-service teacher preparation, action research and elementary teacher preparation. The centrally sponsored scheme also provided funds for a special orientation programme for about 1.8 million teachers in various facets of primary education. Table 22.2 shows the progress made on different teacher education programmes in the recent past.

It is the first time in the post-independence years that teacher education has received so much emphasis from the government of India in terms of funding

Table 22.2 Progress on various teacher education schemes

Scheme	Target	Achievement
Programme for Mass Orientation of School Teachers	2.0 million teachers	1.76 million
Establishment of DIETs	425 by the end of 8th plan period	420
Upgrading of Secondary Teacher Education Institutes into CTEs and IASEs	135	110
Special Orientation Programme of Primary Teachers	1.8 million teachers	1.0 million

Source: Selected Educational Statistics 1998, Ministry of Human Resource Development, Government of India, New Dehli
CTEs = Colleges of Teacher Education
DIETs = District Institutes of Education and Training
IASEs = Institution of Advanced Studies of Education

various projects. However, it is not merely pumping the money into the system that is important, but the impact such programmes have in helping improve training in the field. Commenting on the possible impact of such official endeavours, Seshadri (1993) points out that one should not expect massive resource funding for buildings, equipment and posts, by itself, to work wonders. A state of readiness to receive and assimilate the resource inputs into the system is a prerequisite. What do we do with all the sophisticated computer and educational technology support, when we simply do not have expertise to conceive programme ideas, to formulate and deliver the programme? It is therefore imperative that programmes such as these are monitored meticulously to see that they give the desired results. It may be added that a number of evaluation studies are in progress to see the impact of these centrally sponsored projects, and hopefully they will indicate the impact these programmes had on the school teachers.

Another major development of far-reaching importance has been the establishment of the National Council for Teacher Education (NCTE). NCTE was established by an Act of Parliament in 1993 with a view to achieving planned and coordinated development in teacher education throughout the country. The regulation and proper maintenance of norms and standards in the teacher education system were also in the legislation. In concrete terms, the NCTE has two functions: first, to coordinate and regulate teacher education programmes, ensuring that certain basic standards of professionalism are adhered to by every institution and each programme; and second, to provide academic support to teacher educators and teachers, to ensure that they acquire pedagogical skills and competencies at the pre-service stage and get these renewed at regular intervals.

During the past couple of years of its existence, the NCTE has succeeded in monitoring teacher education programmes through correspondence courses to check low quality. Among the regular institutional programmes, it has succeeded in ensuring that the institutions establish properly equipped laboratories, acquire new equipment, strengthen libraries and above all have a staff–trainee ratio of 1:10. Besides this, it has also carried out a thorough review of the existing teacher education curriculum (NCTE, 1998). In a bold initiative, the NCTE has recommended a swift transition to a two-year programme of teacher preparation at the secondary stage. Essentially, the Council endorses the launching of long-duration integrated programmes for preparing quality teachers in the country.

References

Adiseshiah, M S (1986) Educational perspectives, in *School Education in India: Present status and future needs*, ed P L Malhotra, B S Parakh and C H K Misra, National Council of Educational Research and Training, New Delhi

Avalos, B (1991) *Approaches to Teacher Education: Initial teacher training*, Commonwealth Secretariat, London

Batra, P (1995) Elementary truths, *Seminar*, **436**, pp 20–25

Central Statistics Organization (CSO) (1995) *Economic Survey*, Government of India, New Delhi

Dove, L (1986) *Teachers and Teacher Education in Developing Countries*, Croom Helm, London

Dyer, C (1996) Primary teachers and policy innovation in India: some neglected issues, *International Journal of Educational Development*, **16**, pp 27–40

Kumar, K (1991) *Political Agenda of Education: A study of colonialist and nationalist ideas*, Sage, New Delhi

Lockheed, M E and Verspoor, A M (1990) *Improving Primary Education in Developing Countries: A review of policy options*, IBRD / World Bank, Washington, DC

Ministry of Human Resource Development (MHRD) (1986a) *National Policy on Education*, Government of India, New Delhi

MHRD (1986b) *Program of Action*, Government of India, New Delhi

MHRD (1992) *National Policy on Education and Program of Action (Modified)*, Government of India, New Delhi

Myrdal, G (1971) *Asian Dilemma: An inquiry into the poverty of nations*, Pantheon, New York

National Council for Teacher Education (NCTE) (1998) *Curriculum Framework for Quality of Teacher Education*, NCTE, New Delhi

Parhar, M and Mukhopadhyay (1999) *Indian Education: Development since independence*, Vikas Publishing House, New Delhi

Premi, M K (1991) Literacy dilemma, in *India's Population Heading Towards a Billion*, ed M K Premi, B R Publishers, New Delhi

Raina, V K (1999) Indigenizing teacher education in developing countries: the Indian context, *Prospects*, **24**, pp 1–25

Seshadri, C (1993) Reforming teacher education: can pan-Indian solutions provide the answer?, Professor A C Deva Gowda Memorial Lecture, Regional College of Education, Mysore

Verma, N (1997) India: an unwritten epic, *Biblio*, **2**, pp 6–7

Walia, K and Rajput, J S (2000) *Emerging Priorities in Teacher Education in India*, National Council of Teacher Education, New Delhi

World Bank (1997) *Improving Teachers' Performance: Primary education in India*, World Bank, Washington, DC

23. Changing the face of teacher education in Israel: training a professional reflective teacher

Tikva Zohar

Introduction

This chapter presents an approach that considers teaching to be a reflective occupation, and a new model of teacher education in Israel is described, for training the reflective professional teacher. The aim of this chapter is to point out how training student teachers (STs) according to principles of reflection affects the manner in which they work with their pupils in the classroom. It demonstrates the extent to which STs adopted the principles of reflective teaching and how they used them when they worked with pupils.

The chapter is divided into three parts. The first part briefly describes teacher education in Israel today. The second part presents some of the research findings from a state teachers' college, Seminar Hakibbutzim in Tel Aviv, which examined the use of reflection when implementing assessment in practice classrooms. Some research findings are presented that represent the approach that sees reflectivity as an integral part of good, professional teaching. In the third part, future related issues are presented on the subject of reflection and practical work.

Historical background and processes of change in Israeli teacher education

The Israeli educational system has undergone far-reaching changes since its inception as a result of developments in society, culture, economics, technology and politics. The educational system is expected to answer the various needs generated by these changes, among them the growing demand for education in general, and for higher education in particular (Kfir *et al*, 1998). Until the early 1980s, two systems of higher education existed in Israel. The first was universities, which granted academic degrees, and the second was non-academic institutions, which granted professional certificates after three years. Worldwide reform in teacher training is characterized by lengthening the training period and increasing the requirements for prior degrees. However, in Israel, attempts by non-academic institutions to gain academic standing met with opposition from the universities and the Council for Higher Education, which supervises them (Ariav and Seidenberg, 1995). The universities were not enthusiastic about raising their own training requirements for students studying education, since that would counter the ethos prevailing at Israeli universities regarding the great importance of research (Chen, Gottlieb and Yakir, 1993). However, in spite of the difficulties and the objections of the universities, numerous attempts at change have occurred in teacher training colleges in Israel. These changes focus on two significant processes. One is the academization of the teacher training colleges, and the other, the professionalization of teaching. These two processes indicate one major dilemma regarding teacher training: the extent to which we should focus on academic models rather than on practical teaching.

Academic recognition is the first aspect of academizing teacher training. In 1971, a parliamentary committee proposed that academic training be demanded of teachers in junior high schools (Parliamentary Committee, 1971). As a result, the training institutions had to provide academic training or lose junior high school teacher training to the universities. When, in 1979, the Etzioni committee recommended that the teacher training institutions grant their students a BEd degree (Committee to Examine the Status of the Teacher and the Profession of Education, 1979), the process of academizing the teacher training institutions began. In 1981, the Council for Higher Education changed its position and published guidelines for academic training in teaching (Permanent Committee, 1981). Academizing teacher training anticipated a demand for teachers with advanced degrees, and involved requiring full matriculation accreditation for applicants, lengthening the training period to four years and broadening the knowledge of the discipline. The four-year training awards a BEd degree leading to a teaching certificate.

A second aspect of academizing education involved bringing all underqualified teachers working in the Israeli education system up to the requirements for a BEd degree. Courses were provided by teacher training institutions that were not an integral part of pre-service training programmes. The influence of academization on the change in teacher training has not yet been sufficiently researched. Nevertheless, existing data point to far-reaching changes. Kfir et al (1998) found that curricula had been revolutionized, that changes had taken place both in the student population and in the staff, and that the institutions had changed both structurally and functionally, and had become large and variegated academic institutions. The process of academization is now almost complete.

Professionalization of teaching has already begun and is a continuation of the process of academization. Internship is a concept that teaching, as a new academic profession, newly raised to the level of a profession, has borrowed from such traditional professions as medicine, law and accountancy. The tangible expression of the trend towards the professionalization of teaching is the internship year in teaching. The internship year is the concluding stage of the process of professional training in teaching. At the end of this stage a licence is awarded. The basic assumption is that in teaching too, as in the other professions, a licence to teach will not be valid unless it is preceded by a process of assessment.

This assessment is the responsibility of a committee headed by an inspector from the Ministry of Education. The other members of the committee are the tutor and the head or other senior member of the institution. The committee carries out an assessment of the intern twice in the course of the academic year: a formative assessment in the month of January, and a summative assessment at the end of the internship year. The scope of the assessment covers five areas: teaching, conducting a class, educational tasks, fitting into the life of the school and responsibility.

Israel is probably the first country to run an internship programme in teaching at the national level. In other places in which a similar programme is implemented, it is done at the college or regional level. The university teacher training departments are also expected to join the programme in the near future. In Israel today, there are six universities, each with a department of education that trains high school teachers, and 28 academic teacher training colleges (three of which are in the Arab sector), which train kindergarten, elementary school and middle school teachers in Israel. Most new teachers today receive their training at the teacher training colleges and only a minority at the universities. The training programme of the colleges includes a general liberal arts education, studies in the field of specialization, and education studies including theoretical studies in pedagogy and field experience, the last being the most significant.

Field experience as part of pre-service teacher training

The main model for field experience in teaching in the first three years at the colleges is that of 'practical work' (teaching practice) in various frameworks and in varying amounts, which range, in most cases, from four to six hours a week for each year. These hours are generally concentrated in one or two days a week. In addition, most teacher training colleges arrange periods of 'intensified field experience' in teaching once or twice in the course of the academic year. For the duration of this field experience, the students stay in the practice classrooms continuously for one or two weeks of 'concentrated practice in teaching'.

Field experience provides the student with a realistic environment for trying out the teaching–learning processes, and begins in the first year of training. Though it is only one element of teacher training, it is considered the most significant and, as such, it is the object of interest to researchers in Israel and worldwide. As the trainees are expected to apply in the practice classroom what they learnt in college, field experience for them is therefore the most complex part of the training process. They are required to work simultaneously with the college supervisor, the classroom teacher and the pupils.

The way the trainee functions within this complex system influences the quality of the field experience and the extent of its contribution to creating a professional teacher. The interaction between the students, college supervisors, classroom teachers and pupils offers STs the opportunity to identify their educational skills, to develop a realistic grasp of the subject and to create constructive attitudes towards pupils and the training programme. In other words, the participants are supposed to work as a team. In reality, this is not always the case. STs' expectations from the classroom teacher are shaped by the professional requirements of the college supervisor, but these are not always met. Hoping to be able to model themselves after the classroom teacher, trainees are often disappointed (Lasley and Applegate, 1985).

The teacher must be able to function as part of a multi-professional team in order to generate integrative learning opportunities that will make the material more relevant to pupils (Zohar, 1986, 1996). Most proposals for improving field experience call for the development of alternative training programmes that suit the reflective approach to teaching (Boxall, Gilbert and Qualter, 1999). These presume that the change from the present training model to a practical–reflective model will improve the quality of field experience, and will thus reduce existing tensions. Training by the college supervisor should design and interpret the field experience on the basis of theoretical knowledge and experience. Such training should be an avenue to learning, an interpretation and development of alternatives, both in terms of the quality of the tasks and the way pupils are handled, hopefully encouraging the ST to be more critical. This will hopefully advance the professional education of the teacher. The research findings described below elaborate on these ideas.

Principles of reflection revealed in assessing pupils

In a comprehensive study carried out in a teacher training institute in Israel on the subject of alternative assessment, reflection constituted a central element in the research (Zohar, 2000). The aim of the study was to train STs to assess their pupils in the practice classes by means of alternative assessment tools. In this study, in which 24 third-year students participated, reflection served as a means of learning and as a tool for collecting data. Most of the data were collected by means of such reflective tools as the reflective journal, group discussions, observations, reflective dialogues and self-reports. In the use of reflective tools as a means of improving learning and teaching, there is a certain response for the need to change the whole subject of teaching and systems of assessment. This call for change is in line with the spirit of the times and is based, in the main, on the better understanding of learning processes.

A key question asked in this research probed what examples of reflection the STs expressed by means of the reflective tools available to them, and what principles of reflection they used in order to cultivate it among their pupils. In this part of the chapter, the principles of reflection applied by the students in their work with the pupils are demonstrated. Reflection has many aspects and a wide range of characteristics (LaBoskey, 1993). Therefore, as it was difficult to characterize the examples according to one approach or one definition, the examples discussed below reflect an eclectic and integrative approach to the process of reflection.

Owing to the complexity of the processes, it was not possible to characterize each event according to one principle of reflection. In most cases, events reflected several principles or, alternatively, a principle was expressed in several events. In realizing the principles of reflection, the STs used indirect means that yielded indirect reflection, and direct means that yielded direct reflection. Indirect reflection involves an external factor that encourages reflective cognition, such as literary texts and real events from the pupils' lives. These factors acted as a bridge to the world of the pupil, and filled the role of the 'arbiter' through which the pupils expressed their thoughts and feelings. Direct reflection involves addressing the pupils directly through a question or a remark, in the expectation that in their reflective response the pupils will relate to themselves. Let us therefore examine briefly these two forms of reflection.

Indirect reflection

Indirect reflection is made up of two categories, the first coming from encountering various texts and the other through pupils' peer assessment.

The principle of reflection achieved through creating involvement on the basis of personal experience and past memories was expressed mainly through questions derived from *encountering texts* that were part of an assessment task. The questions aided the pupils to react to events and characters to express emotions, fears, wishes, opinions and beliefs. Below is an example of the types of questions and answers obtained from children:

Question: What, in your opinion, did the little tourist feel when she discovered she had lost her mother? Have you experienced a similar situation in the past? Write about your experience.

Response: Fear. It's like kidnapping a child. It's scary to be alone in a strange place. When I was three years old, I got on to the carousel at the funfair and my parents did not see that I had gone. When I couldn't find them, I cried and thought I'd never see them again. Eventually someone called them on the loudspeaker and everything was all right.

From pupils' answers, one can see how an external event is connected to their internal world and serves as a means of expressing emotions. Through the event, the pupils examine their feelings and actions as if they were there. In certain questions, feelings, thoughts and value positions were examined in light of the pupils' personal experiences. All 24 STs posed questions of this kind to the pupils. The questions were planned in advance and emphasized cognitive abilities rather than being only questions of knowledge. The STs' experiences of reflective processes tend to encourage reflection when dealing with pupils.

With experience, the STs learnt that self-reflection can be encouraged through *peer assessment*. Some STs soon recognized the potential of peer assessment to invite self-reflection. In six classes (involving eight STs), pupils assessed their fellow pupils' compositions and, in four classes, STs included pupils in group observations to assess the cooperative work of their peers. Below is an example where the ST (Hagar) shares her experience of 'discovering' self-reflection through peer assessment, during a group discussion in the college:

Hagar: Listen to what Nira [a pupil] wrote in the observation: 'Ron asks for scissors a few times but no one listens to him. He is not given scissors and he gets annoyed and gets up. Rotem calls out to him but he doesn't want to come back. He was offended because he was ignored. Alon asks if he should write in print or script. Ron sits at the side and looks sad. If I were in the group, I would have convinced him to return. It is not nice that they left him out. Why not call him? Rotem keeps giving instructions and a leader should not act like that... In the end, Ron did not participate.' Nira forgot it was an observation; she identifies with Ron and criticizes Rotem.

Rona: That stems more from her own distress than from Ron's. Her lack of self-confidence is expressed in her interpretation of others' behaviour.

Hagar: In my opinion she is criticizing the group and responding as if she was their mechanic.

That the pupils looked into themselves when providing answers to questions and during observations is also expressed in the use of the reflective language.

Direct reflection

Direct reflection focused on the pupils' self-reflection regarding the assessment objects. The main tool was pupil feedback on each assessment task. The STs approached the pupils individually and directly, mainly in writing. Self-assessment as a tool for encouraging reflection was implemented in various types of tasks and in contexts that emphasized different principles of reflection. The forms of feedback demonstrated below focus on single tasks, the learning process, group work and reflective oral feedback. Each type relates to a principle of reflection.

One principle of reflection is *performance-focused self-awareness* ('the task and I'). As a rule, after carrying out an assessment task, pupils were asked to complete a feedback questionnaire and answer a series of questions connected to implementation of the task. The questions referred to the pupils' ability to deal with the demands of the task, and asked them to note difficulties that arose while carrying out the task. In most tasks, the feedback emphasized enjoyment and difficulties, but STs related to additional topics according to the character of the task. In reading and writing tasks, for example, emphasis was placed on the level of the text and its genre, interest in the topic, new questions that arose as a result of reading the text, and the new knowledge that the pupil gleaned. In tasks that dealt with problem solving, the process of decision making was emphasized. The purpose of the feedback was both to provide the STs with feedback on the activities they prepared and to encourage the pupils to share their difficulties and their preferences. The principle of reflection was to guide the pupils in the cognitive and affective domains. The following is an example of a pupil's feedback on a task:

Pupil A: It was fun because I love interviewing. There were people who asked me all kinds of questions [like] why I am asking and what grade I am in. I was polite. They were too. It took me a while to write, but they waited patiently. One man suggested I use a tape in the future, and that's what I will do next time. We had too many questions and that is not good. It's important to ask briefly and to the point.

From the pupil's words one can see that, in addition to the reference to the task and information on how the pupil carried it out, the feedback shows reflection.

A second principle of reflection is *self-regulation and decision making* ('the personal subject and I'). The results showed that pupils' feedback dealt with reasons for choosing the subject, the planning of the work and assessment of the finished product through reflective reference to the learning process. The reflection focused on an examination of a pupil's choice, abilities, competencies and preferences during the learning process. Reflection focuses on guidance towards metacognitive thought processes regarding personal decisions and different learning strategies. It is seen also in tasks where the emphasis is placed on the selection of knowledge sources, and manners of expressing this knowledge.

A third principle of reflection is *personal competence and self-criticism in a social context* ('the group and I'). Reflection focused on pupils' beliefs and their ability to function as contributing members of a group. In many instances, pupils referred to personal traits, and at times even expressed self-criticism, as shown by the keeping of a reflection journal. Only five STs (out of 24) used the reflection journal in the practice classes. ST Dorit summarizes the contribution of the tool for encouraging reflection:

At first there was enthusiasm but after two or three written 'conversations', only a few persisted. For these, the reflection journal was an open channel, which allowed them to express in writing their understanding of the material, and to relate to everything that disturbed them or was enjoyable. They wrote about everything: friends, family and teachers. They made suggestions, asked questions and, without planning to, I also shared with them thoughts and experiences of my own.

All 24 STs held *assessment and feedback conversations* with the pupils after analysing their assessment tasks, as part of reflection and guidance. Here is an example of part of a dialogue between an ST and a pupil. The ST Mira guided David through self-reflection to formulate an answer as follows:

Mira: Here is your answer, which is very good. However something is missing. First I will read you the question: [she reads aloud] 'Do you think that stories like these should appear in the newspaper?' You answered, 'That people will read and also do good deeds.' What is missing in your answer?

David: I don't know.

Mira: I'll give you a clue. Pay attention to your answer. I'll read it again: 'That people will read and also do good deeds.' If someone reads only the answer, will he know from your answer what the question was?

David: [mumbling] I don't know.

Mira: I have an idea; let's do an exercise. I will ask all kinds of questions and you will just repeat your answer. Here, hold your answer and read it out loud after I ask. First question: what is the point of the story?

David: [reads his original answer] 'That people will read and also do good deeds.'

Mira: Does that fit?

David: Yes.

Mira: Another question: what is the lesson of the story?

David: 'That people will read and also do good deeds.'

Mira: What is your conclusion?

David: That it fits other questions.

Mira: So how can the reader know what the question was? Can you now say what is missing? [the pupil is silent] I think an opening to the sentence is missing. Do you want to try and add an opening, even a short one?

David: It's easier for me to start the answer that way. I can't begin with an opening, because I already have my answer.

Mira: You don't have to begin the answer by writing the opening. You can add it afterwards. Here, read your answer again, and let's suppose that there was a blank line above the answer that you have written. What would you add now?

David: [after a few attempts he looks at the answer and responds] In my opinion stories should… [Mira encourages him with a smile and a touch on the shoulder] So I can leave place for an opening and first begin with the answer.

Mira: That is definitely an option. It's also a solution, which we saw now that you succeeded in. I also suggest that afterwards you read the answer in full in order to be sure that the opening connects with what you have written.

Mira begins with positive feedback in order to create a supportive atmosphere, and uses mediation to direct the pupil to a conclusion that allows him to correct his error. During the entire conversation she does not force him to do anything, and uses his suggestions as a basis for his advancement. In conclusion, on different levels, all the STs made use of the principles of reflection in their work with the pupils. They showed understanding and sensitivity to the use of reflection as a learning tool that contributes to both the teacher and the pupils.

Conclusions and prospects

This chapter has attempted to shed light on a small part of a teacher training programme. The purpose of the programme was to train prospective teachers in the development and use of classroom-based alternative assessment tasks.

Focusing the practical work on one main area (in this case, 'alternative assessment') had a positive effect on the functioning of the STs and the pedagogical adviser, as well as on the STs' patterns of behaviour. This resulted in improved relations between the STs and the classroom teachers. The STs' status and image in the eyes of the classroom teachers increased as a result of their familiarity with the subject of alternative assessment. On the other hand, the status of the training teachers, who displayed a lack of knowledge and interest in alternative assessment, decreased in the eyes of the STs. The lack of a person from the school who could mediate between the STs and others in the school had a detrimental effect on the STs' functioning in the school. An attempt to bridge the gap between the training institute, represented by the supervisor, and the classroom teacher is found in the internship programme at Oxford University (McIntyre, 1993). This model incorporates a third factor: a member of the school staff who serves as the coordinator of student experiential teaching, and as such is also a part-time staff member at the training institute. In Israel, no similar project has been reported but the prospects for this idea might be worth considering.

The prospects for the use of reflection must be encouraged, otherwise it does not occur. Both the STs and the pupils responded to reflection in a positive manner, as a result of being guided toward reflection. Encouraging reflection was necessary because reflection does not occur automatically. Achieving it requires effort, guidance and consistency. In all cases, it was apparent that, the closer to the event the reflection occurs, the more significant the reflective response. It seems that the STs who developed their reflective skills felt that this helped them to become better teachers. Varied tools of reflection increase the reflective potential because different tools fill different needs and yield different reflective responses. The group discussions, feedback conversations and reflective journals were the most effective tools for achieving reflective responses from the STs and the pupils. The more open and less demanding the reflective tool was, the more responsive it was. Because the STs were aware of the reflective processes that occurred during the feedback dialogues, they had a special interest in learning how to use this strategy with their pupils.

The ability to carry out reflective dialogues with pupils demands certain personality characteristics. Only a third of the 24 STs offered suggestions or hints that served as scaffolding (Vygotsky, 1978) to support the pupils' thought processes and expand their learning. Pupils valued these reflective discussions. But because reflective feedback conversations require good teaching skills, high-level communication skills and other individual abilities, most STs had trouble implementing them. However, modelling the reflective discussions and employing reflective dialogue and a reflection journal led two-thirds of the STs to experiment with ways of interacting with their pupils.

To conclude, the rationale for adopting reflection in teaching, learning and training processes is based on the perception that reflection is an important goal for STs, pupils and teacher educators to achieve. Indeed, the findings showed that the ability to reflect is crucial to the development of reflective teaching (Brown, 1987; Tann, 1993). Therefore, the implications and prospects for a more enlightened teacher education in Israel become exciting as well as challenging for the future.

References

Ariav, T and Seidenberg, A (1995) Reform and development in teacher education in Israel, in *Ferment in Education: A look abroad*, ed J J Lane, pp 122–47, University of Chicago Press, Chicago

Boxall, W, Gilbert, J and Qualter, A (1999) Developing a holistic assessment stance in student teachers, *Assessment in Education*, **6** (2), pp 247–61

Brown, A (1987) Metacognition, executive control, self-regulation, and other more mysterious mechanisms, in *Metacognition, Motivation, and Understanding*, ed F Weinert and R Kluwe, pp 65–116, Erlbaum, Hillsdale, NJ

Chen, N, Gottlieb, E and Yakir, R (1993) The academic profession in Israel: continuity and transformation, in *International Study of the Academic Profession*, The Carnegie Foundation for the Advancement of Teaching, Princeton, NJ

Committee to Examine the Status of the Teacher and the Profession of Education (1979) Report, Ministry of Education, Culture and Sport, Jerusalem (in Hebrew)

Kfir, D *et al* (1998) *The Academization of the Teaching Profession and Teacher Education in Israel*, Magnes, Jerusalem (in Hebrew)

LaBoskey, V K (1993) A conceptual framework for reflection in preservice teacher education, in *Conceptualising Reflection in Teacher Development*, ed J Calderhead and P Gates, pp 23–38, Falmer Press, London

Lasley, T J and Applegate, J H (1985) Problems of early field experience students, *Teaching and Teacher Education*, **1** (3), pp 221–27

McIntyre, D (1993) Theory, theorising and reflection in initial teacher education, in *Conceptualising Reflection in Teacher Development*, ed J Calderhead and P Gates, pp 23–38, Falmer Press, London

Parliamentary Committee (1971) *Report of the Parliamentary Committee Examining the Structure of Elementary and High School Education in Israel for the Years 1966–1968*, Jerusalem

Permanent Committee for Academic Tracks in Institutions for Training Workers in Education (1981) *Guideline Programme for the Curriculum for Bachelors of Education Degree*, The Council for Higher Education, Jerusalem (in Hebrew)

Tann, S (1993) Eliciting student teacher personal theories, in *Teachers' Professional Learning*, ed J Calderhead and P Gates, pp 53–69, Falmer Press, London

Vygotsky, L S (1978) Interaction between development and learning, in *Mind in Society: The development of higher psychological processes*, ed L M Cole *et al*, pp 79–91, Harvard University Press, Cambridge, MA

Zohar, T (1986) Primary school teachers' attitude toward the conceptual scheme of curriculum in the humanities, Unpublished MA thesis, School of Education, Tel Aviv University (in Hebrew)

Zohar, T (1996) *Who Needs a Curriculum? Educational anthology for studies at the Open University*, pp 115–31, Open University Press, Tel Aviv

Zohar, T (2000) The education of prospective teachers in the use of classroom based alternative assessment tasks, Unpublished PhD dissertation, The University of Liverpool

Index

Page numbers in italic indicate tables or figures